CONVERSION AND TEXT

The Cases of Augustine of Hippo, Herman-Judah,
and Constantine Tsatsos

CONVERSION AND TEXT

The Cases of Augustine of Hippo, Herman-Judah, and Constantine Tsatsos

KARL F. MORRISON

University Press of Virginia • *Charlottesville and London*

The University Press of Virginia

Copyright © 1992 by the Rector and Visitors
of the University of Virginia

First published 1992

Library of Congress Cataloging-in-Publication Data
Morrison, Karl Frederick.
    Conversion and text : the cases of Augustine of Hippo, Herman-Judah, and Constantine Tsatsos / Karl F. Morrison.
      p.   cm.
    Companion vol. to: Understanding conversion.
    ISBN 0-8139-1359-4 (cloth)
    ISBN 0-8139-1393-4 (paper)
    1. Conversion—Case studies. 2. Augustine, Saint, Bishop of Hippo. 3. Herman, of Scheda, 12th century. 4. Tsatsos, Konstantinos, 1899-   . I. Morrison, Karl Frederick. Understanding conversion. II. Title.
BR110.M67   1991 Suppl.
248.2'4'0922—dc20   91-26972
                                                               CIP

Printed in the United States of America

Contents

Preface: What Is Called Conversion?   vii

Acknowledgments   xix

CASE 1. Augustine of Hippo's *Confessions*   1

CASE 2. Herman-Judah's *Account*
  Introduction   39
  A Translation of Herman-Judah's *Short Account of His Own Conversion*   76

CASE 3. The *Dialogues* of Constantine Tsatsos   114

Summary   144

Abbreviations   151

Notes   153

Index   183

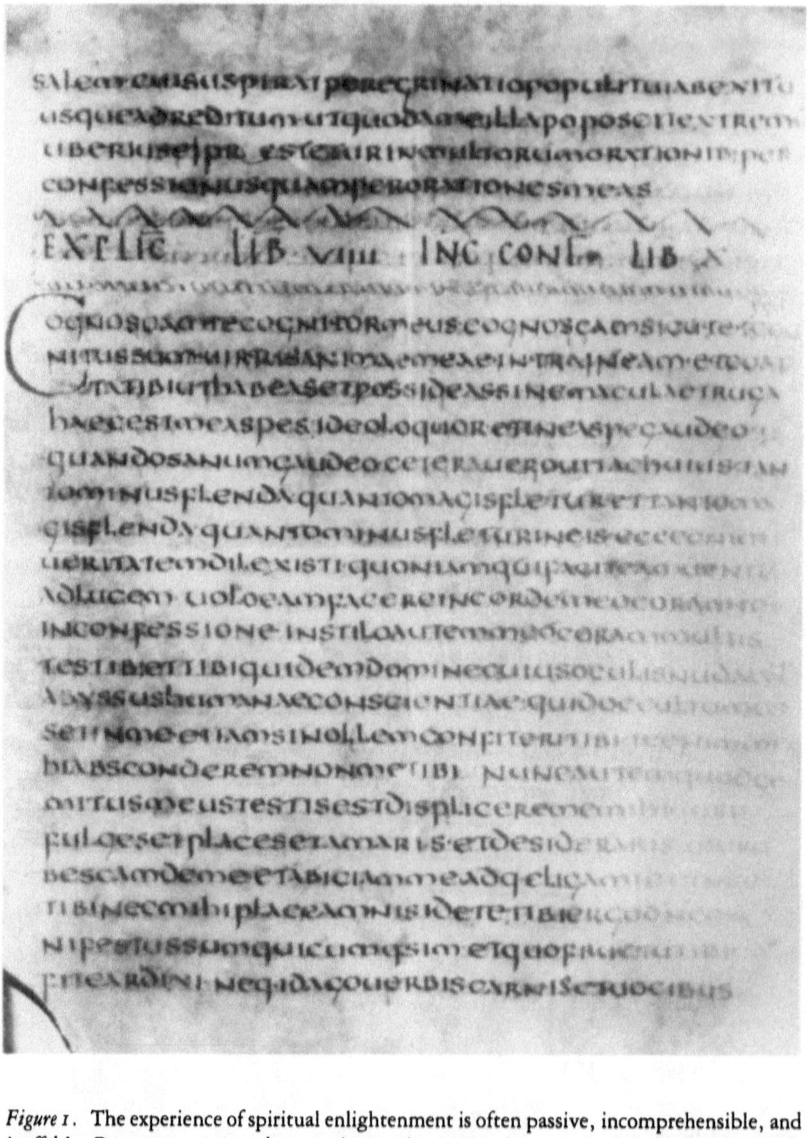

Figure 1. The experience of spiritual enlightenment is often passive, incomprehensible, and ineffable. By contrast, texts about such experiences require conscious, indeed, calculated, action; and, after the moment of composition, they are liable to unpredictable intrusions of editorial revision, artistic adjustment, and copyist's adulteration. This photograph records a (now lost) fragment of one of the earliest known manuscripts of Augustine of Hippo's *Confessions*. The manuscript was dated to the sixth century. It preserved the text of *Confessions*, 9.13.55–10.3.15, the first part of which passage celebrates one result of Augustine's conversion: his acceptance of a life of celibacy. (Lowe Papers, box 117, folder 569, CLA XI (1), for CLA 1640; photograph courtesy of the Pierpont Morgan Library, New York)

PREFACE

What Is Called Conversion?

These case studies of conversion are closely associated with my book *Understanding Conversion*. In order to put them in context, I need, by way of introduction, to say a word about the companion volume.

I originally wrote *Understanding Conversion* as a contribution to the series of Page-Barbour Lectures at the University of Virginia. As it happened, my lectures were delivered during the centennial anniversary year of the death of John Henry Newman, whose conversion, however celebrated (or notorious) an event it may have been, left an indelible mark on literature. Indeed, the contrast between the experience of what was called conversion (something felt) and writings about conversion (things made) gave my lectures their orientation.

Consensus on articles of Christian life through the centuries is often hard to find. However, throughout the history of Christianity there has been unusual consistency among a host of witnesses to this point: that the experience of conversion is beyond thought or words. Equally, there has been no lack of efforts to express the inconceivable and ineffable.

The fact remains that what historians have before them are not vivid experiences but literary compositions, which by their very nature are fictive. The word *conversion* gives a clue to the method of analysis appropriate to the materials. For in the language of religion, it is a metaphor, borrowed from manufacturing processes in numerous arts and crafts (e.g., "converting" copper and tin into bronze). Thus, religious conversion itself—and far more plainly, understanding conversion—were subjects of linguistic or, more exactly, metaphorical inquiry.

Therefore, it is important to ask, What is called conversion? By whom was it so called? What made the specific name, "conversion," thinkable to that person for that particular thing? What was involved in thinking it out?

Uniformity should not be assumed, even among writers who generally moved within the same frame of reference. A comparison of the two theological writers in this book will illustrate this point.

It is striking how rarely Augustine of Hippo employed the verb *convert* or the noun *conversion* in the *Confessions*. In the most general sense, conversion meant, for Augustine, one person's turning toward another. Turning toward (conversion) and turning away from (aversion) were two aspects of the same act. One person turned to another by turning aside from some earlier object of attention. Occasionally, Augustine specifically paired the two aspects, as when he urged that believers should not lose the light that still lay ahead of them by turning away from God (12.2.26; cf. 10.35.59).[1]

There could be bad conversions, as when the human heart fell into idolatry, turning from the Creator to worship the creature (5.3.56; 7.9.54). But, taken as a whole, Augustine's sparing uses of the verb *convert* and the noun *conversion* denote a sequence of action and response: an act of grace (the turning of God toward a person) and the answering turn of that person toward God.

From the beginning of the *Confessions* to the end, Augustine consistently taught that God's "conversion" toward the soul was the precondition of the soul's "conversion" toward him. Analogously, in the act of creation, the Holy Spirit "converted" toward matter in order to form the world, and, in response, the created world must "convert" from its own dark formlessness to the informing light of its Creator in order to find happiness (13.4).

Of course, Augustine's primary concern was to portray this sacred pas de deux in his own life. By far the most numerous instances of the key words concern this autobiographical subject. His use of the words has several interesting characteristics. The first is the degree to which, when it came to conversions of specific persons, he restricted those words to his own spiritual formation.[2] With meticulous care he used them to identify direct action in which God acted and he received. The action could be stretched out for many years, as it was throughout the decades recounted in the narrative. Augustine addressed God in these words: "You converted me to yourself" (8.12.30), even as God thereby "converted" the grief of Augustine's devout mother into joy.

When he wrote about similar events in the lives of others, Augustine used a strikingly different vocabulary. He studiously avoided using the words *convert* and *conversion* when he described how his friend Nebridius was almost, but not yet, Christian, although eventually, through Nebridius, his entire household "was made Christian" (9.3.6). Similar avoidance is clear when Augustine chose to say that even a miracle was unable to bring the empress Justina, God's enemy, to "apply her mind" to the faith that saved, instead of to the Arian heresy (9.7.16). Indeed, when he wrote of his mother's tireless efforts to win his father to God and of their success, he did not write of "conversion." His circumlocutions are particularly obvious in this case, so exceptional in the whole story, for his entire purpose was to declare that God inspired Monica in her proselytizing (toward Augustine even more than toward Patricius) and that on that account God was to be praised, honored, and loved in her (9.9.19, 22).

To be sure, even scrupulous translators occasionally impose the word *conversion* on these passages.[3] But their freedom with the text simply underscores the difference between their thinking and Augustine's. The words *convert* and *conversion* were part of Augustine's meticulously planned witness to God's supernatural acts of grace, especially toward himself.

As a master rhetorician, Augustine commanded a rich vocabulary with which to articulate this action as God's calling, chastening, healing, and stirring the heart, coming ever closer to his elect. But he also employed quite a different glossary to characterize the other side of the relationship: human action, particularly in the outward and formal signs of God's inward, unseen, and unpredictable grace.

Such signs included confession of faith in Christ and obedient submission to Church discipline. Supernatural grace and formal signs converged in the sacraments for all of which baptism was the gateway. "Christians are made, not born," Jerome wrote (*ep. 107,1*). Augustine represented the rhetorician Victorinus declaring, "I want to be made a Christian," as he presented himself to make a public profession of faith and to be baptized in the midst of the Roman congregation (8.2.4). Augustine paired his own "conversion" with baptismal "regeneration" (9.3.6). But neither the profession nor the ritual, neither Christianity nor Church, made the Christian; for, as Augustine insisted, it was God acting through them according to his own sovereign judgment that illuminated souls and brought them to rebirth and that could perfect what the divine call and baptism began (cf. 10.4.5).

What is called conversion? For Augustine, writing the *Confessions*, conversion was the unfolding of a supernatural process, initiated and sustained by God, which empowered the soul to climb out of the valley of lamentations, singing a song of degrees (9.2.2), and, after death, to find rest and full enlightenment in God.[4] In conception and in vocabulary, he distinguished supernatural conversion from its formal signs in partaking of sacraments (including baptism), accepting Christian doctrine, and submitting to ecclesiastical discipline. For conversion was a turning to God, not to Christianity or the Church.

This focus, shining like a spotlight on Augustine himself, is basic to a final characteristic of the Father's use of the key verb and noun, one that bears on the whole organization of the *Confessions*. For, as verbal cues deliberately planted in his narrative, those words lead the reader from the turning of God toward Augustine and his mimetic response (chiefly in the first nine books of the *Confessions*) to the cascade of references to "conversion" in the last, climactic book. Augustine began that book referring to the divine call by which God converted him. He moved on with great intricacy and splendor to conversion as the turning of the world from formlessness to its universal Creator and archetype (13.2.20, 13.4.13, 13.5.6), and finally as the turning of all the redeemed toward God, in the inexhaustible light by which they became light (13.10.8, 13.12.15).

The narrative raises God's turning in grace toward Augustine and Augustine's answering turn in faith toward God to higher and higher levels, subsuming it in the return of the whole cosmos to the Word by which it was made (13.2.20, 13.4.13) and in the renewal, among the sanctified, of God's image and likeness, which restored the original order disrupted by sin. Augustine chose to depict his personal conversion as replicating in miniature the conversions of cosmogony and redemption and as part of them.

Writing more than seven centuries after Augustine and in a different land, my second theological author, Herman-Judah, used the word *conversion* in other, if related, ways. His treatise is by no means as long as the *Confessions*, nor, correspondingly, does it provide a comparable linguistic sample. To be sure, Herman-Judah continued to stress divine intervention as the sole agent of spiritual enlightenment. But the word *conversion* had two non-Augustinian senses for him, the one more general than the Father's meaning, the other, more specific. In some passages his conversion "from Judaism to the grace of Christ" appears to include formal signs of his spiritual transformation, including his public profession of faith and baptism. In this regard, Herman-Judah also appears to retain Augustine's idea that such formal acts were incidents in a longer process of conversion, one that continued after baptism and, indeed, after any events related in the narrative, down to the very time of writing. Evidently, in this general sense, too, he wrote of the "conversion" by which the Apostle Paul changed from the Church's persecutor to its preacher. In other passages, he used the word, more specifically, to refer to his entrance into the monastic life, which he also considered a conversion to penitence.[5] This regard for monasticism as in some way the epitome of conversion was built up incrementally during the centuries between Augustine's day and Herman-Judah's, and its terminology and effects appear in some passages where the word *conversion* could also be interpreted in its wider sense. Here, too, the idea of conversion as a way of life rather than as a specific peripety, or crisis, was telling. For centuries of experience with human frailty had ingrained into ascetic literature the proposition that taking monastic vows was but the "beginning of conversion." Conversion remained to be advanced, perfected, and, after death, consummated. Until the last, each day and hour brought risks of failure.

Even so, the question What is called conversion? has different emphases and answers when applied to Augustine's *Confessions* and to Herman-Judah's *Short Account*, and the scale of difference between their theological connotations and Constantine Tsatsos's metaphysical ones is even greater. Enough has been said, however, to distinguish the supernatural essence of what was called conversion from its formal signs (e.g., professing Christianity, being baptized, and obeying Church order) and, moreover, to avoid confusing either of these with a text that represents them. One comment about Tsatsos's *Dialogues* is necessary. The *Dialogues in a Monastery* is the only one of the three texts considered in this book that does not purport to be autobiographical. For that reason, it underscores the often very indistinct line between the fictional and the fictive and sharpens the question whether texts, as objects that are made by calculated design, can be accepted as surrogates for experience. In what respects does it matter whether Augustine's text suppresses almost his entire career as a Christian, whether the text attributed to Herman-Judah were actually a Christian fabrication, or whether Tsatsos's book is a work of imagination? At least, when we take them into our hands as objects of hermeneutic inquiry, we know that they are, one and all, evidence of critical faculties, of poetics, at work.

Conversion and the other words used to compose texts about that inexpressible experience were historical artifacts. They were used with meanings given them by specific historical contexts, and sometimes gathered into tradition as though intersecting strata in geological deposits. Thus, they became portmanteau words, packed with the meanings that were given them in specific times and places by specific writers. Newman packed his portmanteau, "conversion," with some meanings employed by Augustine of Hippo, but with others as well.

In *Understanding Conversion*, this approach led to some conclusions that I knew other students of religious history might consider experimental. However, the discrepancy between something and the name by which it is called is one of the oldest and most familiar in philosophy. It is also worth recalling that some languages (including Arabic) have no exact equivalent for the mysterious transformation of heart called "conversion" in the Christian tradition. One conclusion seems inescapable. Comparative analysts of world religions often have envisioned a universal morphology of conversion, for example, one that would embrace Buddhism and Islam, as well as Christianity. Such a project would appear more arduous than ever if the study of conversion were seen as a venture in historical philology—that is, analysis of language that made different ideas thinkable and different kinds of texts writable in various epochs and societies, and only in them.

In *Understanding Conversion*, I explored the ideals of ascetic discipline, social myths, and visual arts as components in a vast educational system that defined the process of conversion. I chiefly considered writings from western Europe in the eleventh and twelfth centuries. The educational system consisted of two parts. The one was formal; it was defined by such terms as institutional affiliation, religious obedience, and discipline. Yet the formal aspects of conversion lay within the confines of human nature and institutions called forth by it. They could deceive or be misread. For their validity depended on the second—the actual—level of conversion, which was supernatural. Actual conversion did not mean accepting Christianity, submitting to Church authority, or changing from one way of life within the Church to another. Actual conversion was a turning of the heart to Christ and, in fact, a turning of the heart into Christ by a mystic union or incorporation. It was a matter of empathy. This supernatural phenomenon was instigated and perfected by divine intervention: that is, by grace. Consequently, it eluded the human ability to rationalize. The critical fact was that God elected or "decided for" a specific person before that person could "decide for" Christ. This ensemble of ideas could certainly not be transferred to other cultures without severely modifying or destroying them, as the history of missions and colonialism has amply demonstrated. And it owed its coherence and staying power to the distinctive historical career—social, political, and cultural—of Christendom. All things considered, the case for historical particularism seemed more convincing to me than that for universal morphology.

Throughout those inquiries, I found that concealment was essential to the idea of conversion. Repeating verses from the Prophet Isaiah, the parable of the sower taught that revelations could be understood only by the chosen—by those with ears to hear and eyes to see. The parable of the hidden treasure set forth a model of self-interested deception, in which a person who discovered a treasure (representing the Kingdom of Heaven) buried in a field belonging to another person kept his knowledge to himself until he could purchase the field. Concealment was part of disclosure. The whole hermeneutic project of conversion was summed up in the effort, as the Apostle Paul put it, to see through a glass darkly.

To think of conversion in this way, however, was to consider it a long process of empathetic transformation, one that could be described with metaphors of a patient commercial strategy or the germination, ripening, and harvest of grain. Conversion was not a sudden, cataclysmic event. Even the blinding vision of the Apostle Paul on the road to Damascus, decisive as it was, was by no means a conclusive revelation, a calling rather than a conversion. Empathetic conversion was always probationary, full of discouragement, pain, and temptation, and never sure of final blessedness. It was always proportionate to the capacities of the converted and, above all, to the measure of grace bestowed by God on that specific person. The parable of the wise and foolish virgins was a lesson in how believers could misread their own conversions and not endure until the end.

In *Understanding Conversion* I considered several consequences of regarding empathetic conversion as a long risk-filled process of revelation and concealment, whether it was expected in the mysteries of divine revelation or practiced in spiritual ventures of individual minds and hearts.

At issue was one strategy of composition common to Western culture at a specific moment in its career. A striking aspect of that strategy was the frank recognition that by contrast with the immediacy and truthfulness of the event, understanding required an admixture of fiction. History (as fact) and myth were two distinct things. Myth was the context that made history intelligible. Awareness that understanding conversion was made possible by a fictional, or mythic, element enabled those who reflected on the experience of conversion to apply a wide repertory of devices as they translated suffering into art. Indeed, it enabled them to think of conversion itself as an artistic process, following a template, demanding that beginners learn by doing, and, at every stage of production, risking the destruction of the work at hand. Myth was lived through ritual.

Two other positions recurred throughout the lectures. The first had to do with the idea that, to compel the emotions, art must conceal itself. If the tricks of composition were overt, the truthfulness that could be read into the work was diminished. The magician could not show his hand. In this case the self-concealing art was the interpretation of myth. Due to changes in prevailing myths, the strategy of understanding with which I was preoccupied differed markedly from ideas about understanding in Antiquity, though it employed them. Correspondingly, it represented a profound break in the classical tradition. Of course, through its appropriation of the doctrine of mimesis as the key to artistic process, it assimilated many elements of ancient philosophy and religion. However, its exquisitely ambivalent concept of beauty (*pulchritudo*) as a cognitive norm and its quest for suffering rather than serenity placed it in a world apart from those of ancient schools and cults.

Another distinguishing feature was Christianity's combination of opposites regarding myth. For in declaring its necessary use of myth for the sake of understanding, it also declared war against the myths of other creeds. It was both the servant of myth and an instrument of radical demythologizing, and this double game was nowhere plainer than in its confrontation with Jewish doctrine. To form and direct the emotions, it concealed its artfulness from itself, just as it concealed its assimilation of Jewish methods of exegesis and the conversions of Christians to Judaism.

Faith without works was dead. Myths applied to understanding required that life be brought into line with faith—that the behavior of Christ and the saints be taken as patterns of conduct and enacted in daily life. As the enactment of mythic roles, play—both play ritualized and the ritualization of play—was essential both to understanding conversion and to bringing about its transformative effects in empathy.

But who made these myths convincing by playing them out? Whose play was ritualized? Here, the proportionate character of conversion was important. I found that the cognitive norm of beauty was so defined as to belong to a male esthetic, corresponding with kinds of play open only, or chiefly, to men, not equally to all but proportionately to each according to what the Apostle Paul called "the measure of faith" (Rom. 12:3). Women were also encompassed in the hermeneutic circle of myth, but on the periphery. The roles assigned them were marginal to those of men. Consequently, their participation in the pedagogic ritualized play of myth was also of a different kind, and their share in the drama of conversion was according to a scale of proportion other than that applied to men. The limits and degrees of empathy played out in conversion corresponded with those prescribed by social order.

Pulchritudo (or "beauty") was another portmanteau word. It belonged to the glossary of words used to speak about conversion that were packed with meanings and associations belonging to a class defined by status, learning, and sex: a military, educated, male aristocracy. The empathies learned, taught, and shared in the ritualized play of conversion, including the play of artistic beauty, were those of the same class. The fact that the language and discourse about conversion and its chief educational and bonding devices were controlled by this class and applied to serve its *cultus sui* (or self-image) raised the question of how and (if so) in what proportion the empathetic experience known as "conversion" could actually be had by persons outside the "worship" extended by members of that class to one another.

The last position that I followed throughout the lectures was that the strategy of understanding empathetic conversion under review survived, often in modified form, into recent times. For, like art, tradition must disguise itself to be accepted as what has been believed always, everywhere, and by all right-thinking persons—in other words, as something in the nature of things. Here, I was concerned with the deliberate use of the old as a screen to conceal or disguise the new, as happens in the appeal to primordial rights to justify revolution. Perhaps the most enduring element was the subversive doctrine of conversion worked out with reference to conscience. However, mimetic ways of thinking and arguing, not to mention fundamental propositions of faith, also persisted. The history of thought about conversion was actually built into the idea of conscience as it was used in any given generation. And many contemporary ideas about the transformation of self and society incorporate ideals of reform that were first developed by people who bent their minds to reform the soul through the grind of practice, whether through the arts or through works of justice. Often ancient ideas reappear after long periods of latency in new disguises. In this regard, as in the others, I have learned to be alert to what is unsaid—suppressed, implied, or taken for granted—in the said.

The lectures necessarily moved on a certain level of abstraction; so do the chapters into which they turned. The three case studies of concealment that follow are intended to provide evidence for the general analytic stance taken in *Understanding Conversion*. I hope that they will also suggest what light the hermeneutic program that I pursued can cast on three lives in widely separate social contexts. They are soundings taken in the fifth, twelfth, and twentieth centuries.

I have emphasized that tradition delivered not a single paradigm of conversion but an ill-matched repertory. Some paradigms defined transformations brought about by nature; others, changes possible only with the aid of divine grace. Some projected change as a movement toward future perfection; others, as a reversion to origins. The varieties and incompatibilities were many. But, woven by virtuosos into the intellectual fabric of philological culture, they all had roles in common discourse. Even the few comments on Augustine's use of the word *conversion* with which I began indicate quite distinct paradigms, all called "conversion," applied to personal repentance, the historical unfolding of the Church, and the movements of the cosmos.

Each paradigm had its own origin and vocabulary; each could be extracted from the repertory and launched toward a separate future. Accordingly, to point up modern adaptations of traditional ideas about conversion, I have decided in the last of these case studies to illustrate the blending of ancient, medieval, and modern elements in a work by Constantine Tsatsos. The quiltlike nature of tradition is evident in Tsatsos's recombination of Christian elements with what was essentially a doctrine of conversion drawn from pre-Christian philosophies. Indeed, one fascination of Tsatsos is how he drew not only on traditions conveyed through his Greek heritage but on all strands in European culture, to a degree generally impossible for writers in the West because of their unfamiliarity with modern and contemporary thinking in eastern Europe. In effect, he characteristically discarded Christian paradigms of conversion and reverted to ancient ones in order to make sense of his age.

Although Augustine and Herman-Judah called different things "conversion," they shared a supernatural point of reference. Tsatsos abandoned the supernatural; he retained the kind of speculation on natural being known as metaphysics. But the distance between his metaphysics and any metaphysics accepted by Augustine or Herman-Judah is indicated by the fact that his entire philosophy was existentialist, rooted in the circumstances of individual life being lived, rather than in any presumed eternal verities. Therefore, what he called conversion and what made that thinkable to him as conversion belonged to a realm of ideas quite alien to them.

By means of this comparison with Tsatsos, I hope to cast into sharper contrast than might otherwise be possible the virtuoso manipulation of elements in the repertory of conversion paradigms achieved by Augustine of Hippo, in North Africa under the late Roman Empire, and by Herman-Judah, in the Rhineland at the dawn of the Gothic age. Each deployed elements of the repertory in a distinctive program of manifestation and concealment. As already indicated, I also wish to emphasize the no-man's-land in poetics at which the fictional composition by Tsatsos coincides with the fictive narratives of Augustine and Herman-Judah.

The crux of differences between Tsatsos and the earlier writers is the fact that Christian doctrines of empathetic conversion began with the power of God and theodical questions arising from experiences of evil, while theodicy is almost entirely absent from his text. Moreover, the scope for empathy is very attenuated. For all three writers, however, concealment was a condition of the experience and the narrative of conversion. Despite their extreme differences, the hermeneutic project of conversion remained thinkable for them all because of metaphor, defined by tradition with a repertory of meanings. The project remained for them all seeing through a glass darkly, apprehending an analogical beauty hidden in the human soul through play that few could know. But this also entailed the more pedestrian task of making up something to say. As writers, they took for granted the difference between what was called conversion and a fictive tale about it.

Acknowledgments

In writing each of these studies, I have incurred obligations, which I here gratefully record. Because this collection of studies in some ways supplements a companion work, *Understanding Conversion*, I recall here the thanks that I expressed at greater length there: to the University of Virginia for the honor of delivering the Page-Barbour Lectures (1990), a task that brought both works together; and to the colleagues and friends who read the manuscripts and provided much welcome guidance, Professors Michael Adas, John Van Engen, Jo Ann McNamarra, and Thomas F. X. Noble. As she has often done before, Miss Mary Rall allowed me to draw on her treasury of good ideas.

The study of Augustine's *Confessions* and the translation of Herman-Judah's *Short Account* were completed, at least in broad outline, during my tenancy of a fellowship from the John Simon Guggenheim Memorial Foundation. The essay on Augustine was originally planned as a lecture that I was invited to deliver at Portland State University as part of a commemoration of the sixteen-hundredth anniversary of Augustine's baptism. I am grateful to Portland State University, and especially to Professors Michael Reardon and Lawrence Wheeler, for the opportunity to participate in the Visiting Scholars Program there. Ronald G. Talney, Esq., generously allowed me to print, in this essay, verses from his ode "Portlandia." I also thank Miss Ann Hyde and Mr. William Mitchell, of the Kenneth Spencer Research Library at the University of Kansas, for advice given during the writing of this essay.

The translation of Herman-Judah's *Short Account* is based on the authoritative edition by Gerlinde Niemeyer, *Hermannus quondam Iudaeus: Opusculum de Conversione Sua*, published by the Monumenta Germaniae Historica in 1963 (Series: Quellen zur Geschichte des Mittelalters, 4). Professor Dr. Horst Fuhrmann, president of the Monumenta, kindly granted permission to work from that text.

Four manuscripts of Herman's *Opusculum* exist. One, perhaps contemporary with the author, dates from the late twelfth century; a second, from the early thirteenth; and the remaining two, from the seventeenth century. In the commentaries that followed the publication of Niemeyer's edition, a distinguished scholar, Franz-Josef Schmale, maintained that at points readings from one of the seventeenth-century manuscripts were historically or grammatically more accurate than those provided by the twelfth-century manuscript taken by Niemeyer as the basis of her edition. He proposed that the seventeenth-century manuscript in question was actually closer to Herman's original text than the twelfth-century one (*Historische Zeitschrift* 200 [1965]: 114–20).

Instances are known in which learned and accurate humanists of the fourteenth century and later indulgently corrected what they considered the errors of medieval authors. However, I have been adequately convinced by Schmale's arguments to translate here and there not Niemeyer's established text but alternate readings provided in her critical apparatus. For ease of reference, I have included in the margins citations of corresponding pages in her edition. Citations in the text of the introduction are keyed to these marginal (*MGH*) references.

As indicated, the preliminary work for my introduction and translation was done during my tenure of a fellowship from the John Simon Guggenheim Memorial Foundation. Revision and writing was supported by a grant from the Graduate Research Fund of the University of Kansas. I acknowledge with deep thanks both this institutional support and the emendations proposed by my colleagues Professors Alan Sica and Clinton Howard. Professor Bernard S. Bachrach also gave me the benefit of a thorough reading.

Professor Theofanis G. Stavrou kindly encouraged me to undertake the case study on Constantine Tsatsos and published it, subtantially as it appears here, in *Modern Greek Studies Yearbook* 3 (1987): 99–127. I gladly record my obligation to Professor Stavrou for his encouragement, not on this occasion only, and for permission to reuse the essay here.

CASE 1

Augustine of Hippo's *Confessions*

Introduction

"You know, dear," Mrs. William Blake is reported to have said to her husband, "the first time you saw God was when you were four years old and he put his head to the window and set you a-screaming."[1] Whatever emotions this apparition may have stirred in Blake the child, the memory, reinforced by later experiences, registered a sharp emotional fissure in Blake the man. Alternate versions of one of his *Songs of Innocence and of Experience*, "The Divine Image," indicate this cleavage. In one version, Blake wrote:

> For Mercy has a human heart,
> Pity a human face,
> And Love, the human form divine,
> And Peace, the human dress.

In another, appended to the *Songs of Innocence and of Experience*, he expressed a different vision:

> Cruelty has a human heart,
> And Jealousy a human face,
> Terror, the human form divine,
> And Secrecy, the human dress.

The interchangeability of love and terror as having the "human form divine" is particularly striking.

I mention Blake at the beginning of a discussion of Augustine of Hippo

1

to underscore a connection between religion and art. For anyone who writes about conversion rather than experiencing it, it may be possible to understand (that is, to interpret) conversion. But for those who experience it, conversion is not so much understood as felt. The experience is esthetic, which is also to say affective, and often instantaneous (as seeing a face at the window). Some measure of understanding may come later, but that is understanding of what memory retained of an event, or of a concatenation of events, that is over. As I shall show, Augustine himself distinguished between understanding, as the instantaneous flash of perception, and interpretation, as the process of recollection and decipherment that followed and that could be expressed in words.

The recollection and whatever literary or pictorial representations it may inspire are works of art. Through them, experience has been translated into expression. The difference between experience and recollection, in the mind or in artistic forms, is important. Blake's literary and pictorial works and Augustine's *Confessions* are mnemonic testimonies to the depths of love and terror penetrated in the event, witnesses alike to the esthetic nature of conversion and to the inadequacy of artistic media, within their esthetic limits, to embody and convey that primal feeling. Removed as we are from the event itself, we are in the position of looking over the shoulders of the people to whom the events happened as they put together what had happened to them. Thus, for us understanding conversion through works of art actually means understanding the recollections embalmed in that work, rather than the living event of conversion.

Our task actually consists of several distinct enterprises: (1) understanding the purpose that an author (or painter) drew between the esthetic seizure of conversion and the work of art; (2) understanding the limits that a medium enforced upon the artist (e.g., the medium of painting allows certain kinds of expression but not others, which is why Blake used pictures to expand his text and vice versa); (3) understanding the process of understanding that the artist expected in his audience. To compare two conversions, for example those of the Apostle Paul and Augustine, is actually to compare not experiences that changed lives but narrative strategies of different authors, perhaps recalling, or choosing to recall, some aspects of those experiences on one day and others on the next.[2] Certainly, Augustine's recollections took the form of "attempts at creative writing" in more than one sense.[3]

Understanding (i.e., interpreting) the conversion of Augustine means: (1) understanding the objectives of the *Confessions*, the work of art in which he described his conversion; (2) understanding the deficiencies of language, as Augustine identified them; (3) understanding how Augustine understood understanding.

Any review of these particular subjects is bound to underscore the distinction between conversion (a thing felt) and a text (a thing made). It is also bound to draw a distinction between conversion as a supernatural transformation and the formal signs of such a change, for example the acceptance of a creed, submission to the rule of a particular institution, and commitment to a specific discipline. As indicated in *Understanding Conversion*, supernatural transformation was considered to be initiated, advanced, and completed, if at all, by grace. Without it, formal, institutional acts were a hypocritical charade. With it, believers mystically united with Christ could be called to withstand, or subvert, formal institutions, including those of religion, as prophets had done before them. Conversion was not an abrupt, dramatic peripety, but rather an enduring predicament.

We should also try to be aware of ways in which our understanding of understanding differs from Augustine. In science, observing a phenomenon changes the phenomenon. We shall be observing Augustine observing the phenomenon of his conversion, and change enters into each stage of observation. Clashing interpretive strategies in the minds of scholars explain how we can encounter "myriad Pauls and Augustines, all hotly defended by an appeal to the same data."[4] The disjunction between event and narrative in Augustine's own mind, compounded by the conflicting perspectives of his modern observers, has made it impossible to agree whether his conversion consisted of a single, cataclysmic event or a sequence of two or more "conversion experiences."[5] Of course, posing the question in this way conceals the fact that what a modern scholar calls conversion need not correspond with what Augustine called quite deliberately and specifically "conversion": the supernatural act by which God turned a soul to himself (see the Preface).

Before leaving Blake, I should like to emphasize some ways in which his interpretation of conversion and Augustine's coincided. In the first place, both men considered the works of their maturity to be extensions of great feelings that came to them in childhood. Further, what Blake and Augustine retained of their early visitations were resonances of love and dread. "What is that," Augustine wrote, "which pierces through me with light, and strikes my heart without rending it? I quail; I burn. I quail in as much as I am unlike it; I burn in as much as I am like it."[6] "I trembled," he wrote, "with love and horror."[7] Further, Blake and Augustine conceived of understanding as visual, not linguistic. Blake intended the visual components of his books to be not illustrations but illuminations, irradiating and disclosing the contents of words. "I question not my corporal or vegetative eye," Blake wrote, "any more than I would question a window concerning a sight. I look thro' it and not with it." And again:

> We are led to believe a lie
> When we see *with*, not *through*, the eye.[8]

Augustine, too, considered vision the primary sense. One could not speak at all, he judged, without images formed from memory.[9] He wrote: "We use this word ['to see'] also in regard to the other senses when we apply them to the act of knowing. . . . We say, not only, 'see how it shines'—which only the eyes can detect—but also 'see how it sounds,' 'see how it smells,' 'see how it tastes,' 'see how hard it is.'"[10] Like Blake, Augustine employed the tools of art to expand the medium of words. In his case words were indeed the medium, but the vivid theatricality of his prose constructed a singular rhetorical figure, one "which sets things before the eyes" in such a way that "the case seems, not to be stated, but to be enacted."[11] Thus, Augustine, too, sought to see through, rather than with, the eye of the body, so as to see truly with the eye of the mind. As a small child, Blake screamed when he saw God's face in the window. As an adult, Augustine wrote, he saw a single face in all the words of Scripture, "and I learned to exult with trembling."[12]

Visualizing texts in this fashion incurred the risks of the pathetic and affective fallacies, but such was Augustine's method of spiritual formation. As bishop, he advised his congregation how to sing Psalm 123:

> Those whom we read [about in the text of Scripture] sing exulting. These members of Christ sing this psalm in exultation. And who exults here [in this world] except in hope, as I said? For us, too, that same hope is assured, and we sing with exulting. For they who sing are not alien to us, yet the voice in this psalm is not ours. Hear [the psalm] as though you heard yourselves; hear it as though you were looking at yourselves in the mirror of the Scriptures. For when you look at the Scriptures as in a mirror, your face is transformed with gladness. When in exultation of hope you find yourself like the members of Christ who are singing these words, you will be in the company of those members, and you will sing these words.

The results of such an exercise could be shattering. As he heard the story of St. Anthony of Egypt's ascetic self-sacrifice, Augustine contemplated himself by comparison and saw how foul he was, how twisted and squalid, and, with horror, that there was no escape for him.[13] Was the face that each reader visualized in the mirror of Scripture, with joy and trembling, his own? "Sing," Augustine continued in his advice to his people, "sometimes as one, and sometimes as many; both because many are one and because Christ is one, and, in Christ, the members of Christ make one [body] with Christ." Therefore, it was the same, Augustine wrote, whether one or many sang; for "many men [*homines*] is [*sic*] one man [*homo*], because it (many men) is a unity; and Christ, as we said, is one, and all Christians are members of Christ."[14]

These words of Augustine point toward one last similarity with Blake: namely, the importance of singing in the process of visual understanding. For Blake, as for Augustine, song, and in particular psalmody, was a ritualized means of internalizing experience, of seeing through visual and verbal images and thereby reliving the erotic dread of conversion. One thought that I would like to stress is this: to understand how Augustine's mind worked, one has to understand how he felt art or, in other words, his esthetic. This esthetic may provide some insight into the way in which, as Augustine knew, religion partakes of art to deny it.

With these general observations in mind, I shall now turn to the three aspects of the task at hand: (1) Augustine's understanding of the *Confessions*; (2) his understanding of the limits of language; and (3) his understanding of understanding. My task is specifically to circumscribe, in some way, the passionate experience of which the *Confessions* was an artifact for which it is the only evidence. I shall draw my comments almost exclusively from that book.

Augustine's Understanding of the *Confessions*

Augustine wrote the *Confessions* between thirteen and fifteen years after his conversion. The singularity of the book is indicated by the fact that he never referred to his conversion in any other of his voluminous writings.[15] He began writing the *Confessions* on the tenth anniversary of his mother's death, and he ended the narrative of his spiritual quest by describing how she died in Ostia, as they were returning together to North Africa after his baptism in Milan at the hands of St. Ambrose (387 C.E.).[16] The Father gave no account of the tumultuous years in which, drawn from quasi-monastic retirement, he was ordained, first priest and then bishop, and, though ruling an inconspicuous see, became an eminent contender in

Church disputes. Recollection of his conversion may have been particularly selective given the fact that most of Augustine's closest companions in the years of his conversion had died. Few witnesses remained to add, modify, or contradict. Significantly, he recorded their deaths in the same book of the *Confessions* in which he portrayed his baptism and journey to Ostia.[17] Book 9 was the epitaph for his old life.

Instead of extending his spiritual autobiography to include the years of his episcopate, he provided four books of theoretical discourse on memory, on time, and on exegesis of the account of creation given in the first chapter of Genesis, including God's command to be fecund: "Increase and multiply" (Gen. 1:22, 28). He omitted all but the first weeks of his life after the second birth of baptism.

The *Confessions* has frequently been characterized as an intimate work of personal disclosure, but, if that is so, Augustine's omission of virtually his entire career within the Church indicates that he did not aim at full disclosure.[18] Occasionally he wrote about his confessions as the written text, open to many witnesses.[19] But from time to time he also insisted that his confessions were not the text, not works of the flesh, but that they were silent, words of the soul and the clamor of thought heard by the ear of God.[20] Augustine recognized an even more fundamental distinction: that between what the heart could confess and what it actually had to discuss. The human mind, blind and slothful as it was, wished to lie hidden, even while it wished nothing to be hidden from it,[21] and its great deep contained affects and movements of the heart more numerous than the hairs of the head.[22]

Therefore, his silent confession before God preceded the fleshly words that he uttered before men; but even in the silent confession, he could not confess to God anything that God had not already seen through his tight-closed heart, nor could he declare anything except what God first spoke to him.[23] Although the text of the *Confessions* is cast as a prayerful address to God, Augustine recounted his life and thought not to God but before God to his fellow human beings.[24] Why then did he present his confessions (cast into writings) to human beings, as though they could heal his sicknesses when they refused to hear from God what their own afflictions were? And how, indeed, could they know that he was telling the truth, since no one knows what goes on inside a human being except the spirit within the self?[25]

A fundamental question haunted even the unspoken confession inspired by God and uttered into God's ear. For as Augustine considered the thirty years before his conversion, "the hell of error"[26] when God remained hidden, he grasped the truth that from his hiding places God had broken Augustine's bones with the rod of discipline and smitten him on his open wounds to heal him. God, his tormentor, had laughed at his futile quest for honor, wealth, and advantageous marriage, laughing as his parents had laughed at the torments that when a boy, Augustine suffered from the schoolmaster's rod,[27] mocking Augustine as Augustine mocked God's servants and prophets.[28] Did not God's truth always mock man, even as God could laugh at Augustine, converted and consecrated, as he posed the queries in the *Confessions*?[29]

And so, Augustine asked, "Who made me? Was it not my God, not only good but the Good itself? How is it, then, that I can will to will the bad and will not to will the good? Is it so that I can be justly punished? Who put this in me and grafted in me the shoot of bitterness, since all that I came to be is from my sweetest God?"[30] Where, he asked, was God's right hand for all those long and anguished years, when, as eventually happened, it could draw forth in the twinkle of an eye that free will by which Augustine submitted to the yoke of Christ?[31]

But how much of these reflections was due to the theatrical rhetoric of the *Confessions*? Surely Augustine displayed his sufferings and asked these questions for the benefit of his readers, remembering the distinction between the confession that was felt and the words that were uttered.[32]

For what purpose did Augustine make the sense of his conversion? He wrote for sacramental, evangelistic, and polemical objectives. As "a sacrifice of praise,"[33] the *Confessions* was intended to call forth other sacrifices. It was meant to lead readers to remember his parents, Monica and Patricius, with intercessions at the altar, and especially to arouse many to give thanks to God on Augustine's account and to pray for him, loving in Augustine what should be loved and bewailing what should be bewailed, but always sending up hymns of thanksgiving and tears of lamentation in God's presence from brotherly hearts, his thuribles.[34] Augustine wished to stir up all who adored God to bless God and God's name on hearing his confessions, for they could know from his words out of how great a depth one has to cry out to God.[35] Some part of his evangelistic purpose was served by scriptural exegesis, a confession of what he found in God's books concerning the wonders that God had performed from the beginning, when he made heaven and earth, to their consummation in the everlasting kingdom of his holy city.[36]

Aware of his own celebrity, he had reason to hope that as in the case of the distinguished Roman rhetorician Victorinus, collective joy over the conversion of one person known to many would inflame many to follow his example.[37]

Despite all these objectives the *Confessions* remained, in its author's frame of reference, a gift; the fruit of any gift was "the good and upright will of the giver"—in this case, neither the text nor even Augustine as he was, but rather Augustine as he is and he might yet be, serving his brethren according to God's command not only with words but also with deeds.[38]

Augustine did not declare his polemical objectives as plainly as he did the sacramental and evangelistic ones, but his assertion that the fruit of the *Confessions* was himself demands some reference to the controversies in which he passed his life. "With a fury do I hate those who are enemies [to the great deep of your words, O God]. O that you would kill them with a two-edged sword, and they would not be its enemies. For my love for them demands that they be killed to themselves in order to live to you."[39] The savagery of this brief passage, in which love and hatred converge, is unusual in the *Confessions*, though in another passage Augustine recalled how, just after his conversion, he gnashed his teeth in rage when he could not make the Manichees see the error of their doctrines.[40] This severity has an unspoken link with an observation on idle curiosity. In this life—a vast forest, full of ambushes and dangers, he wrote—he no longer went to the circus games to watch hounds chase hares; but if he were riding through a field and saw such a hunt, it would seize his attention. Often, he said, he would sit at home, watching lizards catch flies or spiders entangling them in their webs. Vagrant thoughts of such things rushed into his mind and destroyed the concentration of his prayer.[41]

The chase of predator and victim was by no means an idle distraction. The Donatist controversy had long since reached a pitch of violence that included the abduction, torture, and murder of hostile clerics. Eventually the Donatist bishops raged publicly and privately against Augustine, arguing "that he was a wolf to be killed in defense of their flock and that there could be no doubt at all that God would forgive the sin of any man who killed him." He escaped several ambushes.[42] The Donatist controversy occupied Augustine for decades; it is not clear when these threats and plots occurred. But factional violence was endemic in North Africa long before Augustine became bishop. He had no need to look abroad, to the attempts in another doctrinal dispute to kidnap and to murder his baptizer, Bishop Ambrose of Milan, by witchcraft and the sword, to believe that he himself served his brethren "in immense danger" that would overwhelm him were he not sheltered by God's protecting wings.[43]

In his polemical zeal against those whom he considered the enemies of God's word, Augustine was both hunter and hunted. The *Confessions* was by no means an isolated work, written in leisurely retrospection. It was composed at the same time as important treatises against the Donatists and the Manichees and in the midst of a series of debates, conferences, and daily skirmishes among religious factions. Like other episcopal sees in North Africa, Hippo was divided between the Donatists and their enemies. Each faction had its own bishop; indeed, inside the walls of his own church Augustine could hear the sounds of revelry from the Donatist cathedral across the street.[44] The serenely retrospective character of the *Confessions* is a conscious dramatic foil to the polemical context in which it was written and in which contemporary readers were intended to place it. In fact, there is reason to think that Augustine himself regarded the *Confessions* as a keystone of his polemical effort, rather than as a diversion from it.[45]

The fruit of the *Confessions*, Augustine said, was himself, as he was at the time of writing and as he might yet become.[46] At the distance of centuries, it is easy to forget that in the heat of the conflicts that engaged him, one practical matter may have been prior to questions of doctrine: namely, the canonical validity of Augustine's title as bishop and, consequently, his authority to preach the word and dispense the sacraments of God.[47] Even as he was completing the *Confessions*, two prominent Donatists impugned his orthodoxy. Despite his alleged conversion, they charged, he was still a Manichee, a fact that he concealed by cynical conjuring tricks with words.[48] Convinced that the moral impurity of a priest invalidated sacraments that he performed, the Donatists considered that Augustine stood in a succession of counterfeit bishops who neither received nor conveyed the gifts of the Holy Spirit. First, he had not resigned his appointment as master of rhetoric in Milan immediately upon his conversion.[49] Thus, while recruited to the army of God, he continued to sit in the seat of lying.[50] This, together with other horrible and deadly sins, he believed had been remitted in baptism. The second possible defect in his title arose because Augustine had been consecrated as bishop while his predecessor was still alive. He became convinced (though in error) that his ordination violated canons of the general council of Nicaea, and he took pains to secure ecclesiastical legislation in North Africa to ensure that no others would repeat his own "uncanonical" accession.[51]

Eventually, Augustine's conflict with the Donatists brought him to frame a comprehensive justification of persecution. While he was writing the *Confessions*, his efforts were directed toward reconciliation. Possibly for this reason, and to evade the painful issue of canon law alleged against him, he did not directly confront canonical challenges to his episcopal title. Instead, he presented his case indirectly. He drew attention to his spiritual credentials. Long before, Quintilian had advised this method of arguing a case, especially in circumstances that made it dangerous to speak plainly, "intimating by some suspicion that we excite that something is to be understood which we do not express."[52]

Augustine took great pains to assert that God had presided over his conversion at every stage and, in fact, that God was, in some sense, the coauthor of the *Confessions*. Monica, he wrote, had striven to make God Augustine's father in place of his genetic father, Patricius, and God assisted her in that effort, though, obedient to divine command, she continued to serve Patricius, even as she also overcame him.[53] The dramatic form of the *Confessions*, an address to God, was designed to emphasize the intimacy of Augustine's relationship to God and to stress that Augustine could confess only what God wished him to utter and, indeed, what God had already spoken to him, that God resolved doctrinal predicaments for Augustine and recalled to his memory events that he had forgotten.[54] When, after his conversion, he recognized the depth and wretchedness of his sins, his heart was troubled; he considered fleeing into solitude.

But God, he wrote, forbade flight and comforted him,[55] implicitly setting him on the road to the episcopate. Throughout, even at times when Augustine seemed furthest from him, God had been close at hand, acting according to the order which he had predestined the course of events to follow.[56]

Analogues to his conversion underscored the effect of divine intervention. The parallels of Victorinus and St. Anthony of Egypt came readily to mind.[57] Chapters describing the latter stages of his conversion are replete with quotations from the letters of St. Paul, whose doctrines, Augustine wrote, he took into his most inward being (*inviscerabantur*) at that crisis.[58] He adverted to the parable of the prodigal son, the widow's lost penny, and the lost sheep, brought home on the Shepherd's shoulders, to remind his readers that there was more rejoicing over the redemption of one sinner than over ninety and nine just persons who needed no repentance.[59] Recounting his departure from the Manichees, he illuminated the condition in which he and his widowed mother found themselves with the miracle in which Christ commanded the dead son of a widow to arise and, when the boy revived and began to speak, restored him to his mother.[60]

Augustine's purpose was not to record a history of his conversion, and the establishment of his credentials entailed the suppression of evidence. Some information, no doubt, was lost, as the Father said, through forgetfulness, and some, omitted for the sake of speeding the narrative along.[61]

Because of Augustine's emphasis on his childhood and parental relationships, his omissions concerning his family are particularly notable.[62] From other sources, we know that Augustine had a sister and a brother, Navigius, who was with Augustine, Monica, and other companions in their retreat at Cassiciacum between Augustine's spiritual crisis and his baptism. In the *Confessions* Augustine recorded that his brother (unnamed) attended Monica on her deathbed in Ostia and was gently rebuked by her. (In contrast, he referred frequently to Alypius, his disciple and companion in the conversion, and eventually his fellow bishop, as "the brother of my heart.")[63]

Otherwise, it would be possible to conclude from the *Confessions* that Augustine was an only child and that his spiritual welfare was the single preoccupation of his mother and his baptism, the only thing for which she wished to remain in this life.[64] In the construction of his self-portrait, Augustine accentuated Monica's piety and the favors that she received from God, notably through years of tearful intercession on his behalf. God, he wrote, was Monica's "most inward master, teaching her in the school of her breast."[65] Augustine thus circumscribed himself with an aura of holiness, especially in connection with Monica's desire that God supplant Patricius as Augustine's father, an idea that resonates with pre-Christian legends of the demigods. But, given his portrayal of Monica's powerful religious devotion, it seems hardly probable that she was indifferent to the spiritual development of her other children, especially since Augustine's sister ended her long life as head of an ascetic community of women. His brother's daughters, also unmentioned by Augustine, became ascetics, too, "likewise in God's service."[66]

Augustine's remarks, including those dismissive of his father, represent dimly, if at all, very large sections of the family context in which his spirituality was formed.

Enough has been said to indicate that in the polemical setting of his life and work, Augustine composed the *Confessions* to vindicate his spiritual title, if not also his canonical one, as a dispenser of God's word and sacraments. It remains, however, to suggest how this hunted hunter shaped the *Confessions* not as personal disclosure so much as evangelistic refutation of his enemies. That shaping is evident in the dominant themes of conversion, suffering, and eroticism, and in the unusual genre of the book.

The most patent refutation is the theme of conversion. The Donatists defined themselves as a closed community of the morally perfect; and, shunning others, they withdrew, as the righteous few, from social exchanges, and much more from ecclesiastical fellowship, with the impure. Against this concept of a clearly defined, exclusive community, Augustine held up the slow and often hidden course of conversion and the need, even of the converted, to continue striving for perfection. All life, he wrote (quoting from the Book of Job), was one temptation.[67] As the dispenser of God's sacrament, he was still beset by sexual fantasies, even when he was awake. In his dreams he followed them beyond delight to relive, in sleep, the lascivious motions of the act itself. Perfection would come when death was swallowed up in victory.[68]

In other writings Augustine referred to the Apostles' catch of good and bad fish in the same net, comparing the Church with a dragnet, containing good and evil until the Last Judgment. Recognizing that the evil might eventually be converted into good, he posed the example not only of his own conversion but also that of Victorinus, in extreme old age, a man with whose eloquent tongue the Devil had slain many, and who, by virtue of his celebrity, served as a model for the conversions of others.[69] Knowledge of saved and damned belonged to God alone. "Look mercifully upon these things, O Lord," Augustine wrote early in the *Confessions*, "and free us who already call to you; free also those who do not yet call to you that they may call to you and you may free them."[70] The fruit of the *Confessions* was not what Augustine had been but what he was and what he might still become.[71]

Suffering, a second major theme in the *Confessions*, addressed the insistence of the Donatists that persecution by the unbelieving world ratified their holiness and, indeed, that they could promote their own salvation by goading their enemies to slaughter them. Later, in his dispute with Pelagius, Augustine greatly hardened his insistence that salvation came through grace, not works; but already in the *Confessions*, there was present the doctrine of dependence that characterized his later teaching and, to be sure, the very sentence that, in Pelagius's view, exalted grace to the exclusion of works. For as he recorded the sexual illusions that distracted him as bishop, he repeatedly appealed to God, who had commanded him to abstain from concupiscence of the flesh, to give what he had commanded.[72]

Accordingly, Augustine developed his theme so as to dissolve any causal connection between suffering and salvation. Part of his tactic was to trivialize suffering by portraying it as an arrow in the rhetorician's quiver and, thus, by reflecting on the calculated effects of the *Confessions* themselves. People took fascinated pleasure in the sufferings of others, he observed.

Lusts for dominance, seeing, and feeling served the lust of doing harm, whether in revenge or in pleasure at a another's misfortune, such as delighted the spectators of gladiatorial combat or those who made others their laughingstocks and butts.[73] Curiosity, one of the most destructive of human traits, drew them to run in droves to gape at a butchered corpse, even if they went pale at the sight and dreaded seeing it in their dreams.[74]

As a schoolboy Augustine had wept over Dido's suicide for love.[75] He had observed in the theater that audiences loved to weep; spectators participated empathetically in the sorrows enacted before them. Their sorrow was their delight.[76] At a higher level of reality, he knew that in actual misfortunes grief and weeping sweetened the bitterness of life, though the reason why eluded him.[77] The autobiographical sections of the *Confessions* are full of pain and awash with tears, in the revenge that, out of envy, an infant took on the world by wailing,[78] in grief at death and parting, in the raging madness of sexual desire, which Augustine felt as though he were beaten with red-hot rods of iron.[79]

Augustine displayed many varieties of suffering to his readers, from the beatings of children by their teachers, of slaves by their masters, and of wives by their husbands to mockery, to the inward agonies of self-hatred and loathing, to physical sickness, to the glorious deaths of martyrs. In all this, he realized that he was manipulating the empathetic snares of tragic theater, in which spectators could not help the sufferer but only witness and delight in his misery.[80] He knew that he would thereby engage the imaginations of readers who were driven by curiosity to pry into another man's life but slow to correct their own. Readers wished to hear him confess what he was within, but neither their eye, nor their ear, nor their mind could probe his heart, where he was whoever he was. They were willing to believe him, but would they know him from his text?[81]

One response to the Donatist morality of suffering, therefore, was to establish that not all pain sanctified, just as not every violent death was martyrdom. In fact, the appearance of suffering could be an illusion, conjured up by tricks of drama and rhetoric.

A second response concerned the suffering that comprised so notable a part of Augustine's relationship with God, as he portrayed it. The Donatists taught that believers could ratify their own salvation by deliberately achieving martyrdom. In the special context of spiritual life, Augustine portrayed suffering as an act of grace, bestowed by God, and, more exactly, a seal of man's dependence for salvation on divine grace, rather than on his own powers. God was Augustine's laughing torturer, a ravenous, consuming fire; he smote and wounded Augustine. God was both torturer and physician. He struck to heal; he killed men that they might not die.[82] He broke Augustine's bones with his rod so that they might rejoice; he struck his open wounds to convert and heal him; he bludgeoned his face until his eyes were swollen shut so as to heal the darkness of his mind; he administered wholesome bitterness to recall sinners to himself. In his consuming fury as fire, he devoured the dead cares of the elect and refashioned them to immortality.[83] Was not Christ crucified the medicine for the wounds of mankind, the medicine, itself tormented, hanging on a tree?[84] It was essential for Augustine that believers participated in the suffering of Christ even as they participated in his glory, that the mystery of themselves was subsumed in his sacrifice and laid upon the altar.[85] Understandably, the nearer God drew to Augustine with his therapeutic mercies, the more wretched Augustine became.[86]

The greatest of all themes for Augustine, in the *Confessions* and elsewhere—more inclusive still than conversion or suffering—was eroticism. In the *Confessions* his development of that theme, like those of conversion and suffering, was shaped by a concurrent polemical program. Although Donatist teachings on sexual purity had a bearing on his account, his thought about eroticism was directed chiefly toward the Manichee doctrine of celibacy. Behind that doctrine stood the same materialistic dualism that so long prevented him from understanding anthropomorphic passages in Scripture as figurative allusions to God as a purely spiritual being and the possibility that Jesus could truly be God incarnate, and not merely an impassible phantom. Augustine's questions quoted earlier—"Who made me [capable of willing good or evil]? Was it not my God, not any good, but the Good itself?"[87]—introduce the chapters in which Augustine described how he found his way out of the labyrinth of Manichee doctrine; and, in fact, the series of questions continues with a sketch of that dualism. If God, good itself, did not make all that was Augustine, did the Devil make him—the Devil who, the Manichees taught, was the principle of action in his character as evil, while God, the principle of good, was passive and suffered evil?[88]

Augustine's realization that there was a spiritual order of being enabled him to grasp that man was made in the image and likeness of God, not in any material sense but in the faculties and dispositions of the soul and, particularly, in the dominant affect, love.

According to the *Confessions*, Augustine confused eroticism with sensuality until his conversion. His ornate portrayals of adolescent lust—of competition with his male peers, of an assignation clinched within the very walls of a church while a liturgy was in progress,[89] and of his long delights in the chains of venery's "death-bearing sweetness"[90]—betray a further confusion of eroticism with sexuality, one that lingered, as I said, in fantasies that overtook the bishop when his guard was down. Yet the scope of eroticism could not be confined to the sexual bonding of men and women, even when the play of lust was given free reign.[91]

There is no hint of affection in the only marriage described by Augustine, that of his parents; and in the calculating discussion of marriage undertaken by Augustine and his closest companions "in the search for truth," the only characteristic specified for a wife was that she should have enough money comfortably to defray their expenses.[92] While he grieved to be parted from his first mistress, the mother of his son, and felt wounded to the shedding of his heart's blood, he quickly took a second mistress and in time realized that he had entered into cohabitation out of a vagrant ardor devoid of prudence. He recorded the name of neither mistress. Only seven women—six anonymous and briefly mentioned—appear in the account of Augustine's spiritual venture, long before, as bishop, he made a practice of keeping his distance from them.[93] Augustine recognized that in Christ there was neither male nor female, neither Jew nor Greek, neither slave nor free; but he was also convinced that God had made females subordinate to males. Women might well be the equals of men in their rational intelligence; but their sexual subordination represented, for Augustine, the proper hierarchy of mental faculties, the acts of appetite being ruled by reason, just as, at a higher level, those of reason, rightly ordered, were subject to the understanding.[94]

Augustine's conviction of women's subordination to men, by virtue of sexuality, is evident in his uncomplaining portrayal of how in his childhood many matrons, the wives of relatively gentle men, commonly went about with their faces disfigured by beatings, while Monica evaded bludgeoning by her fierce husband by not rising up in pride against him. For she understood that in serving Patricius, she served God, who had commanded her to do so.[95]

Thus, even the filial piety in Augustine's description of Monica, whose continual devotion and prayers were paramount in his spiritual venture, betrays distinct limits. In another treatise, written shortly after Augustine's conversion, the Father referred to Monica's occasional use of "vulgar and bad Latin," a passage of interest in light of Augustine's reference, as a rhetorician, in the *Confessions* to those men who hated others and cast them from the company of men because of inelegant pronunciation and errors of the tongue.[96] When his riotous sexuality began to blossom, Monica determined not to bridle him with marriage, advising him only not to fornicate with another man's wife; and for the rest, with Patricius, she had an eye chiefly to what would make him a great and prosperous orator.[97] Ambrose of Milan corrected her for the rustic devotions that she paid at the shrines of martyrs. God himself punished her with the lash of sorrows for her carnal attachment to Augustine.[98] Monica was, Augustine wrote, "a woman in dress, a man in faithfulness."[99]

Eroticism was not absorbed in the ardor of a man for a woman, nor yet in the love of a man for men. At every stage of his progress through degrees of sensuality to spirituality, Augustine's closest companions were other males.[100] He grieved extravagantly at the death in youth of one companion whose friendship was "sweet above all sweetnesses of this life."[101] "Can it sometimes or somewhere be unjust to love God with all one's heart and all one's soul and all one's mind and to love a neighbor as yourself?" he asked. Those shameful acts, contrary to nature, such as the sodomites performed, he answered, were everywhere and always to be despised and punished; and even if such acts were common to all nations, divine law would still condemn them, for God did not make men to use one another in that fashion.[102]

All human loves passed away and perished. His conversion revealed to Augustine that if bodies delighted, one's love should be directed to God, who made them; if souls, they should be loved in God. For true friendship existed only when God fixed it by infusing charity into the hearts of them who cleaved together.[103] All loves must be subsumed in love of God, a supreme eroticism, in which the human soul enfolded in the embraces of God, flowed into God, purged and liquified by the fire of his love.[104]

Profound ambiguities of gender defined this spiritual fusion. Knowing those who devoured by loving, just as they ate bread,[105] Augustine portrayed the soul as an infant, suckling the milk of God and enjoying him, the bread that is not corrupted.[106] Jesus also appeared ambiguously as a bridegroom, going forth from his marriage chamber, the Virgin's womb, a giant to run a race,[107] and again as the wisdom of God, giving milk to nourish the infancy of believers, himself the bread of life.[108] Augustine, the male, imagined his female soul, liquifying with ardor, in God's embraces.[109] Masculine and feminine combined yet again in Augustine's portrayal of the redeemed soul both as a "member of the bride [the Church]" and as a member of Christ, the bridegroom, and "the bridegroom's friend" (*sponsi amicus*),[110] its dross consumed by God, the ravening fire.

These erotic ambiguities, with the associations of eating and being eaten—and thus of the victim's assimilation into the body of the loving predator—were completed by Augustine's paradox that continence was the fecund mother of many children by God, her husband.[111]

When he alluded to his first mistress, Augustine remarked on the difference between marriage, concluded for the begetting of children, and a compact of lust, such as he had entered, in which children might be born to parents who had no desire for them, although, once born, an infant might force his parents to love him.[112] He developed the erotic theme as a progression from the compact of lust, with its intended sterility, to the ecstatic passion of charity, in which, with fecund continence, the womb of the Church brought forth hosts of children for God, her spouse.[113] Augustine portrayed Monica's triumphant joy at his conversion, knowing that what she had desired for him would be fulfilled far more abundantly and in a far more precious and chaste way than it could have been with offspring of his flesh.[114] The transformation of the theme is complete in the ornate discourse on the fecundity of the Church with which Augustine ended the *Confessions*, a fecundity promoted by the dispensers of God's word and sacraments, administering the understanding of divine mysteries and setting forth by their conduct patterns of life that aroused the faithful to imitation.[115]

Here Augustine returned to the themes of conversion and, thus, of suffering. For even in the spiritual subordination within the Church, repeating that of female to male, there existed some uncertainty. The erotic fusion with God renewed the soul in the image of God but did not enable even spiritual rulers to prejudge the results of their fecundation. They could not distinguish between spiritual and carnal men, who "are known to your eyes, our God, and have not yet become manifest to us by their works; so that by their fruits we might know them; but you, O Lord, already know them, and have divided and called them in secret, before the firmament was made."[116]

How did Augustine understand the *Confessions*? Clearly, he considered it a work that in its sacramental, evangelistic, and polemical aspects would enhance the fecundity of the Church. Against the perfectionism of his enemies, he argued that God's plan for human experience had not yet been fully achieved and that, in ignorance of its ultimate form, enemies should come together in the bond of charity. In the din of conflict, one could scarcely hear God's call.[117] Augustine's suppression of evidence indicates that he also considered the *Confessions* a work of art, if not also of artifice, and one designed to attest his spiritual authority. Evidently, the superior skill of some Donatist leaders in rhetoric also challenged him to demonstrate his own mastery of the arts of eloquence.[118]

The meticulous care with which Augustine constructed the *Confessions* is nowhere more evident than in Book 8, the dramatic portrayal of the climactic moment of his conversion.[119] Throughout, he identified materialism as the barrier to conversion, whether in its intellectual aspect, as the doctrines of the Manichees, or, more fundamentally, in its erotic aspect, as his powerful sexuality. The intellectual turning point came first, when, through Ambrose's public teaching, Augustine grasped the idea that material figures of thought and speech could—and, in Scripture, must—be authentically understood as witnesses to spiritual reality. Book 8 sets forth the application of this insight to Augustine's sensual existence.

Thus, he led toward his own conversion across the stepping-stones of three others—those of Victorinus (8.2), the Apostle Paul (8.4), and Anthony of Egypt (8.6). Victorinus, the celebrated Roman rhetorician, he plainly put forward as a surrogate of himself in his secular occupation, without reference to sensuality except for emphasizing the difference between the spoken word and belief, which latter was achieved not because Victorinus read the Scriptures but because the Lord poured himself into Victorinus's heart. Augustine underscored this assertion of dependence on grace by observing that the greatest joy was often preceded by the greatest pain and that the unlikely conversion of a sinner, the Church's victory over a declared enemy, caused greater rejoicing in heaven than the constancy of the good, as exemplified both by Victorinus and, supremely, by Paul. His allusion to Paul, the analyst par excellence of the struggle between flesh and spirit, set the stage for Augustine's assertion that his sexuality remained a great barrier to his conversion. This, in turn, prepared for the account of Anthony's conversion to a life of chastity, reinforced by examplars of others who had imitated him, which Augustine himself immediately took to heart.

The portrayal of the climactic moment then begins (8.8), but, to heighten suspense and draw attention to his main theme, Augustine interrupts his narrative with three chapters (8.9–11) reflecting on the divided wills in the human heart, enacted, above all, in the warfare of flesh against spirit. Dramatic resolution of the narrative is heralded by his elaborate praise of the fecund continence of the Church's spiritual life. Immediately, he moved to the climax itself, for which the entire book—and indeed all earlier books—had prepared. Augustine now replaces his surrogate, Victorinus, embraces both the paradigmatic celibacy of Anthony and the practice of bibliomancy that induced it, and passes through the crisis by absorbing into his very being the words of Paul. His conversion thus subsumes those with which the book began, and in the denouement Monica rejoices in the celibacy by which greater progeny would be given to Augustine than she had hoped for from his flesh.

Apart from Augustine's attention to broad structural lines, many details illustrate his preoccupation with intricate connections that he wished to suggest to the readers' minds. For example, he chose two places in the narrative at which to assert that he became a perplexity, or question (*quaestio*), to himself. The first instance occurs in his discussion of the profound grief that afflicted him in youth at the death of a friend (4.4), a discourse that led to his conclusion that he was cured of his suffering by realizing that all was rightly love of God and that one should love a friend in God and an enemy because of him (4.9: "factus eram ipse mihi magna quaestio"). Augustine repeated the same statement in his great discourse on sensual knowledge (10.33: asking to be cured by God "in cuius oculis mihi quaestio factus sum, et ipse est languor meus"), as he worked toward the doctrine that, in the pursuit of wisdom and piety, Christ was the only true and sufficient mediator.

Two other instances, not plotted out as coordinates identifying the Christological center of Augustine's thought, will illustrate the care with which he designed and executed his narrative. For example, he referred to the public baths twice: first, when describing how his father joyfully observed his sexual maturity in the bath and, again, when recounting how, following his conversion, he went to the bath for emotional release after Monica's funeral.

The second passage is a sequel to the first, for it serves as a prologue to his decision for a life of continence and to the panegyric on the fecund chastity of the Church.[120] It cannot have been accidental that after employing the instance of eating a fig to illustrate the folly of the Manichees' materialism, he portrayed the emotional crisis of his conversion—and, he thought, final emancipation from the Manichees' doctrinal errors—as occurring beneath a fig tree, the allegorical symbol of the conversion of Nathaniel, "an Israelite in whom there is no guile," and the foreshadowing of Christ's second coming.[121]

A greater, overarching design encompassing these incidents is indicated by the symmetry of Augustine's references to peace in the first and the last chapters of the *Confessions* and in the construction of his narrative around the progressive conversion of flaming sexuality, with its intended barrenness, by means of a dumbfounding call to continence, with its spiritual fecundity.

The Limitations of Words

In the main, Augustine developed his linguistic doctrines in works composed after the *Confessions*. Still, in the *Confessions* he did set down in broad outline the guiding principles of his later thought, and these are sufficient to demonstrate his abiding conviction that understanding was not linguistic. It is important to take note of those ideas, however briefly, in order to clarify Augustine's understanding both of conversion and of the *Confessions*.

As noted above, Augustine distinguished between the actual confessions that he poured forth to God in silence and the text that represented them.[122] The differences between them correspond roughly with those between supernatural conversion and its formal signs (demonstrable by human, institutional norms). Augustine frequently lamented the inadequacy of words, as creatures not of God but of human capacity, to convey supernatural knowledge. Words, indeed, did not even arise from human nature as God created it, but rather from human convention. More precisely, the cause of pronouncing words physically was sin—"the abyss of this world and the blindness of the flesh," which cannot see thoughts. The disability of sin made it necessary to speak aloud into the ears.[123] In the world to come, the saints would apprehend each other's thoughts without the medium of words, just as also the very words of the Gospels would be unneeded; even here, as St. Paul wrote, "tongues are for a sign not to them that believe but to them that believe not."[124]

The multiplicity of doctrinal disputes in which Augustine was embroiled, his own slowness in grasping the sense within the text of Scripture as he portrayed it in the *Confessions*, and, finally, the various interpretations that the *Confessions* itself aroused all indicated that authentic understanding of the supernatural could not be linguistic.[125] Many words of commentary could indicate little understanding; to explain more was not to understand more.[126] Words were commodities that could be sold, vessels that readers filled according to their own understanding and not according to the intent of the author.[127] Human beings, too, were vessels, made to honor or dishonor and filled, if redeemed, with the Holy Spirit.[128] They were able to pour into the vessels of words such signification as they themselves contained. The Manichees uttered the syllables of the names of God, Jesus, and the Paraclete, but they had only the sound and racket of the tongue; their heart was empty of truth. Likewise, Augustine himself, in writing his first treatise, *On the Beautiful and the Fitting*, deployed the corporal figments of words but displayed only his own collapse under the weight of pride, since he lacked the sweet truth of God's inner melody.[129]

Words were inadequate even at the descriptive level,[130] inadequate to praise God—can the tongue of one man explain what the thought of no man explains?[131]—and inadequate to enlighten any man who comes into the world.[132] Ambrose's use of the figurative, or "spiritual," interpretation of Scripture freed Augustine from the literal understanding that had intruded materialism into his thinking about God. He realized that, yet more sublimely than rhetoricians, the authors of Scripture had employed words both to conceal and to disclose. What he had once taken to be the rustic simplicity of their style, far inferior to Cicero's elegance, was in fact a tactic of deliberate obscurity, intended to make recovery of the authentic message hard, to bar the lighthearted, and to delight the faithful and persevering readers by the surprise of discovery. When he understood that Scripture's most open words and humble style preserved in profound understanding the dignity of its secret, Augustine also perceived that few could apprehend the depth of the supernatural mystery that God hid from the wise and revealed to the simple.[133]

Augustine recalled that Ambrose had frequently quoted the Apostle's saying, "The letter killeth, but the spirit giveth life" (2 Cor. 3:6). Not words but beauty moves us toward what we love; not words but love in the one kindles love in the other.[134] Understanding was not linguistic but affective. For this reason, the unlearned rose up and took heaven by force, while men of letters lay behind them, wallowing in creatures of flesh and blood.[135] How could readers of Moses and of Augustine know that they had written the truth? Here, too, the answer was not in the text but in the affects of the reader. For those who read the texts in love of one another and of God and in thirst for truth would have the assurance of charity that the authors had not lied, no matter how many and diverse the interpretations placed upon their words.[136]

Augustine's conviction that he wrote under divine impulse and inspiration suggests that the assurance would come to his readers, as to Moses', when the truth that chose to speak through his words also, in the silence in which God speaks, said to the reader in his reading what it had chosen to say to the author in his writing.[137]

When, therefore, our Lord Jesus Christ shall come and, as the Apostle Paul says, will bring to light the things of darkness and will make manifest the thoughts of the heart . . . then, such a day being present, lamps will not be needed. No prophet will be read to us; no book [*codex*] of an apostle will be opened. We shall not require the testimony of John; we shall not need the gospel itself. . . . What shall we then see? I beseech you, love with me; run, by believing, with me. . . . John himself says, and I recalled this verse yesterday, "Most beloved, we are the sons of God; and it hath not yet appeared what we shall be; we know that, when He shall appear, we shall be like him, for we shall see him as he is." . . . I am going to lay down this book [*codex*], and you, too, are going to depart, everyone to his own house. It has been good for us to be in the common light, good to have been glad in it, good to have exulted in it, but when we depart from one another, let us not depart from him.[138]

Understanding Understanding

By now, it is clear that understanding for Augustine was a matter of affective, or empathetic, participation, rather than of verbal communication, and that it occurred, to use Blake's term, by seeing through, not with, the eyes of the body.[139] The distance between the supernatural and human nature and its works (for example, words) is also evident. Commenting on a passage from 1 Corinthians (13:12), Augustine similarly underscored Paul's insistence that in this world we see through a mirror in an enigma. Thus, the Father wrote, the enlightened mind saw through itself to the Trinity, of which it was an image, while the unenlightened saw no farther than the reflecting surface, not knowing "that the mirror that they see is a mirror, that is, an image."[140] The memory, he argued, was the seeing faculty of the soul; the mind, its vision.[141] Understanding depended upon the degree of correspondence between the external world and the picture in the mind formed out of the images stored in memory.[142] Why, he asked, did the external world, accessible to the senses, appear this way to one man and that to a second, speaking to the one and mute to the other? In fact, he wrote, "it speaks to all; but they understand it who compare the voice received from the outside with the truth within."[143] Thus, when, before he submitted to baptism, he wrote *On the Beautiful and the Fitting*, he was led astray by corporeal images, for God had not yet lit the inward candle of his mind and rendered its bodily fictions transparent.[144]

Augustine drew the metaphor of the picture in the mind from art. He employed it to illustrate the contrast between God, whose self-sufficient being and making from nothing were identical, and a human artisan, forming one body from another by a judgment of his soul, "which is able to impose whatever shape it sees inside itself with its internal eye." The artisan, Augustine wrote, was entirely dependent on God's creative act. From that act, the artisan received his mind, body, materials, and the art by which he could see inwardly what he should do outwardly. From God, he received the ability and the norm by which he critically measured the physical work of art against the truth that directed his mind to judge whether the work was well done.[145] The elaborate paradigm of understanding presupposed in the *Confessions* and further developed in subsequent writings postulates the artist imagining, executing, and judging a work.

Augustine defined the conditions, possibilities, and limits that governed the formation of pictures in the mind. The memory, he wrote, was the "stomach," or "treasury," of the mind, in which the materials were deposited. These consisted of several kinds. Some were actually present themselves in the mind. These included the basic elements of literary, dialectical, and mathematical activities, although, to be sure, these principles were dispersed and neglected without formal education.[146] The so-called perturbations—desire, joy, fear, and sadness—were also immediately present, as, indeed, was the blessed life, which was the joy that was God himself.[147] Data "ingested" and "congested" by the senses were present only as "images," through sensory impressions. Still more remote were words, present in the memory as images of images; for example, the word *sun* would be in the memory as the result of a primary image (the visual impression of the sun) perceived through a secondary image ("what the sound of this name signifies").[148]

In view of what has already been said about words, it is important to observe Augustine's argument that the meanings of words were learned kinesthetically and, moreover, by kinesthetic formation of the affects. At every stage of his spiritual pilgrimage, as Augustine recorded it, he learned the sense of words through physical experience. The "sense" of a word was the picture in the mind. It was not a verbal meaning but an association of components in the memory that were prior to any articulated word and prior even to any thought of an articulated word.[149] Sense came before word, the "image of an image," and it was deposited in the memory in infancy by "body language" (or, in Augustine's phrasing, "by the movement of the body, as though by words natural to all peoples"), a glance of the eyes, a gesture of some member of the body, or the sound of the voice.[150] Kinesthesia continued to work throughout life in the blandishments and teasing play of nurses with an infant, the torments and praise visited by schoolmasters on their charges, the exchanges among friends that secured male bonding, the anguish and serenity received from the God of vengeance and mercy.[151] The crucial fact for Augustine was not simply that these experiences trained the mind to recognize, but, far more, that they disciplined the affects what things were to be sought, held to, rejected, and fled from.[152] They educated the soul in associations of love and fear.

However, Augustine's equation of wisdom with piety[153] set the goals and limits of this education. Again and again, he declaimed against curiosity as the vice that had led him into the extravagances of his youth, "sacrilegious curiosity" that had then drawn him from God into the service of demons and that fueled his fascination with theatrical spectacles, idle curiosity that still broke the concentration of his prayers with trifles (a lizard eating a fly or a spider winding a fly in its web), just as it captivated people to run in throngs to gawk at mangled corpses.[154] In killing themselves for God, the learned must cut off pursuits into which the sickness of curiosity plunged them, notably the scrutiny of nature for no purpose other than that of knowledge itself.[155] "Unhappy is the man who knows all these things [i.e., philosophical subjects]," Augustine declared to God, "but knows you not." "But blessed is he who knows you, even though he knows not them."[156]

"It is piety to confess to you," he wrote; just as confession required the silent words of the heart rather than the sounding words of the flesh,[157] so, too, it required the wisdom of piety rather than the ignorant knowledge of human thought.[158] For confession could be made without understanding; and such understanding as it contained was not that which man could give to man, nor angel to angel, nor angel to man.[159]

In the written words of his *Confessions*, Augustine could speak of the formlessness that preceded creation; but he could not compose an inward picture of nonbeing, deprived of all forms, or of nullity.[160] The treasures of wisdom and knowledge were hidden in Christ, and understanding came through spiritual union with him. "I apprehend through him in whom I am apprehended," Augustine wrote.[161] His friend Nebridius, a companion in the days of his conversion, had died and now lived in Abraham's bosom, drinking from the font of eternal wisdom. Had he forgotten Augustine? "I do not think he is so inebriated by that font to have forgotten me, since you, Lord, whom he drinks, are mindful of us."[162]

Augustine spoke at length of the contrast between the incompleteness and variability of human understanding and the perfection of divine, which, for him, was also the contrast between faith and sight. He spoke of the errors that a person's incompetence could intrude into his discussion of philosophical matters, of historical change that made understanding of customs and technical terms relative to the reader's expertise, of the delusiveness of self-reflexive interpretations and of his own susceptibilities to them through the senses and through his sensitivity to praise and censure, and, finally, of the multiplicity of interpretations that knowledgeable readers could place on the same verse of Scripture.[163]

The *Confessions* itself is virtually a graph of this variability. At two points Augustine deliberately paused to identify its stages, from the parts of the memory (sensory impressions) that he had in common with brute animals, to the parts where the affects were kept, further to the very seat of his soul, and finally to the sweetness which God poured into his soul, elevating him to a wholly unfamiliar affect. From that height he quickly fell once more, weeping vehemently, into the accustomed burdens of this life.[164] This hierarchy is the same as that traversed by Augustine and Monica in their extraordinary dual ecstasy, from conversation, to affective exaltation past all corporal things to inward thought and speech and wonder at God's words, then transcending their own minds and entering the region of unfailing plenty where immutable wisdom is. There, they were touched sublimely by a heartbeat (*ictu cordis*) and fell back, returning to the sounding of their speech, where words begin and end.[165]

Evidently, Augustine considered that true spiritual understanding came not as reflection, not as the continued operations of the memory, but rather as an instantaneous flash or heartbeat, which survived by its traces in the memory. "You beat back the infirmity of my sight," he wrote, "shining within me in great force, and I trembled with love and horror. And I found myself far from you in the region of unlikeness."[166] What, he asked, pierced through his heart with light? What was that before which he quailed because he was unlike it, and for which he burned in his likeness to it? "Wisdom—it is wisdom itself, that pervades me with light, ripping open my darkness."[167] At the instant of his conversion, he recalled, his heart was suffused suddenly with the light of confidence, and all shadows of doubt fled away.[168]

Understanding, therefore, was intuitive and instantaneous. In the language of mimesis, it was the reality of which the memory labored to constitute an image, passing through stages of sensory, figurative, and analogical thought. The discursive memory was the image of the incandescent moment when the mind passed beyond sense, figure, and analogy to direct spiritual apprehension and was transformed, then to fall back into the world of types and shadows and spoken words.

Understanding was esthetic, affective, and fleeting. How could Augustine represent it in words on a page, images of its image? Apart from the primary figure of light, three kinesthetic analogues came most naturally to him. One was that of sweetness. Augustine never wearied of contrasting the "death-bearing sweetness" of his sexual practices and the burdens of the world that so sweetly oppressed him with the sweetness of Ambrose's speech and of hymns that drew him to God with penitential tears. He contrasted the evil sweetness of this world with those tears, "the sweet fruit of life's bitterness," and with the sweetness that he imbibed from Scripture. God was the supreme sweetness, sweeter than any pleasure, brighter than any light, more inward than any secret.[169]

Inebriation provided him another allusive image. Alcoholism had a particular fascination for Augustine. He took particular care to affirm that while eating was a sweetness against which he had to fight each day and one that occasionally overcame him, he had never been a drunkard.[170] Three of the few stories he recounted of his parents deal with wine. He chose to recall his father rejoicing with his wine as he described Augustine's maturing genitalia, and two accounts of his mother describe how she was deflected from the reality and the appearance of alcoholism, to which matrons in her place and station commonly fell prey, as they also did to wife beating.[171] Confirmed drinkers, he observed, stimulated thirst by eating salty food, so as to gain the delight of quenching it with drink; he had known drunkards made sober by God.[172] One of the principal reflections on happiness in the *Confessions* was a soliloquy on the happiness of a drunken beggar,[173] and many of Augustine's metaphors for the absorption of knowledge were taken from drinking, both inebriating and not.[174] In spiritual contemplation, he drank Christ. Eroticism fused with spiritual intoxication. "Who," he asked, "will make me this gift, that you come into my heart and inebriate it, that I may forget my evils and embrace you, my one good?"[175]

Finally, the image of play subsumed all of the figures that Augustine employed to portray his understanding of understanding. His passing comments go far toward establishing why he recounted his conversion as a formative process that began in infancy and toward elucidating both his understanding of conversion and the objectives that, as hunter and hunted, he wished the *Confessions* to achieve.[176]

Kinesthetic associations that gave words their sense came by different modes of play because play was inherent in human nature. It was an established pattern, and part of the rite of passage, for children to boil over with playfulness against the strictures that parents customarily imposed.[177] The same impulses underlay the sports and fables of childhood and the great achievements of society: theatrical spectacles ("the games of adults"), the enterprises of governors and kings in acquiring gold, estates, and slaves. Only the stakes, and thus the penalties, increased as one's years multiplied.[178] As a boy, Augustine recalled, he had been driven by "love of playing," which meant in his case love of winning and the torture of losing.[179] The highly competitive instincts of childhood continued in adulthood as he played "quite odiously" with the literary skills that he had learned under the schoolmaster's rod.[180] He competed for and won the orator's crown, which later he discounted in his race for the palm of his heavenly calling.[181] The same continuing fascination with play appears in the metaphor of running, which characterizes so many of Augustine's works, and in the ease with which Augustine was distracted by the chase of predator and victim, even after he no longer indulged his enthusiasm for it by going to the circensian games.[182]

Augustine observed how, by its mimetic power, play transformed those who watched it, as the bloodlust of gladiatorial combat changed his friend Alypius into another man.[183] He also perceived how play changed those who participated in it, as it knit together the friends of his childhood.[184] Because play was stochastic as well as imitative, these transformations could be surprising, as it was in ball games, gladiatorial combat, theater, and the hunt.

Thus, the surprise in supernatural conversion vindicated more rejoicing over one redeemed sinner than over ninety and nine just persons who needed no repentance. Supernatural conversion was no surprise to God, who predestined vessels to honor and dishonor before the firmament was formed and silently laughed at Augustine moving, in ignorance, through the strife of his spiritual journey.[185] But Augustine left no doubt of the imitative, stochastic play that brought him to the incandescent moment of understanding. As his spiritual crisis reached its climax, he heard a mysterious voice—a boy's or a girl's—repeating, singsong, "Take; read. Take; read." On the instant, he could not remember any children's game that used that chanting refrain. But he did recall that Anthony of Egypt's life had been suddenly changed when he felt that a verse, heard by chance from the Gospel, was a command intended directly for himself. Earlier in the *Confessions* Augustine had described how he had turned away from the superstition of bibliomancy.[186] But now, imitating the obedience of Anthony, he raced to the codex of St. Paul's letters that he and Alypius had taken into the garden. He broke open the book. His eyes fell at once on Romans 13:13: "Not in rioting and drunkenness, not in chambering and wantonness, not in strife and envying; but put ye on the Lord Jesus Christ, and make not provision for the flesh to fulfil the lusts thereof." At that, his heart was flooded with the light of confidence. But the risks of play were implied throughout the account, in an unknown children's game, imitative play, bibliomancy, and the dramatic detail that the letters of Paul had lain on a gaming table. All these rhetorical details expose a wide repertoire of play at work in one climactic event.[187] While the light that irradiated his heart scattered the shadows of doubt, other shadows remained and would remain inhering "in the body, which is dead on account of sin until day break and the shadows flee away."[188] Until then, he would burn with love in likeness to that light and quail with fear in unlikeness. Conversion had begun and progressed; it would end with transfigurations from glory into glory after death.

Thus far I have emphasized that for Augustine, the origin of understanding was kinesthetic and that visual understanding (epitomized in theatricality) was dominant. What connection can there be between reading the word and visualizing its contents, between reading, for example, and seeing the face in the text?

My account would be incomplete without some reference to the kinesthetic experience of reading. A central aspect of that experience in Augustine's day was the circulation of written materials in two dominant forms: the codex and the scroll. At his spiritual crisis in the garden at Milan, Augustine had with him a codex of the letters of St. Paul, and his sermons refer to other scriptural texts in codex form.[189] But the use of the word *volumina* indicates that Augustine himself composed his first work (*De Pulchro et Apto*) and one of his latest (the *Retractations*) on scrolls, and statements at the ends of Books 2, 4, and 5 of the *City of God* suggest that they, too, may have been issued first as scrolls.[190] This would have accorded with standard practice, used in copying works of Virgil and Varro (two authors of particular importance to Augustine), of allocating one scroll to each book of a long composition. This likelihood is increased by the fact that Augustine appears to have issued the early books of the *City of God* separately, as they were written. Since he mentioned the response of readers to the early books of the *Confessions* (10.3.3), Augustine evidently issued them, too, before the entire work was completed and, not implausibly, in the form of *volumina*.

Augustine's celebrated description of Ambrose reading betrays some sense of kinesthetic elements in the experience of reading from scrolls. Although Ambrose had fewer moments than he wished for reflection, he spent some of them in a public place. There, Augustine and Monica observed him turning his scrolls. To save his voice, which easily failed him, he read silently, without moving his lips.[191] In his brief description Augustine has captured the physical acts of holding, turning, seeing, and vocalizing, which last Ambrose omitted.

The effects of the physical act of reading scrolls, rather than codices, are plain at many points in Augustine's *Confessions*, and failure to understand the terminology of the scroll has led to misinterpretation of the Father's words and, consequently, to a meager grasp of his metaphorical references. To take one instance: Augustine commonly referred to "the glue of love" or "of charity."[192] This allusion is trivial unless one recalls that scrolls were composed of papyrus sheets which were created by laminating strips of pulp with glue spread between them, the fiber lines of each strip placed crosswise to those on the layer beneath. Sheets were also fastened to one another with glue to form a scroll. Thus, glue was not only a simple adhesive but the element that made the entire structure of the scroll cohere, the unseen bond on which the preservation of the text depended. Consequently, Augustine's metaphor taken from scroll making was by no means trivial when he wrote about a friend before his conversion: "But he was not yet a friend, nor was he later one, as true friendship is, because there is no true friendship unless you [God] glue it together among those cleaving to you with charity spread in our hearts through the Holy Spirit, which is given to us."[193]

Likewise, to understand *pagina* as "page" instead of as one in the running series of columns on a scroll, *volumen* as "volume" instead of "scroll," and its synonym *liber* as "book" (meaning codex) lead to serious misunderstandings of Augustine's intent.[194]

I shall give two examples of how the physical experience of reading from scrolls entered into Augustine's ways of visualizing. The first occurs in his discussion of the firmament "rolled up as a *liber* and now stretched out above us as a hide."[195] Augustine may have taken from Ambrose the figure of the heavens as an extended scroll,[196] but it was characteristic of the bishop of Hippo that he expanded the metaphor by drawing a contrast between the "hide" that composed the "book" of God's firmament and the hides with which God clothed men when, by sin, they became mortal, and which later in the same passage, he compared with "grass," a reference, as I shall argue, to papyrus. Angels, he wrote, had no need to read the book of the firmament, since, without syllables of time, they read their Creator's eternal will directly in his face. Their codex was not closed, nor was their scroll (*liber*) rolled up; for God was eternally present to them. By contrast, the preachers of his word had extended the Scripture over peoples until the end of time. Heaven and earth would pass away, but God's utterances (*sermones*) would abide, since the hide of the firmament would be rolled up. At this point, Augustine referred to mortal humanity not as hides, as before, but as grass; and he went on to make the comparison with papyrus rolls yet more evident by writing that unlike heaven and earth, God's Word would abide, the Son who had looked through the "latticework" (*retia*) of our flesh and inflamed us to run after his fragrance. The word *retia* refers to the network of laminations that comprised the papyrus sheets and which, in fine grades of papyrus, was almost transparent, the best among *scriptabiles facies*.[197] Thus, Augustine implicitly contrasted the hide scroll of the firmament with the grass scroll of human flesh.

My second example is Augustine's celebrated definition of time not as an objective measurement derived from the movement of bodies but as a subjective distention of the mind into the past, by memory, and into the future, by anticipation. There is, he concluded, no measurement of present time, which is an instant, swiftly over, between future and past. His discussion has often been characterized as problematic, but Augustine's intention is readily clarified if one observes that his description of the measurement of time is an appropriation of the experience of reading a scroll.

Augustine's use of the recitation of a song, albeit from memory, suggests the manuscript from which the song was originally learned. His terms make specific the reference to scrolls, rather than to codices. His entire conception presupposes length and, therefore, linearity. Shortness and length, spaces of intervals of time, the swift flight (*transvolare*) or propulsion from future into past, and the consequence of the future out of the past, the running of all past and future from that which always is—all these allusions portray a linear, moving surface. There is also a physical correspondence between the first unfolding of a scroll and Augustine's distinction between the future, which is neither reduced nor consumed, because it is not yet, and the increment of the past, which is no longer. His analogue of all human action, in an individual life or in human experience as a whole, with the distention of the mind carries the metaphor of the scroll to yet another level.[198]

Augustine's references to manuscripts, whether in roll or codex form, naturally allude to a primary mimetic enterprise, the copying of texts, and to its hazards. If the spoken word was an image of an image, the written word was an image once further removed from actuality, and manuscript copies of the written word were images still further away from actuality. The variability of manuscripts through scribal independence and error may be behind Augustine's disregard for the intent of the author and his acceptance of multiple interpretations in manuscript traditions. Indeed, he had good reason to understand this kind of mimetic hazard, given the fact that manuscripts of his own works escaped to copyists before he was able to revise them.

Augustine's reference to the perishability of "grass" underscores the special fragility of papyrus which by contrast with vellum could not be expected to last more than three generations. But his contrast between the "hide" of God's firmament-scroll and the mortal "hides" of human beings underscores the perishability of the text itself, once committed to scrolls. This had to do in part with storage and retrieval. Copying long texts on multiple scrolls—one book of Virgil's *Aeneid* per scroll, for example—[199] meant that individual sections of works could be lost or shuffled into a wrong sequence, especially given the methods of storing scrolls in "hat-boxes" (*capsae*) or in mounds on shelves. This usage no doubt hastened the loss of great segments of Livy's *History*, for example, and promoted extravagant variations in the sequences in which other ancient works are preserved.

The kinesthetic impact of the scroll on Augustine's concept and experience of visualization was not limited to holding and turning the scrolls. The visual image formed in the memory by a codex is very different from that formed by scrolls. The image of the codex is sharply framed; that of the scroll is processual, as columns running in sequence. The introduction of the codex initiated a fundamental change in the character of book illumination and, thus, in the interplay of picture and text. Conservatism prevailed in the early decades of the codex. Just as, after the invention of printing, books were made to look like manuscripts, so, too, in the early decades of the codex, copyists mimetically reproduced in a different format the columnar arrangement of the scrolls and some dominant characteristics of scroll illumination. But in time the format and the materials used in producing codices led to a revolutionary change which has been called the emancipation of the miniature from the text.[200]

Techniques of illustrating scrolls aimed at interpenetration of the sense of the words with that in the pictures. Visualization and reading became, as nearly as possible, one, not only, for example, in the light, sketchy illustrations of scenes from Terence filtered into his text but in the rather more elaborate genre of the *carmen figuratum,* the "figured song." *Carmina figurata* achieved an interpenetration of pictures and words, such as delivered the subject through simultaneous kinetic experiences to the visual and verbal imaginations. Some, indeed, rendered visible the meaning of Augustine's phrase "the face in the words." The object, of course, was not merely to render an author or subject visible but to enable the reader to see himself in the mirror of the pictograph.

I should like to carry this discussion of kinesthetic understanding a step further and apply it to the *Confessions*. The analogue between the face that Augustine saw in the words and a genre of poetic—which is also to say, musical—composition, the *carmen figuratum,* is a good point of departure, for it is a point at which the kinesthetic reflex of imitative play, words, and visualization took place.

Music was of primary importance to Augustine. The *Confessions* is full of references to music, especially to songs and singing, and Augustine employed metaphors of song to illustrate the inwardness of his conversion. When Augustine was a child, the bishop wrote, God sang his words into the boy's ears through Monica.[201] Conversion brought him God's "inward melody," which he lacked when he wrote his first book, the lost *De Pulchro et Apto*. Writing specifically about the time between conversion and baptism, he set the theme of his entire spiritual venture in terms of psalmody. Those days with his friends unrolled (*evoluti,* as a scroll), "seeming long and many, for singing from the very marrow of our bones, 'My heart has said to you, "I have sought your face, your face [O Lord] will I require" ' " (quoting Ps. 27:8). Later, as I said, he found the face of God in the text of Scripture; he anticipated "reading" God's face directly in the Heavenly Jerusalem, as the angels did, without the mediation of any text, without the mediating of images formed in the mind, of memory, or even the act of seeing, "the rays of my eyes."[202]

Ever attuned to "the sweet melodies of songs,"[203] he found psalmody an essential part of his daily physical and spiritual discipline, not as a pastime or as a duty to be discharged but as an act intensifying the devotion of seeing oneself in the mirror of Scripture. In my terms, psalmody was a kinesthetic discipline, a particular kind of education or internalization by ritual. It was not so much an exercise of feeling oneself into a text as it was of absorbing the sense of the words into the pith and heart of one's very being. Just as Augustine strove to penetrate through words to their unspoken and unspeakable senses, so, as he listened to the notes with which a psalm was sung, each occupying its measure of time, he strove to detect "a measure [*numerositas*] standing without time in some secret and high silence."[204]

I propose that these kinesthetic principles of intellectual formation in mind led Augustine to think of the *Confessions* in a particular way. It has often been noted that the *Confessions* constituted an entirely new literary genre. However, I suggest that Augustine's kinesthetic principles overlapped with his literary criticism in such a way as to relate his book to a specific, and entirely traditional, genre: namely, the psalm and, more precisely, to that small cluster of psalms called "songs of degrees" (ps. 119–33). Throughout all his works Augustine testified that the Book of Psalms was a major bulwark of his spirituality. On his deathbed he had the penitential psalms written on pages and fixed to his walls, where he continually read them weeping.[205]

Augustine wrote that he first encountered congregational psalmody in Milan, where Ambrose introduced the practice. But in North Africa the Donatists had long and regularly employed congregational singing both as part of their devotional life and as a means of instruction. Their war cry, "Deo laudes," more feared than the lion's roar,[206] alluded to this usage, which included both scriptural and contemporary psalms. In 393 C.E., while still a priest, Augustine sought to turn the Donatists' weapon against themselves by writing a *Psalm against the Faction of the Donatists*, which he intended to be sung to the people, thereby fixing his case in their memory. In view of the theme of fecundity developed in the *Confessions*, it is worth noting that his *Psalm* concluded with "a sort of epilogue as though their mother, the Church, were speaking to them."[207] By stressing the universality with which the scriptural psalms were sung throughout the earth, Augustine set an implied contrast with the claims of the Donatists, set forth in psalms of their own composition, that the authentic Church was limited to themselves, in North Africa.[208]

It is evident that the historical setting and the objectives of the *Confessions* revived the conception that Augustine had developed in 393 C.E.. God already knew what Augustine was saying. Why, then, was Augustine laying so many stories before him? It was, Augustine wrote, so that he could arouse his own affectionate desire toward God and stir up that of others who read those accounts, so that all might say, "Great is the Lord and greatly to be praised" (Ps. 47:2, 144:5).[209] The very first words of the *Confessions* were this verse from the Psalms. Again and again Augustine recalled that he had celebrated with psalms events described or mysteries revealed for which a simple recounting was inadequate.[210] Was not the recitation of a psalm until all its parts had passed from expectation into memory a paradigm for the whole life of a man, whose parts are all his actions, and for the whole age of the sons of men, whose parts are all the lives of men?[211] In his life, Augustine wrote, he was carried by love wherever he was borne. Converted and restored to God's image, by God's gift, he wrote, "we are kindled and carried upward; we burn within and we go on. We climb the heart's steps, and we sing a song of degrees. By your fire, by your good fire, we burn within and we go on because we go to the peace of Jerusalem above."[212]

Other passages in the *Confessions* record how profoundly Augustine's emotions were stirred by psalmody,[213] but these statements, relating the *Confessions* not simply to prayer but to psalms, together with the historical context in which they were written, enable us to understand another aspect of the purpose and function of that text. The scriptural psalms were a collection of individual works, consisting of hymns of praise, laments, and thanksgivings, a montage and yet regarded as a whole. This model provided the freedom to venture into many subjects which Augustine fully exploited. But it was the unclarity whether the "I" of the Psalms were an individual person or the whole community that best served his purposes. In liturgies this unclarity was dramatically enacted day by day, for a psalm was first sung to the congregation and, then, by the congregation in response.[214] In a comment quoted earlier, Augustine remarked on Psalm 123 as a "song of degrees": "Sing therefore ascending; sometimes as though one is singing, sometimes as though many; for many are one, and Christ is one, and in Christ, the members of Christ make one being with Christ. . . . Therefore, whether one sings or many sing, many men are one man because of this unity."[215]

Prayer isolates the solitary with his God. Augustine designed the theatricality of the *Confessions* to engage his readers with him in his spiritual ascent. He did not wish his readers to observe him praying, as in a theater spectators watched and delighted in miseries into which they could not enter. Instead, he wished them, through the ritualized kinesthetic act of reading, to partake with him in God's praises and, as, by reading, his account passed for them from expectation into memory, to intercede with

God for him in the unity of love. Thus, the song of degrees[216] that was his *Confessions* would not be sung in theatrical solitude.

His commentary on Psalm 123 indicates the effect that he wished the *Confessions* to have.

> And where does he want to ascend, unless to heaven? What does "to heaven" mean? Does he wish to ascend to be with the sun, the moon, and the stars? Certainly not. But eternal Jerusalem is in heaven, where angels are our fellow citizens, from whom we are absent as pilgrims on earth. On pilgrimage, we sigh with longing; in the city, we rejoice. We find companions, however, on this pilgrimage who have already glimpsed that city and urge us to run to it. Before them [*ad hos*] he rejoiced who said, "I was glad in them who said to me: We will go into the house of the Lord." Brothers, remember in charity how, for example, on a festival of martyrs, when a holy place is named, when crowds flow together on the appointed day to celebrate the solemnity; how those crowds stir themselves up, how they admonish one another and say, "Let us go! Let us go!" And they ask, "Where are we to go?" And the answer comes, "To that place, to the holy place." They talk together and, though they are kindled one by one, they make a single flame, and a single flame made by the give-and-take of those drawing near seizes them up to the holy place, and holy thought sanctifies them. If, therefore, holy love seizes them thus to a worldly place, what sort of love ought it to be that seizes into heaven those who are of one accord and say to one another, "We will go into the house of the Lord"? Therefore, together let us run, let us run, because we will go into the house of the Lord. Let us run and not be weary, for we go to that place where we shall never tire.[217]

Summary

By now, it is clear what Augustine called conversion. I have explained what made that name thinkable to him for that subject. Some aspects of the process by which he applied the name, the calling of it, in the *Confessions* have also been detected.

Understanding the conversion of Augustine is a matter of seeing darkly through a hall of mirrors. First, there is the mirror of the understanding constituted by the work of art itself; then, the mirror consisting in the possibilities, demands, and limits of the medium, in this case, of words;

and, finally, that of the understanding of understanding. Above all, readers look at Augustine through the refractions of their own minds. Augustine himself asked the fundamental question. How, he asked, could his readers know that he was telling the truth? But he readily placed the origin of understanding both in the thought and words of the writer and in the apprehension of the reader. Prompted by extreme divergences in scriptural interpretation and the controversies that they stirred up, he also asked how readers could know that Moses had told the truth. It was not necessary, he wrote, to recover the intent of the author, Moses. In fact, if he, Augustine, had been Moses and had had to write the Book of Genesis, he would have wished to have such skill in eloquence and such a mode of discourse as to enable every possible interpretation to be found in the few words of his text.[218]

Augustine's answer to the question of veracity ignored the task of verifying historical facts, for truth was not in the information conveyed so much as in the piety enkindled, not in understanding so much as in charity, not in the reading so much as in the vision. Thus, neither he nor his readers saw truth in one another, but rather in the light of God that enlightened them all, which is also to say, in the charity that bound them, even if strangers, one to all. Understanding was prior to words; and affective affinity, prior to understanding. In this union the love of play was irradiated and transferred into the play of love and fear and, at the last, of love casting out fear.

An elaborate chain of mimesis, drawn from the ritualized visual and performing arts of spectacle, provided Augustine the coherence for his way of thinking about understanding. For historical writing, the brightest link in that chain was his sense that through a common humanity, the supernatural conversion of the individual replicated the conversion of the world. Individually and collectively, the "one person" comprising the body of Christ followed the same mimetic passage from image to presence. As a "song of degrees," the *Confessions*, beginning with Augustine's travails, ends with a panegyric on the fecundity of the Church and the peace by which God enters into the redeemed, and they, into him, their joy. This same ascent was the outline that Augustine followed in his account of "the most glorious city of God," living by faith in this passing time, a stranger among the ungodly, and at length delivered into the peace that passes all understanding. There, kindled into flame by beauty, the redeemed would be filled with God, and being one with the end without end, they would not understand but rest and see, see and love, love and praise.[219]

Augustine's understanding of understanding did not exhaust itself in the mimetic play of the saved, nor, to be sure, was this the most provocative aspect of his hermeneutic doctrines. The saved were the fewest of the few. Augustine was driven by a passionate need for wholeness, denied in this life but consummated in Paradise. Such was the power of his need that the reprobate, the great majority of humankind, and their evil works were encompassed in a single pattern with the saved. Plato, too, dominated by a need for the ultimate wholeness of things, perceived that tragedy and comedy sprang from a common origin, witnesses to a common beauty. Augustine's mimetic doctrines included both the soul's chaste, voluptuous coupling with its celestial bridegroom and the fornication that it committed, seeking apart from him what it must return to him to find pure and limpid. "All they perversely imitate you, who put themselves at a distance from you and rise up against you. But by imitating you even in this way, they indicate that you are the creator of all nature and, consequently, that there is no place at all to which one may withdraw from you." In the playful theft of pears, Augustine continued, he had viciously and perversely imitated his Lord. He had given a dark likeness of omnipotence, as a prisoner, in his powerlessness, rendered an impaired imitation of freedom, delighting to do something forbidden because it was forbidden.[220]

The esthetic that led to one conclusion in the mimetic likeness of the saved to God led to another in the perverse imitation of God by the reprobate. "Justice," Augustine wrote, "is the supreme and true beauty."[221] By that justice, God had elected some as vessels of wrath, giving to them the punishment that they deserved, and others as vessels of mercy, giving them the grace that they did not merit.[222] Evil was not a defect in the world to be eliminated, for it functioned much as silences did, establishing with elegance and beauty the intervals between words as they unrolled from future into past and accumulated into discourse. The subjection of earthly things to heavenly, in their temporal sequences, resembled a song of the universe. Likewise, God created and moderated the counterpoint of good and evil, as though it was a great poem. The right imitation of the few saved and the perverse imitation of the many reprobate were not mutually exclusive. Rather, they were antitheses that God used in composing history as an exquisite poem, achieving its beauty "by the opposition of contraries, arranged, so to speak, by an eloquence not of words but of things."[223] The endless agonies of the damned, melting as wax before the face of the inextinguishable fire, sufferings yet more incredible than the bliss of the saved, had their place in this composition, whose principles were hidden in God's inscrutable wisdom.

There is perhaps an unconscious cross-reference between Augustine's account of his playful theft of pears and his doctrine that by the wound of sin, the human race had been placed under the Devil's power, "as though by right he plucked the fruit from his own branch."[224] God had created the Devil; the Devil and those belonging to him were in God's power. Demons could do among men only what, and when, God's high and secret providence allowed them to do. The work of the Devil was in and passed through the work of God, and, to be sure, the human race had been made the sport (*ludibrium*) of demons.[225] Was not God, who ritualized the play of the game, also its ultimate and only player, while people were played by him as a musician plays an instrument or, at least, played by the game—that is, by the understanding of understanding that was supernaturally given or withheld from them?

The highly competitive "love of play," which impelled Augustine in his youth and took one form in fascination with the killer instincts of predators, reached its highest pitch in these doctrines, which also constituted one of the most enduring legacies of his conversion. After more than a thousand years, John Calvin, reaffirming Augustine's teaching, wrote: "When the ungodly hear these things, they cry out that God with inordinate power abuseth his poor creatures for a sport to his cruelty."[226] But Calvin's "ungodly" were only repeating questions about supernatural conversion that Augustine had abandoned as unanswerable when in terror and in love he gazed upon the face unrolling from the text of Scripture.

CASE 2

Herman-Judah's *Account*

INTRODUCTION

Text and Event

By contrast with Augustine's *Confessions*, the account to which I now turn is obscure; but it is also an astonishing and singular witness to the relations between Christians and Jews in the Middle Ages.

Even if the author completed his account earlier than the 1150s—that is, before the renewed attacks upon Jews in the Rhineland during the Second Crusade—it would be hard to consider it in any sense "a typical autobiographical narrative."[1] Rather, if it is what it purports to be, it is the first autobiographical account of conversion extant in the Latin West after Augustine's *Confessions*. It is certainly, in many regards, a *"unicum* in medieval religious literature."[2] Readers differ concerning the degree to which it can be praised for its "rare loftiness of spirit" and "complete sincerity." One, at least, has denounced it as a fabrication, a twelfth-century document, to be sure, but a pious fraud made by Christian hands.[3]

Occasionally, on different grounds, Jewish and Christian scholars have found it an embarrassment. Some critics have openly questioned the historical value of the text, suspecting the degree to which self-interest may have biased Herman-Judah's account. Attention has been drawn to the long space of time that elapsed between baptism and the time of writing and to the possibility, given the large number of scriptural quotations from the Vulgate in the text, that his new religion had so thoroughly impregnated Herman's vocabulary as to warp the way in which he reconstructed the evolution of his thought.[4] Having succumbed to so many other temptations, did he entirely resist that to humor Christians who were eagerly anticipating the conversion of the Jews as a harbinger of Christ's second coming?[5]

The most sweeping of all doubts is that the account is not autobiographical at all.[6] Manuscript evidence leaves no question that it was composed in the late twelfth century. Affinities to other texts demonstrate that it was composed in the Rhineland, and specifically in the ambit of the Augustinian canonry of Cappenberg. However, at least one critic has resolved the anomalies in the text by concluding that its author could not have been born and bred in Jewish society. The *Opusculum*, it is argued, contains "not a scrap of evidence of any acquaintance with the inner or outer Jewish life beyond the knowledge of an averagely intelligent contemporary Christian."[7] Thus, the work could not have been written by a Jewish convert of learning and respected status in his native community.[8]

For the task at hand—understanding how conversion was understood—the text has value whether or not it is a genuine autobiographical account. Unlike Augustine's, Herman-Judah's existence as a historical figure depends entirely on this treatise; and since all literary portrayals, including Augustine's, are "fictions," the account was unquestionably shaped to serve specific ends and composed by selecting, omitting, and editing materials conformable to those ends. The question whether the author were, in fact, the subject is important for assessing the text as a measure of the degree to which conversion entailed a particular convert's assimilation to the dominant Christian society. It also has a bearing on any effort to recover the kinds and extents of dealings between Jewish and Christian communities in the Rhineland during the twelfth century. However, here especially, the purposes for which the treatise was written militate against a display of affinity to, or affection for, Jewish traditions and norms.

A modern scholar may well be "disappointed" not to find such evidence.[9] But one should take into account the possibility that a convert, always under suspicion, might well wish to avoid the consequences of appearing to have remained a Jew in monk's clothing. Caught in attacks of anti-Semitism, Jewish converts in other eras of Western civilization have sought to defend themselves by minimizing the residue of their pre-Christian commitments and maximizing, in stereotypes familiar to their attackers, the degree of their assimilation. It would not be implausible to find a similar use of protective coloration in the general atmosphere surrounding the Second Crusade.

Whether the imaginative fancy of one bred a Christian or the apologia of a Jewish convert, the *Opusculum* is a "fictionalized account," composed with an undeniable subtlety. My task is to reconstruct what can be found of the ways of understanding that lay behind the text.

According to the text, its putative author was born into an eminent Jewish family of Cologne. He was known as Judah (or Judas) ben David ha-Levi before his baptism. Then, as a sign of his new life, he took the name Herman. Exact chronology is not a virtue of this account. At any rate, its subject is represented as living during the first three quarters of the twelfth century (c. 1107–1181), in the section of the Rhine valley dominated by Cologne, Mainz, and Worms, the same area that had witnessed the devastating slaughters of Jews by Christians that attended the First Crusade, ten years before Herman-Judah's putative birth.[10]

Evidently, many aspects of Herman-Judah's career remain ambiguous or unknown, despite meticulous research.[11] For example, it has not been determined when or, correspondingly, how long after his baptism the treatise was written. The baptism is represented as taking place in 1128 or 1129; the account may have been written in the 1150s or later.

Unlike Augustine, the author gave no account of his childhood and education. Only one important allusion to those years is recorded. When he was in his thirteenth year, according to the treatise, he had a dream that was misinterpreted at the time but that anticipated his acceptance of Christianity. The biographical materials provided chiefly belong to the period 1127 (or 1128)—1129 (or 1130). Though, given the dream, the narrator believed that his change of faith was foreseen by God at least from 1120 (or 1121) onward, the process of change, as reconstructed for admiring or curious Christian readers and for Jews wavering in their beliefs, actually came when he was an adult; it lasted two years, a short period of spiritual conflict by comparison with Augustine's thirty-two years.

Acting as an agent of a family enterprise, he went to Mainz, where he made an unsecured loan to Bishop Egbert of Münster (1127 or 1128; Egbert reigned 1127–32). Outraged at the financial recklessness of their twenty-year-old son, his parents ordered him to attach himself to Egbert's household until the debt was repaid in full. To guard their child against assimilation to the Christians among whom he was being sent, they also attached to him an elderly tutor, or custodian, of good repute and impeccable orthodoxy.

The poetic narrator, Herman-Judah, was a member of the bishop's household for twenty weeks (from early December 1127 or late November 1128 until late spring 1128 or 1129). He attended Egbert when he visited the Augustinian canons at Cappenberg, near Münster, a monastic house recently established by Norbert of Xanten, the founder of the Premonstratensian order. Always avid for knowledge, he overcame his distaste for Christian churches as pagan temples, full of abominable idols and impure rituals. He visited churches and listened to sermons. He fraternized with members of the bishop's official entourage who turned on him the full beams of their evangelistic fervor. Indulging what appears to have been a wide enthusiasm for pitting Jews against Christians in debate, he engaged in a public disputation with the celebrated Abbot Rupert of Deutz.

Once the debt was repaid (late spring 1128 or 1129), according to the narrative, Herman-Judah returned to Cologne, but he had contracted a spiritual malaise that took several months to run its course. In June he married, satisfying demands from inside the Jewish community. By late summer, after a time of rigorous fasting and seclusion, he had the spiritual assurance for which he had yearned. His own community secretly passed against him the dread sentence for the sin of idolatry: death by stoning. He intercepted and destroyed the order for his execution, kidnapped a younger brother whom he consigned to a monastery, took refuge from the pursuing authorities in another monastery, and late in November presented himself for baptism in Cologne (25 November 1128 or 24 November 1129). Not much later, he entered the Augustinian house at Cappenberg. After five more years, when he had mastered the Latin language, he was ordained as priest. Although he identified his father-in-law by name and recalled that his wife came to him a virgin, he did not relate his wife's name or the means by which their marriage was dissolved.

The poetic narrator's subsequent career cannot be reconstructed from this account. On other evidence Herman-Judah has been identified with a man who served for a time as provost (or head) of the Augustinian canonry at Scheda, and he may also have held other positions in Bonn and Cologne.[12] The date of his death, like that of the composition of the treatise, is conjectural.

Disclosure and Concealment in
Herman-Judah's *Account*

It is important to distinguish from the outset between the hermeneutic scenario that the author, putatively Herman-Judah himself, constructed in the narrative for readers and the hermeneutic methods that he employed prior to the writing of the narrative. My concern is chiefly with the unstated, poetic methods, instead of with the written narrative. But both were firmly rooted in events and attitudes of the previous century. I must begin, therefore, by recounting part of the prehistory of the text that the author did not acknowledge.[13]

In 1096, a decade before Herman-Judah's putative birth, elements of the expedition that became the First Crusade swept through the Rhineland. Inflamed by their objective, snatching Christ's tomb from the grasp of the infidel, they realized that the Jewish people, who to them were greater culprits, the actual slayers of Christ, were present in the cities and villages around them, and not only in distant Palestine.[14] The motive of revenge quickly enlarged to include Jews in Germany, neighbors of some Crusaders, as well as Saracens in the Holy Land, especially when preachers declared that a Christian warrior could gain pardon of all his sins by killing a Jew.[15]

The bishop of Speier succeeded in protecting the Jews in his city from the full vigor of the attack. But by weakness and betrayal other bishops abandoned the Jews subject to them. Some Jews submitted to forced baptism; others were slain by Crusaders. Inspired by traditions of martyrdom, still others killed their children, kinsmen, neighbors, and themselves according to the prescripts of ritual slaughter. The number of the slain is not known, but estimates in two cities familiar to Herman-Judah—800 in Worms and between 900 and 1,300 in Mainz—are thought reasonable. Although the bishop of Cologne dispersed the Jews of his see into seven villages in an attempt to save some, at least, they, too, were gathered up in the sacrificial carnage.

The decimated communities reconstituted themselves. They rebuilt synagogues. The survivers remembered these events. They commemorated them in solemn liturgies, portions of which are preserved in the *Chronicle* of Rabbi Eliezer bar Nathan, who lived in Mainz and Cologne. They told them to the young; and some of what he heard from eyewitnesses, chiefly concerning the slaughters in Mainz and Cologne, is recorded in the *Chronicle* of Solomon bar Simson (fl. 1140). These writings call for vengeance with a burning intensity matched by the motive of revenge that impelled the Crusaders. Neither abated in Herman-Judah's youth; both, indeed, were refreshed by the attacks on Jewish communities in the Rhineland that accompanied the Second Crusade (1146).

Thus, when, before his baptism, Herman-Judah began to make the sign of the cross over his heart or forehead (*MGH*, 105–6, 115), he was seeking power through the very symbol of common purpose that had marked the Crusaders' clothes. He was seeking power through a symbol that his community condemned as an abomination, a contaminant that holy persons within recent memory had killed their children and themselves rather than venerate.[16] At his baptism, in the eyes of the Jews, he submitted to defilement with "the putrid and profane water" of despicable enemies, murderers, "the slime of the road."[17] Quite naturally, the Jews bewailed him "inconsolably, with a most bitter sorrow, as one perfidious and lost" (*MGH*, 120).

Concealment was a fundamental part of revelation in New Testament parables of conversion; it remained primary in the experiences of later Christians who hoped to fulfill the "form of conversion" in their own lives. What may be concealed, of course, is the old life, or at least aspects of it that could jeopardize the serenity of the new one. Suppression of information can be a protective measure, and not merely a tactic for advancing the narrative. So employed, as in Augustine's *Confessions*, it may be an imaginative reconstruction of history. However, suppression may also serve positive objectives in the game of communication. Those moving in a suspect or hostile environment may encode their ideas for others like them in that environment. Indirectly, by allusions, ambiguities, and frames of reference that were unobjectionable to the untrained or insensitive, they can express one meaning for those who know the code and another for those who do not. Christian exegetes thought that this was precisely the way in which the Holy Spirit had written the Scriptures and in which they were required to interpret it.

Herman-Judah's *Account* exemplifies both kinds of concealment. (I shall refer to the poetic narrator [Herman-Judah] as the real narrator [the author]. However, the possibility that this alleged identity was false should always be kept in mind.) The narrator suppressed facts about his past life. More important for my purposes, he portrayed his spiritual odyssey with a pattern of allusion and analogy that was obscure to Christian readers but manifest to Jewish. Insofar as he wrote for the purpose of encouraging Jews to follow his example of accepting Christianity, he was using concealment not to hide the buried treasure that he found but rather to identify for a specific audience the measures by which it could be recovered. He portrayed a way by which one could be assimilated to a menacing Christian society and still preserve one's ancestral religion. It must also be said that for Herman-Judah the Jewish audience for which he wrote was at least as ambivalent as the Christian one; for it, his toying with Christianity and subsequent baptism was apostasy, a crime that carried the sentence of death. Although

Signs of Contrivance

Conversion is often portrayed as a positive event, a turning toward. It also has a negative aspect, a turning away. The event of formal adhesion may consist of this flight toward the future and from the past. But the process of understanding which follows the event is rather different. For whether the convert is a solitary person or a whole people, the old life overshadows the understanding of the new. The event may produce a transformation; but something resistant to change informs understanding it, and retention of the old may indeed have been a condition without which there could have been no change.

The transference of devotion from gods to saints during the conversion of the Roman Empire has long been recognized. John Donne referred to the conservatism of imperial Christianity as an analogue of his own classicizing poetry, written after he abandoned his earlier ways of luxury and vice and became a priest:

> Temples were not demolish'd though profane.
> Here Peter Jove's, there Paul hath Dian's fane.
> So whether my hymne you admit or chuse,
> In me you've hallowed a pagan Muse.
> (To the Countess of Bedford: "T'have written then," ll. 13–16)

Plainly, there is nothing constant through the centuries about this resistance to change. Quite different ways of thinking about conversion were available to Augustine of Hippo, who came to Christianity from a mélange of currents in late Roman philosophical paganism, and Herman-Judah, who interpreted his conversion in the light of materials given him by his Jewish heritage. When he portrayed the actual moment of illumination that sealed his formal adhesion to Christianity, Herman-Judah took Augustine's description of his own climactic illumination as his model and (without acknowledgment) used some of the Father's own words to describe his experience. But he construed those words in the context of his, not Augustine's, tradition.[18]

Both Augustine and Herman-Judah labored against their communities' suspicion of converts. But it must be said that while Augustine's speculative powers led him to diminish the institutional aspects of his conversion (including his ordinations as priest and bishop) and ornately to expand its supernatural context, Herman-Judah's strategy made very considerable room for demonstrable evidence of institutional obedience; it was important for him to prove the rightness of his faith by his conduct. He assigned the supernatural intervention of grace a prominent but simplistic character in his narrative. Augustine drew unmistakably the distinction between supernatural conversion to Christ and its formal signs in acceptance of Christianity and submission to the Church. Herman kept these distinctions but rendered them less sharp. I have already indicated some differences between what Augustine called conversion and what Herman-Judah called by the same name (see the Preface). What made the name thinkable in a particular way to a Jewish convert in twelfth-century Germany?

Herman-Judah characterized his narrative as a history; he constructed it by a highly selective use of facts. He offered no theological (or philosophical) speculation as such, but only the "descriptive business of history," with some digressions, to be sure, which he intended to be edifying.[19] Yet no more than Augustine did he intend to present a complete account. Because materials by and about him are meager, it is not possible to gain so clear a sense of suppressed materials as it is in Augustine's case.[20] However, one instance may suggest their scale.

According to his narrative Herman-Judah began his journey toward Christianity while waiting in the entourage of Bishop Egbert of Münster for the repayment of a loan.[21] While attending the bishop, he gained new spiritual insights at the Augustinian canonry of Cappenberg, which he entered himself after his baptism and where eventually he became a priest. He dilated on the sanctity of the brothers, counts Gottfried and Otto, who had founded the canonry in their castle and humbly submitted themselves to its rule.

In his panegyric on them and their monastery, he did not state that Egbert's financial difficulties arose in large part because he had to rebuild Münster, including his cathedral, after the city had been burned by the sainted counts (1121). The catastrophe that they perpetrated followed from the bitter local factionalism entailed by the conflict, at a more exalted political level, between empire and papacy. They put Münster to the torch as an episode in the Götterdämmerung of the Investiture Conflict, which ended the following year (1122) with the Concordat of Worms. Indeed, the foundation of Cappenberg appears to have been an act of penance for the colossal desolation. Gottfried had lately died (1127) when Herman-Judah's connection with Cappenberg began, and the mills of the local hagiographical cult had begun to grind. Apparently, loyalty to the founders of his house kept him both from recording the connective tissues of history and from praising Egbert for his enterprise of renovation, as might otherwise have been expected.

There are other omissions. During his lifetime the accusation that use of religious images idolatrously violated the Second Commandment was not limited to Jewish polemics against Christians. In 1152 a dispute broke out in Herman-Judah's former synagogue in Cologne over a window decorated with pictures of lions and serpents. The resolution engaged a rabbi in Mainz, who judged against the window because its presence in the synagogue suggested that it was there for veneration, and another in Regensburg, who judged that these and similar representations were licit.[22] Although the dispute followed Herman-Judah's baptism by some years, it may have preceded the composition of his treatise. At any rate, the window was installed before 1152, and, given the long continuing Jewish disdain for Christian "idolatry," the installation may well have followed a period of debate.

Less hypothetically, Herman-Judah reports nothing about the possibilities of religious art, as they must have arisen in the reconstruction of synagogues after the desolation of 1096. And this silence, by its association with the slaughter of hundreds of Jews, may impinge on other omissions, such as the portrayal of God as a loving torturer, so pronounced in Augustine's *Confessions*, and the ideal of blood martyrdom as imitation of Christ, conspicuous in Christian literature from the beginning and generally invoked as a motive for holy acts by other writers in Herman-Judah's era. The imitation of Christ as suffering victim was not a motif for Herman-Judah. He did not explicitly appeal to the imitation of Christ in blood sacrifice; yet, he tacitly shaped his narrative around other priestly ideals in his ancestral faith that had been enacted by Jews in 1096 and that the survivors of that catastrophe recalled with awe.[23]

These factual omissions and Herman-Judah's careful organization of the treatise as an exercise in interpretation indicate that his historical materials were included and excluded to suit a calculated hermeneutical program. The narrative is a kind of detective story, in which the author constructed a hermeneutic gap to ensnare the reader. It begins with a mysterious dream that according to the account came to Herman-Judah when he was in his thirteenth year. Puzzled, he sought elucidation from a kinsman who (wrongly) interpreted the dream in a carnal way as foretelling a prosperous marriage, fame, and fortune. Thus, Herman-Judah opened the hermeneutic gap for his readers. The balance of the narrative slowly closes the gap by relating a sequence of experiences (between 1127 or 1128 and 1128 or 1129) crowned by his spiritual enlightenment, a second revelatory dream and his baptism.

This sequence amounted to an education in figurative interpretation, which enabled him at length to explain his childhood dream correctly. Finally, he understood that it prophesied the spiritual honor that he would win as a follower of Christ.

The planned movement of the reader from the dream that opened his hermeneutic gap to the one that closed it, from question to correct answer, resembles the dialectical passage in scholastic exposition from the *quaestio* (the first dream), to contrary arguments (the carnal interpretation), to positive arguments (the spiritual interpretation), and, finally, to the scholar's own conclusion (Herman-Judah's concluding apostrophe on the eucharistic feast).

I propose that the hermeneutic strategies by which Herman-Judah shaped his materials by inclusion and exclusion did indeed derive from a form of scholasticism. Writing within a hostile Christian society and addressing a Jewish audience of some ambivalence, he deployed a Hebraic scholasticism that markedly differed from the strategies that Augustine of Hippo used in the *Confessions* against his enemies, the Donatists and the Manichees. For Herman-Judah used concealment not simply to exclude factual inconveniences but more particularly to convey his stance. I shall also attempt to demonstrate that while Augustine's hermeneutic was visual and esthetic, Hermann's was auditory and intellectual.

The Credit of the Author: Ambivalent Disengagement from the Old Life

With an eye toward the Christian society into which he had moved, Herman-Judah, "once a Jew," had a single clear apologetic purpose: to dissociate himself from the "Jews and Judaizers" whom many Christian exegetes condemned for rejecting spiritual (or figurative) interpretations of Scripture in favor of exclusively literal ones.[24]

One effect of Jewish literalism—namely, the prohibition of religious images according to the letter of the Second Commandment—was often linked with debate over exegetical method. This was the case in Herman-Judah's account of his debate with Abbot Rupert of Deutz (*MGH*, 76–83) and, indeed, with Rupert's own rendering of an earlier "duel under the guise of dialogue" with an anonymous Jew.[25]

The great movement of Herman-Judah's spiritual journey is precisely his conversion from the carnal (literal) misinterpretation of his childhood dream to the correct (spiritual) understanding of it, and he drew particular attention to this movement by setting forth the first great barrier to his journey as Christian "idolatry." And yet his comments on exegesis and sacred art indicate that he was unable entirely to lay aside his literalist principles. Augustine had argued that Christ was actually present, though hidden, in the text of the Old Testament as pith is in the husk of chaff (below, n. 57). Likewise, in his account of a debate with a Jew, Rupert of Deutz asserted that he was not swathing the Law in his own interpretation but that the relation between the Gospels and the Old Testament was the same as that in the Prophet Ezekiel's vision of "a wheel inside a wheel."[26]

Herman-Judah's acceptance of Christian exegesis went as far as acknowledging the anagogic, or prophetic, relations between the two Testaments, but not so far as to accept the principle that the two could stand in the relation of prophecy and fulfillment precisely because they were, in some mystic sense, identical.

Likewise, his comments on art hew close to the literal issue of idolatry without verging on the empathetic participation that in Christian cult characterized the devotional veneration of images. He betrayed no hint of the character of religious art in the synagogues known to him, at least two of which were rebuilt after the devastations in 1096, or of the debate, with its preliminaries, that divided the synagogue in Cologne over the use of religious images in 1152.[27]

He was writing amid readers prepared to believe that Jews mutilated crucifixes and images of Christ in majesty, only to be struck dumb when the sacred likenesses bled. A century later Matthew Paris expressed the same stereotype of iconoclasm and cruelty. He recounted how Abraham, a rich Jew of Berkhamsted, put a beautiful statue of the Virgin and Child in his privy and compounded the blasphemy by begriming it. When, because of her pity for another woman, Abraham's wife removed the statue and cleansed it of its filth, he impiously strangled her.[28] Writing against such stereotypes and in the midst of such feeling, Herman-Judah calculated his remarks carefully.

His objections, as he recorded them, extended to one subject: that is, to representations of Christ. Among all the artful varieties of carvings and pictures that he saw in Münster, his attention was caught by one particularly "monstrous idol." The painting consisted of two registers. The lower register showed a man wretchedly hanging on a cross; the upper, the same man enthroned as though he had been deified (*MGH*, 76). Herman-Judah recalled that in his debate with Rupert of Deutz, he had charged that the image of the Crucified violated the literal prohibition of idolatry and that veneration perversely flaunted the specific assertion, "Cursed is every man who hangs on a tree" (Gal. 3:13; cf. Deut. 21:23). Rupert's rebuttal was that the crucifix was a mnemonic device, serving the illiterate commons much as books served the learned. Like the altar raised by the Reubenites and Gadites (Josh. 22), it was a memorial and a witness; it was also a devotional aid by which pious reflection on the outward image of Christ's death could kindle inward love of Christ. Thus, he said, Christ had voided the curses of the Law in his death, and through the form of the cross believers adored not the image but Christ's redemptive Passion (*MGH*, 80).

One misses in Herman-Judah's account the great range of subjects that, Rupert recorded, were carved over "all the walls of churches," the visual realism of paintings that seemed to stand out from the wall and walk,[29] and, finally, the sense that, penetrating the work of art, a worshiper could participate in, and become one with, its subject.[30] Herman-Judah had not assimilated the iconic devotion of his adversary.

Even as he wrote his apologia, he may have perceived differences between his ways of thinking and those that dominated the society into which he had moved. Indeed, this awareness may have influenced the choice of analogues with which the former merchant-scholar illuminated his position: an Old Testamental figure, Naaman the Syrian, a mighty and exalted Gentile, who, being cured of leprosy when he heeded the Prophet Elisha, confessed "there is no God in all the earth, but in Israel" (2 Kings 5:15); Nicodemus, who concealed his faith in Jesus out of fear of the Jews; the merchant who sold all that he had to acquire one pearl of great price; and the Apostle Paul, suggested to him, Herman-Judah said, by others.[31]

Indeed, a script in the Fleury playbook, *The Conversion of St. Paul*, illustrates the analogies that Herman-Judah incorporated in his account: Paul's preaching to the Jews the truth of Christ's incarnation by the Virgin and the sentence of death passed against Paul by the "prince of the synagogue" at Damascus.[32]

To this list of analogues at the confluence of Jewish and Christian pasts may be added the prodigal son. In the *Anulus* Rupert characterized Christians as the prodigal son and Jews as the elder brother.[33] Perhaps he repeated this view when he encountered Herman-Judah. At any rate, a response, seeming accidental, is present in the facts that Herman-Judah ended his treatise, as Rupert had ended his, with reference to the homecoming feast for the prodigal and that he characterized himself, a Jew, as the returning son, the one who "was dead and is alive again," and for whom the father killed the fatted calf, ate, and made merry.

Quite naturally, Herman-Judah's apologia was intended to establish the credit of the author, but in this regard, too, the ambiguity of his position made itself felt. One part of his defense led him to affirm an extensive inventory of Christian prejudices. The adder and the scorpion were two symbols frequently employed by Christians to designate Jews or Judaism. Herman-Judah may indeed have seen them in the paintings and sculptures adorning churches or in the manuscripts that Christians placed in his hands.[34]

Herman-Judah applied the symbol of the adder to himself and that of the scorpion to his father-in-law (*MGH*, 82, 99), and he accumulated testimonies to the characteristics of deafness to truth, treachery, and malign intimidation conveyed by them. In the early days of his quest, he wrote, he mingled with Christians, though he was not yet a sheep of their fold, still bearing in himself, as a goat, the stench of error (*MGH*, 73).

Throughout, he testified that if not in alliance, the Jews and the Devil worked to the same end when, by fraud and terror, they impeded his adherence to Christian faith. Did not the Jews actually constitute "the Synagogue of Satan" (*MGH*, 97)? Herman-Judah rounded out what Christian readers might have expected from such a convergence of human and demonic interests by affirming not only that the Jews were blinded by perfidy and malignity to Christian truth but that they repudiated the faith, art, and rituals of the Church as abominations cast up by an impure, mad, and execrable superstition (*MGH*, 79, 99, 105).

Finally, Herman-Judah titillated his readers with the conflicting stereotypes of laziness and rampant sexuality among Jews when he described how he succumbed to lust in his marriage and languidly abandoned himself to what he judged supreme pleasure of the flesh, which was also its corruption (*MGH*, 102).[35]

When he turned to his own conduct, Herman-Judah did not hesitate to affirm that he had deftly employed stereotypical evasiveness and deceit against his fellow Jews as he edged his way out of "the most filthy and nefarious sect of Jewish superstition."[36] Nor in this self-portrait of calculated deception did he scruple to balance violence with violence when he described how, having thwarted the plot of the Jews to kill him, he kidnapped his half brother and deposited him in a monastery to be baptized and educated (*MGH*, 114–16).[37] In this way he coerced his brother into baptism, although in 1096 Jews had ritually slaughtered their children to protect them from baptism.

Herman-Judah evidently judged that conforming to Christian stereotypes of Jews and performing corrective acts redounded to his credit. Though, as an Augustinian canon, he had ascetically renounced world and self, he associated his works of cunning and violence with a large array of other testimonials to robustly secular goods in his pre-Christian life: to the wealth and authority of his family, who could, among other things, be creditors to a bishop and interpreters of dreams (*MGH*, 70–72), and to his own wealth, education, intellect, adroitness, piety, and wide esteem among Jews and Christians.[38]

Above all, he sought to enhance his credit by enlarging upon the favors that he deservedly received from God between the time of his first dream, in his thirteenth year, and the time of writing. God punished an enemy with sudden death (*MGH*, 93–94) and revealed to Herman-Judah the death sentence that the Jews of Mainz had issued against him (*MGH*, 111–112). He sped Herman to proficiency in Latin (*MGH*, 76, 122) and, at length, raised him from the dung heap and seated him among the princes of his people by calling him to the priesthood (*MGH*, 122, 124–26). Even in kidnapping his half brother, Herman-Judah served the ordinance of God (*MGH*, 115).

Herman-Judah's assent to stereotypes hostile to Jews and dilation of his own credit, emphasizing the favors that he had earned from God, was ambiguously complemented by his experience, indeed expectation, of Christian hostility. God had exalted the Jews as more worthy of honor and dearer to himself than any other people. He considered them alone worthy to know his holy name, and he not only prescribed to them the Law by which they became holy, but he even wrote it for them with his own hand on tablets of stone (*MGH*, 77). After his enlightenment Herman-Judah understood that the Jews had been worthy to receive among themselves Jesus Christ, the author of eternal salvation and the general good of all (*MGH*, 87).

How was it, then, that Christians spat on Jews as though they were dead dogs, with curses and abhorrence (*MGH*, 77)? Jews were commanded to love their friends and hate their enemies, but Christians were obliged to love their enemies and to do good to all, including those who hated them. Yet Jews had every reason to expect Christians to detest them as "enemies of their sect" and to spit on them (*MGH*, 83–84, 87). When a moment of liturgical confusion arose at the very instant of his baptism, Herman-Judah believed that the Christian clergy had set him up as a laughingstock in the baptismal font (*MGH*, 121). It may have entered his mind that within

Introduction to Herman-Judah's *Account*   53

living memory, at such a font in the same city, an exultant mob had slaughtered a Jew for resisting what he believed the defilement of baptism and that Jewish women, dragged to the door of "the edifice of idolatry" and fumigated with clouds of incense, had been cut down with axes when they refused to enter.[39]

Herman-Judah complained that on that late November day, he was frozen rigid by the cold water in the font. Bishop Otto of Bamberg, baptizing Pomeranians in the winter, had the water heated.[40]

Hermeneutic Objectives

The method of exegesis that Herman-Judah practiced, his Old Testamental idea of reciprocal dealings with God, and his concept of spiritual illumination give soundings in the depths of his understanding. From them one can learn some of the unspoken ways of thinking by which the narrative in the text was constructed. They also elucidate how aspects of formal adhesion to Christianity and Church and the monastic profession became thinkable to him as conversion.

Herman-Judah's account contains a varied sample of interpretive exercises from which one may extract dominant elements of the method that guided him in the construction of the narrative. The architectonic unity of the narrative depends upon the hermeneutic gap between the first dream and its misinterpretation, and, at the end, the correct interpretation that came to Herman-Judah in his Christian state. Yet in constructing this major narrative gap and closure for the reader, Herman-Judah did not deploy an elaborate hermeneutic method. The method that he applied was a quite rudimentary version of all figurative, or metaphorical, discourse: understanding one thing by another.[41]

In Herman-Judah's hands this method amounted to the simple equation of prophetic components in the vision to spiritual blessings, achieved or anticipated. The method used to establish equations between individual elements of prophecy and fulfillment (that is, between signs and circumstances) was identical with the method employed by his kinsman Isaac at the first to interpret the dream as anticipating material blessings.

Herman-Judah resorted to Daniel as an exemplar in his quest for divine illumination (*MGH*, 94–96), but a comparison between Herman-Judah's two visions and those recorded in the Book of Daniel casts into high relief the difference between the allegory that clarifies unknown signs (as did Herman-Judah's simple equations) and the allegory that, with ornate methods of association, used paradox to solve and explain enigmas.[42] His first dream was a *praesagium* (*MGH*, 124); it presignified (*MGH*, 122). Herman-Judah's second dream required no interpretation (*MGH*, 116–18). There, even the method of equation used by Isaac was unneeded. Herman-Judah was never far from the Jew whom Rupert of Deutz represented as saying, "What else ought I to know, except what the clear face of the letter plainly says to me?"[43]

At one stage, Herman-Judah recorded that he had skillfully deployed Christian allegories to silence Jews. They, he said, were mouthing old wives' tales pieced together by the third-century scholar Gamaliel III, who completed the redaction of the Mishnah (*MGH*, 113). The point of conflict is not evident in this passage. But Herman-Judah's comment that it hinged on prophecy, taken together with other interpretive exercises in his account, suggests that there, too, he was performing equations between prophecy and fulfillment that included both the Old Testament and the New or asserting simple analogies between circumstances, such as those that he saw between Naaman the Syrian's purification of leprosy in the Jordan and his own baptism.[44] Paradox and enigma were not his chosen element.

Some brief comparisons with Augustine's dialectical methods of understanding will serve as a point of departure. They will also prepare for a distinction between Augustine's implied polemics against the Donatists and the Manichees in the *Confessions* and the very different kind of hermeneutic program that Herman-Judah had in view as he addressed ambivalences among Christians and Jews.

Evidently, Augustine's *Confessions* and Herman-Judah's *Opusculum* are so different in conception and in scale as to be incomparable. The absence from Herman-Judah's work of long sections on the nature of thought and on scriptural exegesis, corresponding with the last four books of the *Confessions*, make it hard to discover how he thought about how the mind worked or about the conditions, limits, and possibilities of scriptural study as a way to truth. The absence of passages concerning the formative years of his childhood and education precludes other lines of inquiry. Comparison is possible on individual points, but there is no broad category on which it can be pursued.

The dialectical give-and-take that dominates Augustine's account was erotic. Augustine employed eroticism as a major theme that, together with conversion and suffering, served the implied polemical assault in the *Confessions* against the Donatists and the Manichees.[45] His elaboration of the theme of dialectical eroticism enabled him to construct a progressive narrative unity as in his spiritual quest he passed from infantile sensuality, to sexuality that sought sterile pleasure, and at last to the fecundity of holy continence. Though his life was far from solitary, only seven women figured in his account; his mother was the chief among them and the only one named. In the great sweep of eroticism from sensuality to continence, his companions were chiefly other males, bound to him by the assimilating give-and-take of friendship (*amicitia*).

Although Herman-Judah rejoiced to have left behind the "Pharisaism" of his literal methods (*MGH*, 75), discrepancies as wide as those between his visions and Daniel's gape between the samples of Herman-Judah's exegetical method and the models of Augustine's that lay before Herman-Judah, with their unmoving Christological center and careful attention, with abundant scriptural references, to the relations of the part and the whole.

It is not enough to assert that Herman-Judah's account has no human interest, that it delivers only "cardboard" figures and never any human being of flesh and blood.[46] For grievous circumstances lay behind his "schematic and abstract" portrayals of character. While Augustine continued, even after his baptism, with friends of his childhood and youth, Herman-Judah's baptism severed earlier associations. With his conversion Herman-Judah turned aside from enduring friendship with other males, except under the aspect of fraternal charity among Christians and, particularly, in the Augustinian communities where he lived (*MGH*, 87, 122). For Herman-Judah, as for Augustine, women, notably wives, stood outside the erotic circle in which bonding occurred.

For Herman-Judah love was far from untrammeled, self-forgetting passion. He equated love with charity and works of love (or charity) with works of piety. Even when he wrote of actions impelled by ardors of holy love—including his own abandonment of world and self for love of Christ—he cast them either under the aspect of the pursuit of knowledge or under that of an obligation owed to Christ for the love through which he submitted to his ignominious but redemptive death (*MGH*, 80, 82, 88, 112).

Two devices that Augustine used to great dramatic effect could offer little to a story of love as pious obligation. The pathos of unrequited love has no place in Herman's understanding of reciprocity between God and those who loved him (e.g., *MGH*, 90). For much the same reason, only a bloodless vestige of the anguish of conflicting loves, elaborately developed by Augustine, appears in Herman-Judah's characterization of scruples that afflicted his conscience as he weighed transgressing the Law by his contact with the impure and execrable rites of the Gentiles (*MGH*, 105–6).

Both writers recorded a time of inward conflict just before the moment of illumination. Augustine characterized that conflict as a struggle between two wills (*voluntates*) in the same mind. The one, he said, inclined to concupiscence of the flesh; the other, to chastity and continence, "but not yet." This controversy in his heart was nothing other than a struggle with himself against himself.[47]

By contrast, Herman-Judah encountered a predicament that concerned not a basic division in human nature (such as body and soul) but a dilemma over ritual observance (*MGH*, 105–6).[48] He was torn between his desire for authentic understanding (which he still thought could come before faith) and the commands of the Old Testament Law that the chosen people in no way imitate the Gentiles' rites, impure as they were and execrable before God. Moreover, Herman considered that this quandary arose through scruples of his conscience against himself as a transgressor of divine Law. He thus set forth a juristic notion of conscience far from Augustine's.

In the *Confessions* Augustine recounted the long trials of his ventures without referring to a juridically scrupulous or remorseful conscience. He introduced conscience after his spiritual illumination, and even then he left it far from the center of narrative action. Conscience was, he wrote, a great abyss that, despite its hidden depths, was naked to God's eyes. He also described it as a knowingly passionate faculty that enabled him to utter his confessions, more confident in hope of God's mercy than in his own innocence. "I love you, Lord, not with a doubtful, but with a sure, conscience. You smote my heart with your word, and I loved you."[49]

Finally, while Augustine described his inward division as grounded in his own nature, deformed by sin, Herman-Judah characterized his as a visitation of the Devil "transfiguring himself into an angel of light," struggling with all guile, as ever, to prevent his adherence to Christianity. Herman-Judah was familiar with theological arguments of original sin and the corruption of the flesh.[50] But there is no evidence that he had absorbed the fundamental Augustinian argument that the corruption of the will preceded and brought about that of the flesh. He referred to the corruption of the flesh only in regard to the carnal delights of marriage, but in no way did he imply the depravity of mind and heart by sin.

Thus, while Augustine was able to narrate the impediments to his submission to the Church as resulting from a flaw intruded by sin upon human nature, Herman-Judah consistently ascribed the impediments that he encountered to the malice and craft of Satan, seconded by the perfidious malignity of the Jews.[51]

The primary moment in both narratives is the account of climactic illumination. Although Augustine's *Confessions* were not universally available—they were not present in Thomas à Becket's library, for example[52]—Herman-Judah knew at least the Father's description of his spiritual crisis late one summer in a garden at Milan; he paraphrased it as he composed his own.

A comparison of the two incidents gives a sharp measure of the differences in understanding that lay behind them. With theatrical vividness and detail, Augustine portrayed the inner tumult that beset him as he collapsed in tears of abandonment and insufficiency. Suddenly recalling an oracular use of Scripture in the life of Anthony of Egypt, he ran with his friend Alypius to a copy of the letters of the Apostle Paul which lay on a gaming table near at hand. The illumination came when his eyes fell, as though by chance, on Romans 13:13–14. There was no wish or need to read further, for as he came to the end of the Apostle's sentence, something resembling light flooded his heart with confidence, and all the shadows of doubt fled away. Alypius then read the next verse (Rom. 14:1), which he likewise interpreted as referring to himself in an oracular sense, admonishing him to change his life. Together, the friends went to Monica, who exulted that God had done more than any of them could ask or understand, more, indeed, than she had implored him to do through the years of pitiable weeping with which she had interceded for Augustine's conversion. God had converted her sorrow into joy more abundantly in Augustine's decision for celibacy than she had wished in her hope for children of his flesh.[53] Though he did not at once resign his chair of rhetoric, Augustine was afflicted by illnesses that prevented his teaching, an incapacity concealed by the timely arrival of the summer holiday. The entire party—Augustine, Alypius, Monica, and others (including Augustine's son)—withdrew for discourse and contemplation prior to baptism of catechumens the following Easter.

The thirty-two years of Augustine's leisurely spiritual voyage preceded this heartrending moment. A few intense months between the heat of midsummer and the rigid cold of late November anticipated the corresponding moment in Herman-Judah's narrative. Herman-Judah provided no details that could enable his reader to visualize the scene. Furthermore, while Augustine was distraught by inadequacy, Herman-Judah recalled displaying immense resourcefulness, tailoring means to end. Because he considered sin a juristic act, rather than a deformity intruded upon human nature, as Augustine had done, Herman-Judah was free to confide in the efficacy of human works. "Therefore," he wrote, delicately paraphrasing a collect, "what I faithfully sought from [God] I deserved effectively to obtain" (*MGH*, 107).

As a Jew having the legal status as a "servant" (*servus,* translated by some as "serf") of the king,[54] he reasoned by analogy that God could be induced to show favor to a person of servile status by the intercessions of those close to him, just as could an earthly king. This thought, he wrote, came to him by divine inspiration. Lacking companionship of family and friends, he calculated that the prayers of two sisters celebrated throughout Cologne for their sanctity would have more merit than he before God. He sought them out in their monastic retreat. With many tears he disclosed to them the temptations that plagued him. Answering his tears with copious weeping of their own, they promised to pray as long as it took for him to become worthy to receive the consolation of heavenly grace. Not much later, in undescribed circumstances, the brilliant light of Christian faith suddenly irradiated his heart and put to flight the shadows of his earlier doubt and ignorance.

It was entirely fitting, Herman-Judah commented with satisfaction, that one who fell because of woman should be raised up by the prayers of woman. To edify female readers, he added that they should imitate the example of his intercessors, knowing how effective their quiet prayers might be before God; for he had been drawn to the faith of Christ neither by reason nor by disputations with great clerics, but by the devout prayers of simple women. He supplied no counterpart to Monica's bitter, theatrically portrayed, anguish.

Instead of disclosing his new beliefs with joy, he for a time kept them secret out of fear of the Jews. At the same time, he desired ever more ardently to be baptized with the waters of regeneration, and so to enter the Kingdom of Heaven. Finally, after the Jewish community had issued its judgment of death against him, he kidnapped a younger half brother, whom he consigned to a monastery, and he himself submitted to catechesis and baptism, having been inwardly confirmed in his decision, shortly before baptism, by the second dream (*MGH*, 108–20).

Augustine related that heavenly visions were vouchsafed to Monica; he claimed none for himself.[55] It is a measure of the distance in thinking between the two accounts that at this juncture Herman-Judah claimed to have seen himself seated in heaven, delighting with Christ's most excellent friends in contemplating him while he contentedly watched as the souls of two cousins who had scoffed at his Christianizing were first tormented and then cast forever into the outer darkness (*MGH*, 116–17).

Throughout Herman-Judah's narrative an Old Testamental assurance of collaboration between God's supernatural power and human initiative is repeatedly expressed in stories of reward and retribution (e.g., *MGH*, 89–92, 93–94). Herman-Judah evidently did not consider himself utterly dependent on grace, as did Augustine, but rather in give-and-take with it. God would, he thought, reward those who loved him according to their works. Augustine acknowledged his obligation to Monica, whose prayers, offered without his knowledge and contrary to his own purposes, conformed with God's own hidden plans for him. Herman-Judah portrayed the two sisters as agents in a plan that, albeit under divine inspiration, he himself had devised to procure grace through merit. His comments on the exemplary devotion and simplicity with which they reversed the baneful work of Eve emphasize that in his view they had played well the roles in which he had cast and directed them. Yet the beginning of his journey, the dream given to him when he was still a child, was a call of grace, not an act of human knowledge or will. Consequently, the entire unfolding story, with the dialogue between divine grace and human nature, had the supernatural origin of vocation and election, and perhaps also of predestination.

The kind of dialectical fusion of souls such as Augustine described between himself and Monica in their wordless discourse at Ostia is entirely absent, together with the conceptions that made it thinkable. Herman-Judah's sense of partnership between God and himself invites one to understand the light that enlightened his heart not as the astonishing infusion of divinity sensed by Augustine but as the "flashes" of true opinions, the "secrets and mysteries of the Torah," as Maimonides portrayed them, withheld from the ignorant, incommunicable in writing, and disclosed only to the perfect, only to the few who, being wise, could understand by themselves.[56]

Herman-Judah used a term familiar to Jewish exegetes for centuries when he remembered that at one stage in his venture, he had feared that he would never attain "a mystic understanding of the Mosaic Law . . . on the bright summit of [his] mind," where he might also penetrate, as the prophet Daniel had done, the mysteries of dreams (*MGH*, 94, 104; cf. *MGH*, 78).

He recognized that before the light of truth dawned upon him, he was, "by a preposterous order," seeking faith through understanding (*MGH*, 104). Although eventually convinced that faith must come before the toil of rational understanding, he never lost his conviction that grace might come through works.

Other allusions to Augustinian texts likewise illustrate the fact that Herman-Judah's way of understanding both those texts and the critical event of enlightenment was by no means that of Augustine.[57] To be sure, as is indicated in his account of how he and a Christian agreed to test the rightness of their faiths in an ordeal of hot iron (*MGH*, 84–85), confidence in demonic power and in the magical aspects of religion (here combined in the ritual of exorcism), and in the efficacy of works, was by no means confined to Jews.[58] Other passages suggest more specifically that the substratum of his thought derived from Hebraic schools of thought[59] and that his thought and actions were molded by the social condition of the Jews.[60]

Hermeneutic Methods: An Exercise in Cryptography

Thus far, I have outlined the hermeneutic method that left as its souvenir a text describing how Herman-Judah understood his spiritual metamorphoses. That method differed markedly from the one that enabled Augustine to understand his and, by inclusion and exclusion, to mold understanding into narrative. Some of the reasonings that made "conversion" thinkable in different meanings to Augustine and Herman-Judah have been recovered.

Herman-Judah's method was epideictic, not dialectical. It was cognitive, not esthetic, and as such excluded the possibility of empathetic participation together with the devotional practices that, above all others, served the cultivation of empathy: namely, the *imitatio Christi*. Finally, it hewed close to literalism. For its purpose was to clarify unknown signs, rather than, by deploying paradox, to solve and explain enigmas. When used to construct his apology, Herman-Judah's hermeneutic methods led to ambiguous results. Without conspicuous heroism, Herman-Judah attempted to certify his own credit by confirming with his own experience hostile stereotypes of Jewish character and life. By portraying Christians as bound under the law of charity but fervid in loathing toward the Jews, he also implied questions about the circumstances into which conversion had brought him and the reception that Christian readers might give his account. Clearly, there was something unsaid in what Herman said about his religious adventures and, thus, at a deeper, pretextual stage of thinking, a provision in his hermeneutic method for covertly expressing the unsaid.

The facts that Herman-Judah is known to have suppressed point to things that he did not wish to say. My argument, however, has brought me to things that he wished to say but not to utter. At some junctures Herman-Judah deliberately used his invisible hermeneutic method to enhance the flavor of his narrative.

Such is the case in the thinking behind the narrative of three events late in the process of his Christianization. The first was the climactic enlightenment in answer to the prayers of the sisters, Glismut and Bertha. Herman-Judah commented that it was right for one who had fallen on account of woman to be raised by the prayers of woman (*MGH*, 108). In a previous chapter he had referred to "the first parent [Adam]," to whom a woman administered "the taste of death" (*MGH*, 98); but without specific names Herman-Judah left it unclear whether his reference to the one who had fallen meant Adam or himself in his recent marriage. However, the second term of his contrast—he who was raised by woman's prayers—was plainly himself. And this is the point at which the unsaid in the uttered becomes apparent.

In conventions of Christian exegesis, the woman through whom the human race fell was Eve. The woman through whom it was raised up was the Virgin Mary. By using the singular ("woman's prayer"), Herman-Judah implied a dramatic cross-reference between the Blessed Virgin, who gave carnal birth to Christ, and Glismut and Bertha, the "simple women" whose "devout prayer" brought Herman-Judah to spiritual rebirth by another virgin mother, the Church (*MGH*, 109, 120). He underscored this correspondence by deliberately contrasting carnal birth and spiritual rebirth (*MGH*, 109).

A second instance occurs at the same point in Herman-Judah's narrative. He recalled that when God commanded the Hebrews to leave captivity in Egypt, he also ordered them to provide for the journey by despoiling the Egyptians, taking with them on the exodus plundered gold, silver, and precious raiment. Leaving the Egyptian darkness of Jewish unbelief, he wrote, he determined not to go empty-handed but to take away "rational booty": that is, to kidnap his half brother, so that they might have the same virgin mother, not according to the flesh, but according to the spirit, and become the "holy temple of God" (*MGH*, 109, 120).

It is not clear that Herman-Judah had in mind, besides the text of Exodus, the celebrated commentary in which Augustine invoked that text as authority for Christians to appropriate the treasures of Greek and Roman learning in scriptural interpretation. However, Herman-Judah's term "rational booty" (*rationalis praeda*) plainly did imply other cross-references, not only to St. Paul's admonition that Christians render their reasonable service to God by presenting themselves as a "living sacrifice, holy, well-pleasing to God" (Rom. 12:1–2)[61] but also to the prayer of consecration which preserved the ancient reference to the eucharistic elements as a "reasonable sacrifice," "reasonable" in the sense of "fitting" but also in the sense that Christ, who was being offered up, was a living sacrifice endowed with the human faculty of reason, (as Herman-Judah wrote) a living price paid for redemption (*MGH*, 106).[62]

Finally, Herman-Judah's references to himself imply similarly Christological references. This is true of the passage just cited, in which he obliquely applied to himself, as well as to his brother, the figures of "rational plunder" (or sacrifice) and temple. It is implied in the parallel evident to every Christian reader between Herman-Judah's first intimation of heavenly calling in his thirteenth year and Christ's discourse in the Temple at the age of twelve. As he closed the hermeneutic gap for his readers, Herman-Judah drew the parallel yet tighter. He equated the palace of the king where he feasted in his vision with a temple: "the place of [his] conversion," the ascetic community at Cappenberg. (See also the note at *MGH*, 124.) There, as priest eating the salad of the gospel, he glutted himself at the altar on "the flesh-meats of the immaculate lamb, Jesus Christ, and [became] drunk from the cup of his sacrosanct blood." He also became part of the sacrificial and eucharistic feast, for Christ fed on the sweetness of his spiritual advancements (*profectuum nostrorum; MGH*, 71, 124). The lines of implication are complete when the flesh of the eaten is transformed into the body of the eater, a fact on which rested the whole weight of Old Testamental laws against dietary pollution.

Throughout these three instances, Herman-Judah constructed a pattern of said but unuttered associations for his Christian readers. Evidently implying but not uttering the association of himself with Christ, the narrative gratified those who could delight in it but held it tantalizingly out of reach from hostile critics.

Though they also shaped the narrative, other yet more crucial instances of the same covert method occurred at a more hidden level. There, he invited readers into his process of understanding, and it is evident that the readers who could follow him furthest were not Christian. To explore this aspect of his understanding, I turn to the dreams of deliverance and retribution that dominate his narrative.

The less complex of the two dreams is the second, retributive one. A few days before baptism, Herman-Judah reported, he dreamed that he was sitting with Christ's best friends in Paradise, delighting in contemplation of him. Two cousins who had scorned Herman-Judah's attempts to win them to Christ also appeared, tortured by seeing the glory of the saints, which they were unworthy to enjoy. After a few words vindicating himself, Herman-Judah watched them, with remorse on their lips, whisked out of sight to hell.

The unsaid in the vision is implied in a detail of Christ's regalia. Instead of a scepter, Herman-Judah wrote, Christ held the triumphal sign of his cross above (or upon) his right shoulder. The double painting that Herman-Judah saw in the cathedral at Münster, depicting a crucifixion in the lower register and, in the upper, Christ "most handsome and sitting as one deified," may have suggested this representation.

A contemporary variation on the theme occurs in one of the most celebrated manuscripts of the twelfth century, the Gospel Book of Duke Henry the Lion of Saxony. There are important discrepancies. Christ stands; he holds the standard of the cross in his left hand and, in the right, a placard with verses from the Old Testament witnessing that God had taken him by the right hand, led him according to his will, and received him with glory (Ps. 73:23–24). However, the illumination does correspond with Herman-Judah's description in two important regards: namely, it places Christ, holding the standard of the cross as a royal ensign, among his "most excellent friends"; and by subordinate representations of kings resting scepters on their shoulders, it establishes parallels both between scepter and cross and between the kings' crowns and Christ's nimbus of glory.

This representation refers iconographically to another in the same codex. The standard of the cross and its banner held in triumph corresponds with the spear held in dejection by the Synagogue in a picture of the crucifixion. Synagogue's spear, not flourished but resting on the earth, carries the same banner as the glorious standard of the cross. It was common for paintings to represent the Church with her victorious standard symmetrically confronting the Synagogue with her dejected one. In the Gospel Book the two illuminations are separated. But it is possible that the double painting that Herman-Judah saw consisted of a lower register depicting the crucifixion with the defeated Synagogue and an upper one with a heavenly court, both much like those in the Gospel Book.[63] Therefore, what is said but not uttered in the dream of retribution is the historical degradation of the Synagogue and the glorification of the Church, a universal event represented in the narrative by the particular cases of Herman-Judah and his kinsmen.

The first dream, one of deliverance, is altogether more complex than the later one. Supposedly sent to Herman-Judah in his thirteenth year, it represented him given signs of honor by a great king and endowed with the faculties of a mightly prince who had died. The king led Herman-Judah with him on horseback into his palace and, despite the envy of other princes, gave him the place of honor next to himself at a banquet. As though his dearest friend, he ate with him from the same platter.

Thus far I have mentioned ways in which Herman-Judah could have expected Christian readers to expand his text. But the first dream of deliverance displays traces of how, in writing, he did not expand but rather contracted the text from the range of association in his mind. Those traces are enticements for readers to re-create the path his thought had taken; but here Herman appears to have had in mind such "semi-Christians" as he had once been in the eyes of Jews (*MGH*, 114).

The first clue is the connection between feasting and the real subject of Herman-Judah's account, the search for truth,[64] which is related to his frequent metaphorical references to the bowels. Feasting is a recurrent motif. In the structure of his account, Herman-Judah began with this dream and concluded with the correct interpretation of it, relating the dream-feast with the eucharistic banquet of the altar and the celestial one of the saints, both alluded to, in his experience, by the feast of the fatted calf celebrating the return of the prodigal son. Maimonides also testified to the association of knowledge with eating. "Inasmuch as this use has become so frequent and widespread in the Hebrew language that it has become, as it were, the first meaning, the words meaning hunger and thirst are likewise employed to designate lack of knowledge and of apprehension."[65]

Nor, for some, were *feasting* and *knowing* merely verbal synonyms. As commentators on the Book of Esther pointed out, regarding Ahasuerus's feast, "the essential difference between Jewish and pagan festivities [is that] when Jews are gathered about a festal board, they discuss a Halakah or a Haggadah, or, at the least, a simple verse from the Scriptures. Ahasuerus and his boon companions rounded out the banquet with prurient talk."[66]

The arresting detail that God feasted from a salad platter with one of his chosen brings us closer to the said but unuttered. Yet a further trace of Herman-Judah's debate with Rupert of Deutz may be evident here. For in his own account of a debate with a Jew, Rupert gave considerable attention to Jewish dietary laws and surveyed the gustatory landmarks in the history of salvation, beginning with Satan's temptation of Eve to eat and live forever and the combination of eating, drinking, and play in the worship of the Golden Calf and passing through other examples to conclude with a blending of the feast for the prodigal son and the eucharistic banquets at the altar and in heaven, not unlike the conclusion of Herman-Judah's treatise. In a commentary on the Book of Revelation, Rupert specifically referred to the example of Daniel and his companions who, for the sake of God, turned aside the royal banquet that was offered to them and ate vegetables.[67]

That the king and Herman-Judah feasted on a platter of vegetables[68] leads again to the prophet whom Herman-Judah took as his model in fasting to prepare for interpreting the mysteries of dreams. As Herman-Judah demonstrated by fasting for three days instead of three weeks,[69] he did not strictly apply the paradigm of Daniel to his own efforts. This license was also plain in the fact that none of the dreams interpreted by Daniel concerned Daniel himself.

There, however, are many points of correspondence between Herman-Judah's account and the Book of Daniel. One very evident correspondence is the refusal by Daniel and his companions to violate Jewish laws by eating the king of Babylon's food and their decision to restrict their diet to vegetables and water. Attentive readers could believe that Daniel kept to this resolve even when he joined "the banquet of the King and was honored above all his friends" (Dan. 14:1; see Herman-Judah, *MGH*, 71).

Daniel and his companions were young Jewish men of noble descent, handsome, educated, and agile of mind. They had been taken captive at the fall of Jerusalem and lived in exile among idolatrous Gentiles. Through the favor of their conqueror, the king of Babylon, they were chosen to assist in his government. Thus, they were maintained at his expense and educated in the literature and language of the Gentiles. They became more adept than all the exorcists, magicians, wise men, and Chaldaeans at his court in the interpretation of dreams.

Despite terrible risks, they refused to break both Jewish dietary laws and the laws of their religion against idolatry and blasphemy, although by their faithfulness they incurred the severest penalties under the laws of their Gentile rulers. Condemned and subjected to punishment, they were unharmed. By contrast, their Gentile enemies were destroyed in traps that they had laid for them. The faithfulness of the Jews and their miraculous deliverances won the reverence of Gentiles for the God of Israel. Throughout the Book of Daniel run the themes that God, who had the power to raise the humble and cast down the proud, preserved Daniel and his companions in their hostile environment by revealing secrets and that he disposed and ruled all kingdoms, even those of the Gentiles. One vision contains the further note that a time would lapse between the giving of the prophecy and its fulfillment; the book (understanding) would be sealed, but the time would come for the prophet, Daniel, to draw his lot of vindication (Dan. 10:9).[70]

Written after Jerusalem had been laid desolate by Babylon, this account of a young Jew who refused to be polluted by assimilation to Gentile society, even though he served Gentile rulers, and who would eventually be vindicated, had a certain timeliness for Herman-Judah. Those who kept the massacres of 1096 fresh in memory recalled that Crusaders had attempted to force Jews to eat illicit food, which was called "the King's food."[71] Among the Jewish martyrs of 1096, some had earlier been invited to dine with priests (and had apparently agreed in those happier times). Once the massacres began, Jews shunned what was for them the disgusting food of their enemies and ate in purity.[72] Herman-Judah no doubt knew that for centuries, "according to the example and precepts of the holy Fathers," Christians had been forbidden to eat and drink with Jews, though these laws, like others, were often evaded.[73]

There were, of course, other instances in which Jews had kept their faith even while wielding power over idolatrous Gentiles. Did not the Gentiles themselves still honor "Joseph raised up in Pharaoh's chariot, Daniel adorned in the king's purple, and Mordecai mounted on the royal steed"?[74] Indeed, there were incidents in the Book of Esther that reinforced and multiplied lessons that Herman-Judah derived from Daniel. Apart from the pervasive esteem for the Book of Esther in Jewish communities, there are some specific reasons to think that his debate with Rupert of Deutz and his perusal of Christian books may have drawn Herman-Judah's attention forcibly to Esther.[75]

Like Daniel, Mordecai was a Jewish exile amid idolaters.[76] Like Daniel, he strictly observed Jewish dietary laws, even at the royal court and at the king's banquet. Raised to honor by a Gentile king and invested with the powers of disgraced and fallen officers of state, he was conspired against by Haman, an envious Gentile, who fell into his own trap. Haman had engineered a plan for the slaughter of the Jews; but his fall enabled the Jews to reverse roles and, by royal decree, rise up and massacre the Gentiles who, according to Haman's plot, would have slaughtered them. Just as the vindications of Daniel and his companions won honor for the God of Israel, so, according to the Book of Esther, dread of impending death prompted many Gentiles to convert to Judaism before the day appointed for slaughter. Refusal to violate the law by assimilation, the deployment of power by Jews in a Gentile environment, and the endurance of envy, mortal danger, and revenge are recurrent themes in both books.

Together with the detail that Mordecai was mounted on the king's horse,[77] deliverance as set forth in the Book of Esther provided elements that occur in Herman-Judah's account but that are not present in Daniel. One of them was that deliverance came through the agency of a woman, acting, to be sure, at a man's direction, a woman who, according to some legends, also refused food from the king's table and lived on a diet of vegetables.[78] Legend also enlarged the text to have the king's Jewish guests discount his feast and anticipate, by contrast, "the banquet [that] God will prepare for the righteous in the world to come."[79]

Finally, and perhaps most important, the version of Esther available to Herman-Judah and used by his debating opponent, Rupert, provided the organizing scheme that Herman-Judah employed in his narrative: namely, the strategy, for the reader, of hermeneutic gap and closure.[80] It began with a dream (the dream of Mordecai), imperfectly understood, and it concluded with a detailed interpretation of the dream. Rupert's own interpretation of Mordecai's dream portraying Esther as an allegorical anticipation of Christ may have been fresh in his mind when he locked horns in debate with Herman-Judah (*MGH*, 76).

In view of the Christian malevolence toward Jews that he had found a social norm, Herman-Judah's recourse to Daniel and Esther was a marked affirmation of the community whose tradition he had imbibed from his mother's breasts (*MGH*, 100).[81] It is also a powerful commentary on the association that he drew between his own circumstances and the great Jewish figures, recorded in these books, who lived among idolatrous Gentiles and, at any cost, avoided pollution by their abominable ways and execrable superstitions.

A paradox of similar magnitude is presented by the exceptionally elaborate parallels that Herman-Judah drew between his baptism and the sevenfold immersion in the Jordan by which Naaman the Syrian was cleansed of leprosy and brought to confess that there was no God in all the earth except in Israel. The same acknowledgment of piety among Gentiles prompted the comparison that Herman-Judah drew between the conversion of Nineveh, the Assyrian city, to penitence when the Ninevites heard Jonah's preaching and "believed God" (Jon. 3:5) and the discipline of continual penance at Cappenberg (*MGH*, 91).

The examplars of Daniel, Esther, and Naaman have in common one feature that also elucidates the purpose for which Herman-Judah wrote his text. For in different ways they record that with grace, unbelievers were brought to Christian faith through the counsel and actions of the pious. Herman-Judah wrote to delight his readers and to proclaim "the grace of him who [had] called [him] out of darkness into his wonderful light," and to the priesthood as well (*MGH*, 70, 122). But he demonstrated his settled evangelistic intent by urging Christians to seek Jewish converts by examples of charity (*MGH*, 87), his exhortation to simple women to imitate the examples of Glismut and Bertha whose prayers drew him to the faith of Christ (*MGH*, 108), and his final invitation to the reader to join him in rejoicing over his restoration from death to life and in magnifying the Lord (*MGH*, 127). The evidence thus far reviewed indicates that he wrote with "semi-Christians" among the Jews particularly in mind, affirming the antecedents that he had in common with them and inviting them to follow where he had gone. It also indicates that he wrote in full knowledge of the hatred of the Jewish community toward apostates and that he recognized the difficult task of establishing his credit in the eyes of Jews who could be as hostile toward him as were some Christians.

A survey of extremely fragmentary materials has led one scholar to conclude that between the ninth and the thirteenth centuries, there was in western Europe "an intensive activity of Jewish propaganda and proselytism."[82] Indeed, conversions to Judaism—including perhaps that of an archbishop of Bari ignored by contemporary Latin writers—are recorded.[83] It is possible that Herman-Judah retained the spirit of proselytism, as he did the examples of Daniel and Mordecai, from his life as a Jew and that his Christian admirers, by repeatedly asking him to recount the tumultuous course of his search for truth (*MGH*, 69), channeled that residual impulse into the service of Christian evangelism.

The connection between conversion and sacrifice was also grounded in Herman-Judah's ancestral legacy, as assimilated into Christianity. Herman-Judah identified himself as an Israelite from the tribe of Levi, following the example of Paul, an Israelite of the tribe of Benjamin (*MGH*, 70; Rom. 11:1). By his day Christian allegorists took it as axiomatic that if it were figurative, a passage in Scripture had to refer to Christ. Rupert of Deutz insisted on this rule. As noted above, Herman-Judah deployed some striking Christological references to himself. And yet the fact that so many of the scriptural coordinates that he chose—from the books of Daniel and Esther, for example—were not in the standard repertory of Christology sets Herman-Judah's way of thinking apart from usual patterns in Christian exegesis. The link between conversion and sacrifice was inescapable for him, a juncture at which Christology could not be evaded. If his text is an account of his passage from literal to figurative (or spiritual) interpretation of the Scriptures, it is equally an account of his acceptance of the doctrine that Christ's crucifixion was a sacrificial act and of his own vocation from the Levirate to reenact that sacrifice at the altar (e.g., *MGH*, 127). Stating a common position, John of Salisbury wrote that the Christian clergy had succeeded to the privileges of the Levites. If this were not so, he added, "the Apostle [Paul] is void and all interpreters of the Scriptures, false."[84]

In retrospect Herman-Judah recalled that his first step toward Christianization was his disgusted fascination with the double painting of Christ crucified and enthroned: that is, of the sacrificial moment (*MGH*, 75). The entire portion of his debate with Rupert of Deutz that he chose to re-create turns on the allegorical equation between representations of the cross and the altar that the Reubenites and Gadites built, never to be used as an altar but always to remain a memorial to the one altar where sacrifices were actually and licitly presented (*MGH*, 78–80, 82). Thus, the debate also presupposed an equation between actual cross and actual altar. Likewise, the overarching structure of the treatise begins with a vision of a royal banquet and ends with an interpretation of that vision as a sign of the eucharistic feast. There are other indications of the link between conversion and sacrifice in Herman-Judah's pre-Christian use of the sign of the cross to obtain power and vision (*MGH*, 105, 115) and in the implicit theological dependence of baptism on Christ's redemptive death.

But, in the end, did Herman-Judah deserve to be loved or hated by God? His pairing of conversion and sacrifice belonged to a wider network of association in Herman-Judah's mind, one that included a conviction of his own sinfulness and unworthiness. He was uncertain that though among the called, he was also in the narrower company of the chosen, uncertainty from which vivid belief in God as the Lord of vengeance permitted no easy release (*MGH*, 70, 93, 116–18, 126).[85] It is possible to relate this network of ideas to the implied association of the "rational sacrifice" that was Christ, "the price of redemption" (*MGH*, 80, 82; cf. "vitale pretium," *MGH*, 106) with the "rational booty" that he offered in the forms of his half brother and, indeed, himself as priest, if not as victim (above at n. 62).

The web of sin, impending vengeance, and propitiating sacrifice belonged to the Old Testamental heritage of Christianity. For Herman-Judah and his Jewish contemporaries in the Rhineland, including the "semi-Christians" among them, it belonged to ways of understanding not only

Scripture but also recent experience. The massacres of 1096 (and 1146) were interpreted as acts of vengeance visited by God upon his people because of their sinfulness. Those who ritually slaughtered others or themselves were regarded as discharging the sacrificial office of priests. One father, indeed, specifically enacted that office as he slaughtered his children in the synagogue before the Ark and sprinkled their blood on its pillars with a prayer for expiation.[86] Those whose blood was thus sacrificially offered on the altar of God were thought to walk with the righteous in the Garden of Eden and to sit with Rabbi Akiba and his companions, martyred of old, and feast with them.[87]

The phrase "God of vengeance" and the statement that God was Lord of vengeance recur in accounts of the massacres in 1096 written by Herman-Judah's contemporaries. They expressed, on the one hand, the submission of the Jews to divine punishment for their sins and, on the other, the call for divine revenge on the murdering idolaters. This combination of guilt and revenge, of abasement and vindication, is reproduced in Herman-Judah's characterization of his own motives. What distinguishes his text from these others is his association of sacrifice, not with steadfastness in Judaism, but with going over to its deadly enemies.

The identification of conversion with sacrifice marks a division between the hermeneutic strategy that Herman-Judah constructed for readers in the text and the hermeneutic method that he followed prior to the writing of the text. It leaves a trail of familiar signs for "semi-Christians" who might follow him in abandoning Synagogue for Church and who might also harbor suspicions of him as an apostate. And finally it releases the pathos in the words of the Jewish convert in whose footsteps Herman-Judah himself had followed: "I say then, hath God cast away his people? God forbid. For I also am an Israelite, of the seed of Abraham, of the tribe of Benjamin. God hath not cast away his people which he acknowledged of old as his own" (Rom. 11:1–2). It is the pathos of a man who, converting, found himself among people who placed an interpretation on the Book of Daniel quite different from his, interpreters who took the account of Daniel and his companions in the fiery furnace as a type of the hellish furnace in which God would torture his deniers, the Jews, forever.[88]

Conclusion: Serious Play

Writing about the city of Christ, Otto of Freising commented: "The perfidious city of faithless Jews and Gentiles [i.e, the Muslims] still remains;

but by comparison with the more noble kingdoms held by our people, hardly any things done by them in their realms (vile as they are before God and the world) are found to be worthy of writing down or of commending to posterity."[89] In a small way Herman-Judah escaped this sentence of oblivion; he succeeded by describing how he was assimilated to the enemies of his people.

The presence of a covert message between the lines is not surprising. For quite regularly authors write so as to invite, or compel, readers to expand a text encompassing such a message. Readers move from the letter of the text to the expanded interpretation of the text. By contrast, as authors move from interpretation to text, they also leave marks of how the text was formed by distillation and contraction within a wider, and unwritten, range of association. Nor was deliberate concealment astonishing, given the charged environment in which Herman-Judah lived, and given also the deliberate practice of obscurity and concealment that belonged to the tradition of Christian exegesis. It was wrong, Otto of Freising wrote, to make great matters contemptible by spreading them out for all to see.[90] This practice was also warranted in the synagogue by the distinction between the large majority and the few wise, to which Maimonides was not the only or the least authoritative witness (above at n. 56).

As in the case of Augustine's *Confessions*, a student of Herman-Judah's account needs to make numerous distinctions. These include the supernatural phenomenon of conversion: the formal signs of conversion (acceptance of faith, submission to baptism, obedience to Church discipline); the hermeneutic methods employed to interpret the supernatural event and what were taken to be its formal signs; the way of life and spiritual charismata required after baptism to perfect the conversion process; and, finally, the text that memorialized understanding conversion. In both cases, the recollective text was written a time, perhaps many years, after the events recorded. It is also clear that both texts served sacramental, evangelistic, and militant objectives. They were addressed to audiences that were, actually or potentially, hostile. But what Herman-Judah called conversion was not what Augustine called by that name. What made the naming thinkable to the one differed from the other's processes of cognition and recognition. The dominance of eroticism in Augustine's text and its attenuation in Herman-Judah's was a crucial symptom of their divergence in methods of understanding behind the divergent uses of the same name.

Eroticism enabled Augustine to serve his sacramental objectives with the high mysticism of dialectical participation between God and the faithful (both individual and collective). It permitted him to conceive his evangelistic task as conducive to empathetic participation among the faithful of every epoch in world history. Finally, together with his episcopal office as "dispensor of God's word and sacrament," eroticism brought Augustine to identify himself so closely with the magistracy of the Church that an apology on his own behalf was indistinguishable from polemics in defense of the Church. In all regards, although he changed theological systems, Augustine employed the same forms of thought and language before and after union with the Church.

By contrast, the meager place of eroticism in Herman-Judah's account excluded participatory bonding, whether dialectical or empathetic. Whatever causes for this may have lain in the temperament of the man, the loneliness of the Jewish convert in Christian society also played a role. As he worked out his sacramental and evangelistic objectives, Herman-Judah's thinking did not move from the manifold of community to the bonding of communion. For he was still guided by the highly individualistic exemplars of personal accountability provided by the Old Testament, and not, as Augustine was, by unitive principles of ontology and metaphysics derived from Neoplatonism.

Herman-Judah's militance also is individualistic, a personal apologia rather than doctrinal polemics sheltering under the magistracy of the Church. Furthermore, his apology was drawn from the traditions in which he had been nurtured, and which were despised by the tradition to which he was converted. It was set forth in Latin, a language alien to his community, one that Herman-Judah learned at the cost of five years of study after his baptism and after, renouncing family, friends, world, and self, he had entered the religious community at Cappenberg (*MGH*, 122).

One measure of the absence of participatory bonding from Herman-Judah's account is that he did not follow Augustine in asserting that God was coauthor of his work. Another is in the discrete problematics in the two works. With his metaphysical equipment, Augustine found his problematic core in speculative matters, such as the origins of good and evil, human nature, the freedom of the will, the relations of the individual to the whole, the character of time, and the mysteries of Incarnation and Church.

The problematic core that Herman-Judah encountered was by no means speculative, even in its exegetical method. Though preoccupied with the distinction between literal and figurative interpretations of Scripture, he left no trace of passing beyond the anagogical linkage between Old Testament prophecy and New Testament fulfillment and the moral application of scriptural models to contemporary life to the more rarified atmosphere of mystical interpretation. Certainly, he spoke of "mysteries" in the Scriptures, but he appears to have meant "secrets," such as Maimonides asserted were revealed to the wise in flashes, and not metaphysical hierarchies of being.

Herman-Judah's problematic was composed of practical matters: the application of the Mosaic Law (*MGH*, 71, 76–83, 94–96, 103–6); the riddle of why the Jews were exiled and dispersed if their faith were authentic and the Christians prospered if theirs were wrong (*MGH*, 92); how to overcome the tricks of the Devil; how to maintain life, fortune, and status among the Jews while moving toward baptism; and, after baptism, how to reconcile the command given to Christians to love their enemies with the habit Christians had of spitting in derision upon the Jews (*MGH*, 77, 87). He did not pose the speculative questions posed by Augustine (and repeated by Otto of Freising) of why there was evil and suffering in the world if its divine Creator and Governor were good and why, since God could at any instant reveal his truth, he permitted the Jews to languish in their ignorance.[91]

If the absence of participatory bonding was a symptom of a nonspeculative way of thinking, the lack of speculative tools and methods constituted a yet more fundamental difference between Augustine's hermeneutic methods and Herman-Judah's. It was telling that Augustine identified the spoils of the Egyptians with the appropriation of pre-Christian ideas and methods, while Herman-Judah identified them with the kidnapping of his brother. Augustine employed a metaphor of violence; Hermann committed an act of violence, which extended but did not spiritualize the letter of the scriptural text. The difference between the two authors regarding art likewise hinges on the power of understanding abstractly by visualization. For Augustine, painting and metaphors drawn from painting were universal aids to belief and understanding. For Herman-Judah, disciplined from infancy to mistrust graven images, visual art was an enterprise to be mentioned only as an obstacle encountered early in the sequence of events that led to baptism. Art and metaphors drawn from it did not serve his methods of understanding.

This may have been true because, unlike Augustine, he did not consider thought a process by which sensory experiences were transformed into images in the memory (pictures in the mind) and then abstracted and transformed again into thought. There was no need for him to state his epistemological principles in an account of his conversion. However, one point is evident in his comments on religious art, the ascetic discipline at Cappenberg, feasts (including the Eucharist), and the emotional sufferings that beset him. In no regard did he characterize sensory perceptions as kinesthetic materials to be internalized, digested, and visualized into knowledge. He used Augustine's habitual distinction between outward (physical) and inner (spiritual) vision, thus becoming able to confess that as a Jew he was physically sighted and spiritually blind (*MGH*, 82–83). But when he used the iconographical symbol of the adder to represent himself, it was to point up the difference between the ear of the body and the ear of the heart, which was also that of intellect (*MGH*, 82, 102).

The distinction between epistemologists who give first place to hearing and those who consider vision primary is an ancient and continuing one. The striking aspect of Herman-Judah's account is that hearing is represented only by the spoken (or written) word. Music, which was so pronounced an aid to spiritual understanding for Augustine and for Herman-Judah's contemporaries, is absent from Herman-Judah's own account, strangely absent even from his feasts. Psalmody, the form of music most often invoked as an instrument of understanding, was normally a collective enterprise.

I return, through the primacy of the word and the concreteness of nonspeculative thought, to the smallness of love in Herman-Judah's understanding. Much can be told from analogues and metaphors of play, especially in the language of ritual. To describe Christian life and work, the Church Fathers assembled a repertoire of such figures. Some, drawn from amphitheater and circus, emphasized conflict and individual skill. Others, taken from the theater (and painting) elucidated the emotional bonding that came by imitation.[92]

Herman-Judah employed some figures drawn from that repertoire. He entered the religious community at Cappenberg, he wrote, for spiritual combat—"to fight naked with the naked Enemy" (*MGH*, 121). He challenged Rupert of Deutz to join him in the conflict of disputation (*MGH*, 76). He used the analogue of a solitary runner, straining himself to no avail, but watched by others who could, if they wished, set him on the right track (*MGH*, 89–90). He discounted the "lies" of painting (*MGH*, 75), and his distance from imitative bonding is further indicated by his allusion to acting. For he used the metaphor of an actor transforming himself into the persona of another to illustrate deception.[93]

Another visual metaphor of play crept into Herman-Judah's vocabulary when he described the ordeal by hot iron, once vainly proposed to determine whether he should be baptized. He spoke of the proposed trial as "this spectacle of faith" (*MGH*, 85). But Herman-Judah's sense of conflict with the Devil and the "Synagogue of Satan" makes it evident that he intended, not the mimetic sense of the theater, but the conflictual one of the amphitheater, as Rupert of Deutz had done when he wrote of his debate with a Jew as "a festive spectacle for boys," a "conflict," and a "duel," for which Scripture provided the weapons.[94]

Above all, Herman-Judah's account was dominated by the terrible, unseen play of Satan, so strikingly absent from Augustine's. At every turn, the deceptions, enticements, and malicious guile of the ancient Enemy were what threatened to thrust Herman-Judah back into the pit of perdition, even as the waters of baptism ran down his head. The diabolic power loosed upon him was part of the continuing game of war between God and Satan. In the *Confessions*, Augustine avoided delivering up to his earthly foes the Manichaeism potentially implied in such a narrative strategy.

These metaphors of play, ritualized into thought about becoming and being Christian, may indeed express a kind of bonding, one by malevolent sympathy that, as in a feud, binds rivals together in such a way that the hostility of the one is necessary to the self-understanding of the other.[95] For Herman-Judah, understanding conversion in the light of Jewish hermeneutics, and for the "semi-Christians" whom he may have wished to encourage, metaphors of conflict and aggressive imitation must have silently echoed Rupert's mocking recollection of how the idolatrous Jews had played, eating and drinking before the Golden Calf, and his vengeful joy in the punishment visited upon them for persecuting Christ and the early Church as if at play.[96]

A Translation of Herman-Judah's
Short Account of His Own Conversion

A Letter by Herman

To his dearest son Henry, Herman, who by the grace of God is what he is, sends heartfelt love in Christ.

Many religious, both men and women, persist in trying to find out from me how I converted from Judaism to the grace of Christ and whether, among the first beginnings of my conversion, I endured temptations of the malign Enemy. Indeed, recently, when you were present, the devout request of some women of holy lives compelled me to unfold its whole sequence of events. For I was not converted with that ease with which we often see many unbelievers, whether Jews or pagans, converted to the catholic faith by a swift and unanticipated change.[1] In such cases, those whom we yesterday lamented as faithless we rejoice with today as believers, made coheirs with us in the grace of Christ.

But, by contrast, my conversion was gained in the face of powerful waves of temptations, which ever mounted at the beginning, of many treacheries that the ancient Enemy laid to arrest it, of long-suffering amid continual ebb and flow, and, finally, with the greatest toil. For these reasons, it ought to be all the more delightful for pious ears to hear, as it is amazing in light of the difficulty with which it came to pass.

Thus, aroused by the devotion of many and, most of all, given heart by your pious urging, dearest brother, I have thought it a worthy task to commit it to writing and, through it, faithfully to proclaim to believers of the coming age, as of the present, the inestimable grace of him who has called me from darkness into his wondrous light, and thus to serve his everlasting praise and glory.

Here ends the letter.

IN THE NAME OF THE LORD. *Here begins the brief account of his conversion given by brother Herman, of good memory, who was once a Jew.*

Chapter 1. *Concerning a vision which he saw while still a boy concerning the future grace of Christ toward him.*
Now, then, I am a sinner and an unworthy priest, Herman, once called Judah. I am of the Israelite people and the tribe of Levi[2] and I was born of David, my father, and Sephora, my mother, in the metropolis of Cologne. While I was still held pinioned in the net of Jewish unbelief, God showed me by a most joyful premonition the blessings of his grace that were to come to me.

The vision was of the following kind. In the thirteenth year of my age [1120 or 1121], what I saw in a dream was as though the Roman emperor Henry [V], who was ruling at that time (the predecessor of the glorious King Lothar [III]), had confiscated all the holdings of a certain overmighty prince who suddenly died. That king (so it seemed) came to me and gave me a horse, white as snow and wonderfully muscled, and a belt woven of gold with consummate craftsmanship, and a silk purse hanging from it that held seven very heavy coins. All of this he gave over to me.

"Know," he said, "that my dukes and princes take serious umbrage at the benefice that I have conferred on you. Despite that, I shall add to these many more benefices by far, and I shall give you the entire inheritance of this dead prince to possess, by perpetual right, as a heritage."

Then, returning due thanks for this regal generosity, I buckled on that noble belt.[3] Having mounted the horse, I accompanied the king, at his side, to his palace. There, as he splendidly feasted with his friends, I reclined next to him, as the dearest of friends. From the same vessel [*scutella*] as he I ate a salad [*olus*] made up of many kinds of herbs and roots.[4]

And so, awakening, still in the joy of this vision, I did not—even though a child—judge the most extraordinary things that I had seen to be empty, as the lightheartedness of a child might have indicated. Instead, I was sure that I had foreseen by that premonition some great thing in store for me.

I betook myself to a certain relative of mine, named Isaac, a man then of great authority among the Jews.[5] I entreated him to interpret the dream for me in whatever way he could, and I recounted it to him step by step.

"Knowing" only those things "that are of the flesh" [cf. Rom. 8:5], he set forth for me a conjecture that made sense from the perspective of carnal happiness. He said that the great white stallion signified that a noble and beautiful wife would fall my lot; the coins in the purse, that I was to have great riches; the feast celebrated with the emperor, that I would in future be highly honored among the Jews.

But, much later, divine grace fulfilled this vision for me more than plainly with spiritual benefits, as the interpretation of this vision which follows [chap. 21] will indicate and the outcome of the matter will prove. Now, however, I shall unfold in order what sort of beginning the circumstances surrounding my conversion were destined to have.

Chapter 2. *On what occasion he first joined the Christians and how much he profited by their company.*

In the seventh year after these events, therefore, I arrived in Mainz to do business with various associations of merchants [1127 or 1128]. Indeed, all Jews are enserfed to commerce. The glorious King Lothar was there at the same time, having with him Egbert, the venerable bishop of the church at Münster and a man of all counsel. Because the king kept him there, occupied with affairs of the kingdom, the bishop had been detained longer than he planned. The money in his coffers had been exhausted.[6] He was compelled by need to borrow silver from me. However, I took no security from him, as the practice of the Jews demanded, thinking the good faith of so great a man a pledge of great value.

When this became known, my parents and friends chastised me with a rebuke that was sharp enough, saying that I had been grossly negligent in taking it upon myself to make money available to anyone without security and above all to a man frequently distracted by many administrative undertakings. By the custom of the Jews, which I knew very well, I ought to have exacted a pawn twice the amount of the loan. And so they were of the opinion that I should betake myself to the aforesaid bishop and stay with him as long as it took for me to recover the entire debt from him. However, fearing (which actually happened) that going about with Christians, I might be turned away by their stimulus from following our fathers' tradition, they retained a certain Jew named Baruch, a man well advanced in age, and with care and resourcefulness, they committed me to his custody.

And so, yielding to the advice of my parents and friends, I went to Münster, which city was the see of his bishopric [early December 1127 or late November 1129]. There, when I found the bishop, I raised the matter of the debt with him, saying that I did not dare enter my parents' sight again until I had the money in hand.

At the moment he lacked a sum from which to repay me. Thus, he kept me with him for almost twenty weeks. In that space of time—since often, as he was used to do, that good Shepherd administered the fodder of God's word to the sheep committed to him—I mingled with the herd of those sheep, led on by a friendly inquisitiveness common to the young, or rather by a brazen impudence, since, on account of the stench of error, I as yet deserved to be numbered among the goats instead of the sheep.

And so, there I heard a "scribe learned in the Kingdom of Heaven bringing forth new and old from his treasure" [cf. Matt. 13:52]. Linking the Old Testament to the New and vindicating the New with apt reasoning from the Old, he taught that some precepts of the Law—"Thou shalt not commit adultery; thou shalt not steal; thou shalt not bear false witness; honor thy father and thy mother" [Exod. 20:12, 14–16]—were to be kept only according to the surface of the letter but others—such as "Thou shalt not plow with an ox and an ass together; thou shalt not seethe a kid in its mother's milk" [Deut. 22:10; Exod. 23:19, 34:26; Deut. 14:21]—were fatuous according to the letter. Nevertheless, through a most beautiful way of reasoning, he translated [the second kind of precepts] into allegorical meanings. Using this kind of distinction, he adverted to the example of the Jews, like some beasts of burden, content with the letter of the precepts alone, as with chaff, and Christians, like men using reason, refreshing themselves with spiritual understanding, as with the sweetest pith of the straw.[7]

As the bishop discoursed among the people on these and like matters, I listened with so much the greater eagerness and delight, as I retained in my own memory those things which he was recalling from the histories of the Old Deed [*Instrumentum*] and which had often been read in Hebrew codices. Knowing also that animals that do not chew the cud are numbered by the Law among the unclean, I transferred to the stomach of memory for frequent rumination with myself whatever things I had heard in his preaching that pleased me.[8]

Dumbfounded with amazement, Christians perceived that I listened most attentively to the things that were being said. When they asked whether the bishop's sermon had pleased me, I answered that it had, some parts more than others. But wishing well for my inquisitiveness and, at the same time, pitying, with pious feeling, my error, they urged me most devoutly to join myself to the catholic union. They affirmed that their Jesus was most merciful and would send away none who turned to him, according to the testimony that he himself gave in the gospel, saying, "If anyone come to me, him will I not cast out" [John 6:37].

To give credence to the bounty of this grace, they also set before me the example of their Apostle Paul, in whose honor the smaller basilica of that city had been built and dedicated, saying that he had first been a Pharisee and so great a follower of the Law that having received authority from the chief priests, he persecuted Christ's faithful with an insatiable cruelty. But in the midst of his attempt to accomplish this crime, he was hurled to earth by a bolt of heavenly light, and when from on high Christ forbade the savagery that he intended, he was wonderfully changed through God's clemency from Saul into Paul, from wolf into lamb, from persecutor into preacher. Stroking me with these and similar words, as though—so to speak—with certain enchantments,[9] Christians urged me to cast off the burdensome yoke of the Mosaic Law and to shoulder the easy one of Christ.

And so, as time went on, their intense conversations made me increasingly eager to inquire quite diligently into the sacraments of the Church. I was not yet entering the basilica out of devotion so much as out of curiosity. Earlier, I had shrunk from it as from some pagan temple. Examining everything in it with more than some care, I saw, among the artful varieties of carvings and pictures, a particularly monstrous idol.

To be exact, I discerned one and the same man abased and exalted, despised and lifted up, ignominious and glorious. Below, he hung wretchedly on a cross.[10] Above, by means of painting's lies, he was enthroned, handsome enough to seem to have been deified. I admit, I was struck mute, suspecting that effigies of this sort were such likenesses [*simulachra*] as, by a many-formed delusive error, paganism normally dictated for itself. The Pharisaical doctrine that once was mine easily persuaded me that this was true.

Moreover, my tutor, whom I recalled above, craftily looking into what I was doing, caught up with me frequenting gatherings of Christians as often as I could and repeatedly crossing the thresholds of churches. He sharply rebuked me, as one given over to his custody, and he affirmed that he was going to report to my parents' ears all the follies of my illicit curiosity. As though deaf and not hearing his threats and arguments at all, I gave every day over to my new curiosity, so much the more as, living under the care of the bishop, I was entirely free from almost all business. Frequently, also, entering the schools of the clergy, I received books from them, in which I diligently considered the properties of individual elements [of grammar] and wisely studied names. I began at once, without a teacher and to the immense astonishment of those who heard, to join letters to syllables and syllables to expressions; and so, in brief, I came to know how to read Scripture. This would, perhaps, seem incredible to anyone if it were ascribed to me and not to God, to whom nothing is impossible.

Chapter 3. *Concerning the disputation held by him with Rupert, abbot of Deutz.* At that time the abbot of the monastery of Deutz, a man named Rupert, was staying in Münster.[11] He was subtle in temperament, learned in eloquence, and most accomplished in sacred as well as in human letters. I saw him. I invited him to lock horns in debate. To use the Apostle's words, he was "ready to give account to everyone who asked him about the faith and hope that is in Christ" [cf. 1 Pet. 3:15]. He promised, with God's help, to give me satisfaction at the agreed place and time on whatever matter I wished, both by reason and by authority of Scripture.

Then, I arose and spoke to him in the following way.[12] "You Christians bear a great prejudice toward the Jews. You spit upon them with curses and loathing as though they were dead dogs, although you read that of old, God chose them for himself, as his own people, from among all the nations of the world. He considered them alone worthy to know his holy name. For them alone, he deigned [to give] the most perfect rule of his justice; and in observation of it, they live and become holy, as he is holy. He not only commanded that rule by proclaiming it, but he even wrote it with his own hand on tablets of stone. [He gave the Law] to them alone, I say, for this Scripture itself, which is daily ruminated by your own mouth, testifies, saying: 'He declares his word to Jacob, his works of justice and judgment to Israel. He has not done so to every nation, and he has not manifested his judgments to them' [Ps. 147:19–20].

"But you, blinded by vast envy of the divine benefits toward us, consider loathsome above all mortals the very ones whom, as you have read, you know to be more honorable and beloved to God than all other human beings. But let that be.

"We bear patiently, indeed, and with equanimity the invectives and mockery of men, all the while faithfully persevering in God's law and ceremonies. Certainly, it is better for us to fall into the hands of men than to abandon the Law of our God. What is more fearful: to bear the wrath of men or that of God, to be spat upon by men or cursed by God? In the divine Law, it is written as follows: 'Cursed be everyone who does not stand fast in all the things that are written' in this volume. Doubtless, in these words our righteousness, which is from the Law, is defended by insuperable authority against all your yapping.

"So also that pride is manifestly condemned by which you fatuously boast of observing the Law while impiously derogating us for keeping it with a straightforward observance, as we received from our fathers. For, indeed, nothing is qualified, nothing excepted, when the universal rule is laid down: 'Cursed be he who does not stand fast in all the things that are written' in this volume [Gal. 3:10; cf. Deut. 27:26].

"You are not doers of the Law, as you say, but plainly judges of it. Laughable as it is to say, you correct it just as you want. You accept some things but reject others. Among the latter, you decide some are superstitious and others, said in a mystic fashion, are to be accepted, not in the way in which they were actually said, but according to whatever stupid, asinine, and depraved fictions anyone pleases. Plainly, it is stupid temerity and madness worthy of unrestrained derision for human beings to wish to correct what God established and, under a terrible curse, commanded them to observe.

"You Christians are particularly liable to the curse, since while you presume to be judges of the Law, you are also condemned as its prevaricators. For the moment, let me select from among the many one thing that would suffice for your total damnation. Why do you, who vaunt yourselves on the observance of the Law, defy it with the impiety of manifest idolatry?

"For look at what I have seen with my own eyes. In your temples you have set up as objects of adoration for yourselves huge images elaborately wrought with the arts of painters and sculptors. O, if, to consummate your perdition, you worshiped the likeness of anything besides that of a crucified man![13] For since, according to the authority of the Law, 'cursed is everyone who hangs on wood' [Gal. 3:13; cf. Deut. 21:23], how much more are you accursed for worshiping one who hangs on wood? Moreover, if, as another passage in Scripture testifies, 'cursed is everyone who trusts in man and makes flesh his arm" (Jer. 17:5], how much heavier is the sentence under which you fall, since you even place your hope in a crucified man?

"Not only do you not hide the madness of this superstition of yours, but you even—which is the greater crime—glory in it. You preach your sin as Sodom. Choose whichever of these two options suits you. Either set forth for me the authority for this abominable worship of yours, if you happen by some chance to know it, or, indeed, the logical consequence, if you cannot do that, confess openly instead that you cannot, bearing the shame of this damnable error, which is entirely contrary to the Law."

Chapter 4. *Rupert's answers to Judah's charges.*[14]
To these remarks Rupert answered: "I find nothing at all daunting in any of the arguments that you have, as the occasion allows, set up for me to oppose. Indeed, there is an abundant supply of authorities out of your own books with which we can defend and confirm the truth of our religion. Fully armed with them, as with an invincible shield, we may be able safely both to dodge and to cast back the darts of your objections.

"From them, I shall now show you by a conclusive argument, if you are disposed to give me your patient attention, that what you call our idolatry is most full of piety and religion and radiant with the light of all truth.

"Therefore: We abhor and execrate in every way the crime of idolatry that you are trying to foist on us. We faithfully embrace the cult of the one and true God. Nor do we, as your slander maintains, worship as a divinity the image of a crucified man or of anything else. Rather, through the adorable form of the cross, we represent to ourselves, with pious devotion, Christ's Passion, by which 'to snatch us from the curse of the Law, he made himself a thing accursed for us on the cross' [cf. Gal. 3:13]. We do this so that while we externally image forth his death through the likeness of the cross, we may also be kindled inwardly to love of him and that we, who continually remember that entirely untainted by any sin, he endured so ignominious a death for us, may always consider with pious reflection (wrapped up in many and great sins as we are) what a great obligation we owe for his love. This is the general rationale for the images that you see among us.

"There is also a specific rationale. Images were devised to benefit the simple and uneducated so that those who could not learn the Passion of their Redeemer by reading in books could see the very price of their redemption through the visible appearance of the cross. What codices represent to us, images represent to the uneducated common folk.[15]

"To keep the ritual of our religion from seeming to be built up only by human reason, let me demonstrate its support in the authority of the Old Testament.[16] For ancient history recounts to us something very similar to this. When the children of Israel were led into the promised land, 'the sons of Reuben and the sons of Gad and half the tribe of Manasses' [cf. Josh. 22:9–10], as they went to the land that had fallen their lot and came to the hills along the Jordan, built there an altar of immense size. However, the Lord had commanded in the Law that all the children of Israel should have one altar in common for celebrating the rite of sacrifices and that that altar

MGH, 80

MGH, 81

should stand in the place that he had chosen for invoking the power of his majesty. That place was then, as everyone knew, located in Shiloh.

"And so, when this act of the Reubenites and the Gadites was reported to the children of Israel, they were profoundly stirred up against them, as prevaricators of the Law, and seized weapons to punish the brazenness in them that had led to this monstrous deed.

"And yet, taking provident counsel, they for a time withheld their hands from spilling the blood of brothers until, envoys from each tribe having been sent ahead to them, they could learn through the inquiries of the envoys what had been the occasion of such great effrontery. When the envoys had arrived and rebuked them for having presumed to build up an altar contrary to a prohibition of the Law and to the scandal and ruin of all Israel, they received the following kind of response from them.

" 'The Mighty One, God, the Lord! The Mighty One, God, the Lord! He knows, and lets Israel itself know! If it was in rebellion or in breach of faith toward the Lord, spare us not today for building an altar to turn away from following the Lord; or if we did so to offer burnt offerings or cereal offerings or peace offerings on it, may the Lord himself take vengeance. Nay, but we did it from fear that in time to come your children might say to our children, "What have you to do with the Lord, the God of Israel? For the Lord has made the Jordan a boundary between us and you, you Reubenites and Gadites; you have no portion in the Lord." So your children might make our children cease to worship the Lord. Therefore we said, "Let us now build an altar, not for burnt offering, nor for sacrifice, but to be a witness between us and you, and between the generations after us, that we do perform the service of the Lord" ' [Josh. 22:22–27].

"So, therefore, they had constructed the altar, not to sacrifice victims and holocausts on it, but to demonstrate by such a testimony that they and their posterity belonged to the lot of God's people. Thus, we also, for a like reason, hold the cross of Christ in great reverence because of the one hanging on it, but in no way do we render it the worship owed divinity. As the altar was made for them, so also is the cross made for us as a witness to the end that while we consider that the price of our redemption hung upon it, we may rejoice that through that price we belong to the company of saints and to the eternal heritage of the Heavenly Jerusalem."

Rupert in this way met all my objections both with the most beautiful arguments and with the most valid authorities of Scripture. With the brilliant rays of his answers, he cast my objections aside as though they were shades of darkest night. But, wretched as I was, like an adder,[17] deaf and stopping up his ears [cf. Ps. 56:5], I did not perceive the words of Rupert's most sweet incantation with the ears of the heart,[18] and I was not able to detect the light of truth with my mental eyes, darkened as they were by a cloud of Jewish blindness.

Since it would take a very long time for us to unfold the whole course of our debate, let it suffice to have touched on it here in part. Now let us pursue the business in hand: namely, historical description.

Chapter 5. *That the charity and faith of a certain man greatly stirred him to the faith of Christ.*
At this point, the memory comes back of something that I think ought to be inserted here. One reason is that, by its sweetness, it served me as a great stimulus of conversion. Another is that it can give to readers an outstanding example of perfect charity and unfeigned faith, and one to be imitated.

Egbert, the pontiff already mentioned, had, as the purveyor of his household, a certain man called Richmar, who was—as was well proven to me—strongly religious in his whole manner of life. One day the bishop, in the midst of dinner, sent him half a loaf of white bread and a portion of roast pike by his butler, as lords do.[19] But because he was completely filled with feelings of piety, he set before me, with love's supreme alacrity, what had been sent to him (for I was sitting beside him). He contented himself only with bread and water, according to the religious practice habitual to him.

Not only did I greatly rejoice on account of this deed, but I was also powerfully wonderstruck that a man whom thus far I thought beyond the Law and without God could have the virtue of charity in such great measure, especially toward me. For he could likewise have detested me as the enemy of his sect, rather than loving me, especially in view of the just sentence in which the Old Law says, "Love your friend and hold your enemy in hatred" [Lev. 19:18].[20] But he acted as a disciple of the true law of the gospel, in which it is said, "Love your enemies, do good to them who hate you": that is, do good not only "to those who belong to the household of his faith" but also "to all" human beings [Matt. 5:43–44; Gal. 6:10]. Wherefore, he assiduously showed his love to me in good deeds, although I was unworthy of them, and he labored tirelessly with gentle conversations, both exhorting and beseeching, to draw me away from the error of my fathers and to win me for Christ. He knew indeed, as the Apostle James said, that "he who makes a sinner convert from the error of his way, saves his own soul from death and covers a multitude of his own sins" [James 5:20].

But when he saw that with these acts of piety, he could not soften the iron hardness of my heart to obey the true faith, he took my measure as the Apostle testifies in a certain place, saying "that the Jews seek signs" [1 Cor. 1:22]. He proposed to me, with the greatest steadfastness, this bargain: that if, in proof of his faith, he sensed no burning while carrying (as is customarily done) a scorching iron in his bare hand, I would faithfully submit to the cure of holy baptism, the dark cover of all unbelief washed from my heart. But if, to the contrary, his hand were branded, it would be again up to my judgment what I wished to do or choose but that he would not bring any further persuasions to bear on me in this matter.

I joyfully took this most stalwart proposal of his to heart. As though already sure of my conversion, he could not have been happier. Eagerly, he raced to ask the bishop graciously to exorcise the iron to be used for celebrating this spectacle of faith.

But since the time of mercy had not yet come for me, the outcome of his pious petition was just the contrary of what he hoped. Indeed, the bishop, although he admired and praised the great constancy of faith in him, yet censured this petition of his as not so much pious as inordinate. Weighing it on the higher scale of his discernment, the bishop rebuked him with a mild response. He said that he had had, in this matter, the zeal "of God, but not according to knowledge" [cf. Rom. 10:2]. God was on no account to be tested by examinations of this sort. But rather, the bishop continued, he was to be entreated to the end that he "who wishes all men to be saved and to come to knowledge of truth" [1 Tim. 2:4] would deign to untie the knots of unbelief by his own most merciful piety when and as he wished and make a master of error into a disciple of truth.

For the rest, he said, you are never to ask or, above all, to yearn for some sign from God to promote this change. Certainly, it would be the easiest thing for his omnipotence to convert whomever he wished without any miracle, but only by the secret visitation of his grace. A sign which is displayed visibly to the external sight would be idle if he did not work invisibly through grace in the heart of a human being. And, indeed, we read that many have been converted without signs but also that countless others have stayed fast in infidelity after seeing miracles. Besides, he added, it has to be known that faith which is won over by miracles has either no or very little merit but that faith which is undertaken without any incitement of miracles, but with simple piety and pious simplicity, has the most excellent merit before God and the highest praise. To this, our Lord himself, the author of this faith, bore witness in the Gospel when he made clear the rule of unbelief. He said, "Unless you see signs and prodigies, you do not believe" [John 4:48]; and the faith with which the centurion believed before he saw a sign—or rather through which he became worthy to receive a sign—[Christ] so extolled with the glorification of his praise as to say that he "had never found such great faith, not even in Israel" [cf. Luke 7:9]. In this way, too, after his resurrection, [Christ] looked askance at the unbelief which kept Thomas from being able to believe unless he touched the scars of his [Lord's] wounds. [Christ] said, "Because you have seen me, you have believed" [John 20:29]. By adding "Blessed are they who have not seen and have believed," he commended the faith of those who, he foresaw, would be believers in him only through the preaching that they heard.

Thus, the eminent teacher invalidated the pact of our agreement (to the outcome of which we were both bound with equal eagerness), not by using his episcopal authority to forbid, but by dissuading us with the manifest truth of rational arguments.

[I have digressed here] so that those reading this brief treatise with pious intent may gain some useful fruit that is not of the least and may imitate the example of great discernment in the bishop and the example of wonderful faith and, especially, of perfect charity in his steward. For [Richmar] did not curse me as a man of perfidy, unworthy of Christian companionship; but, instead, he most devotedly communicated to me works of charity and piety as though I were his fellow Christian. With similar zeal of piety, neither man abominated [adherents] of the Jewish or any other human error, spitting upon them as some customarily do.[21] As truly Christian men (that is, imitators of Christ who prayed for his crucifiers), they in goodness opened to adherents of error the embrace of fraternal charity. For "since," as the Savior himself says, "salvation is of the Jews" [John 4:22]—his Apostle Paul also bearing witness that "by their sin, salvation is gone out to the Gentiles" [Rom. 11:11][22]—there is a reciprocity entirely worthy and pleasing to God in Christians' striving with all their might for the salvation of those from among whom they have rightly received the author of eternal salvation, Jesus Christ.

If they are commanded to extend their love to those from whom they receive evil, how much more ought they extend it to those through whom came the general good? Let them confirm their love of them, therefore, as much as they can, sharing necessities and being for them the pattern of all piety, to the end that those who cannot be won by word may be won by example. For truly, as some person says, anyone is taught better by example than by word. Let them pour out earnest and suppliant prayers for them to the "Father of mercies," if it happens, as the Apostle says, that "God gives them penitence to recognize truth and cast aside the snares of the Devil, by whom they are held captive to his will" [cf. 2 Cor. 1:3; 2 Tim. 2:25–26].

But from these comments by way of digression (not idle, I hope, or useless), let us now return to the sequence of events that I had undertaken.

Chapter 6. *How, when he came with Bishop Egbert to the monastery of Cappenberg (where he was later converted), he was stricken with compunction on seeing the religious way of life followed by the cenobites.*

I was still attending the same venerable bishop in expection of repayment of the debt and went with him in his frequent visitation of different places in his diocese.[23] One time it happened that I arrived with him at the monastery of Cappenberg. The site of this distinguished place was on the summit of a mountain in a castle that once had been the most celebrated throughout all Westphalia. Its counts, Gottfried and Otto, were men of magnificence and regal generosity. They were brothers, flourishing [until they embraced the monastic life] in the rosy blossom of their earlier lives and abounding in riches and the delights of all worldly pomp.[24]

Inflamed by the fire of divine love, they abandoned, with eager devotion for Christ, whatever pleasures they had or could have had in this world. They turned that castle, with the most ample lands of their patrimony, into that monastery of clerics holding to the rule of St. Augustine, gladly making the oblation to God in the simplicity of their heart. Knowing, however, that the perfect relinquish not only what is theirs but also themselves, these most fervent emulators of gospel perfection denied themselves alike with all that was theirs. Having put on the habit of that same perfection, they bent their necks most meekly to the yoke of rule by another, striving to outdo the other brethren in humility of total surrender, as they had formerly outdone them in worldly dignity.

As I began to say, coming to that place, in that society of Christ's faithful assembled from persons of varied conditions and diverse nations, I saw the prophecy of Isaiah concerning the times of Christ spiritually fulfilled, though, to buttress my error, I thought carnally that that prophecy was to be accomplished in the coming of the Christ [i.e., the Messiah]. Isaiah said, "The calf, the lion, and the lamb will feed together and a little boy will lead them" [Isa. 11:6]. On the basis of this prophecy, the Jews defend their perfidy. They do not see that this, which is carnally predicted, has been fulfilled. They deny that he has already come whose advent was predicted in these words.

But how did it come about that in that place wise and uneducated, strong and sick, noble and baseborn alike ate of the sustenance of the divine Word, except that "the calf, the lion, and the lamb were feeding together"? The little boy also led them, in as much as a spiritual father, a little child in malice but perfect in understanding, governed them in Christ's place.

And so, observing the ignoble (as I understood) religious way of life followed by the counts and monks, I saw removal of hair by razor or shears, manifold renunciation of freedom to leave the monastery, torment of the flesh, and continuance in prayers and vigils. Wretched and pitiable as I was, I accounted the cenobites all the more unhappy as I judged that they persevered in their labor in empty hope, without reaping any fruit in recompense. To take an example: If I saw a man who did not know the road running quickly through the byways, I would judge him the more miserable the farther and farther I saw the very speed of his running carry him away from the right track.[25] Accordingly, I thought these men to be pitied rather than despised. They were powerful runners through their various strenuous labors. But I thought them more pitiable than all men, since (so I thought) they had departed from the royal way of observances prescribed by the Law. They seemed to be afflicting themselves with empty labor in this life, and yet not to find any consolation before God, the Judge, after this life for their past affliction, but rather to incur from him a sentence of eternal damnation as skeptics and unbelievers.

Wretched myself, I was sorry for them from my inmost being because of human feelings, and drawing deep sighs from the depths of my heart, I began to argue within myself about these questions, as though I were arguing against God, as though they were the wretched.

"Of what sort, Lord, is the abyss of your judgments, so great and so unsearchable, such that you repel from your commands these, your most devout servants, who are seeking you with all their heart, and hide from them in their error the path of your truth, the path by walking in which they could be saved? Despising all delights of the world to follow you alone, they have chosen you as the object of their love. In faith, they have cast all their care upon you for love of whom they ceaselessly persist in the martyrdoms of immense labors, more burdensome than death.[26] 'You judge the world in equity' [cf. Ps. 95:13]. 'All your ways are mercy and truth' [Ps. 24:10]. It is not your way to obstruct the advancement of your servants, to abominate your lovers, and to hide yourself from those seeking you and striving to know you. Your voice, instead, is that which says, 'I love them who love me, and those who watch for me will come to me' (Prov. 8:17).

"By the mouth of the prophet, you also have declared that word full of mercy: 'I wish not the death of a sinner, but rather that he convert and live' [Ezek. 33:11]. Therefore, showing that you desire the life of sinners, you invite them to conversion, so that they can live. It is altogether worthy and fitting for your goodness, 'of whose mercy there is no reckoning,' that by your most kind mercy you turn again to these brethren who, with strict penitence, have already turned to you. For elsewhere by the prophet you deigned to promise: 'Turn again to me, and I shall turn again to you' [Zech. 1:3].

"According to the word of this promise, you once accepted the three-day penitence of the Ninevites and spared them, mercifully turning aside the sword of your vengeance. By this example, you evidently demonstrated with what fatherly feelings you desire the penitence and salvation of sinners. 'For you, Lord, are sweet and mild and of much mercy to all who call upon you' [Ps. 85:5]. And, if to all, then to these your servants, who perform, not a penance of three days, as once those Ninevites did, but continual penance, and who, for your love, despise in all humility and abasement not only 'the world and things that are in the world' [cf. 1 John 2:15] but even—which is much harder—themselves."

While, groaning within myself, I considered these things and (if it is pious to express it this way) after a certain fashion wrestled with God for judgment in favor of these monks, straightway a heavy scruple of doubtfulness arose in my heart concerning the mutually contrary and diverse laws established by Jews and Christians. For since God's nature is goodness and his judgment, mercy, I saw that it would be most appropriate for him to show the way of truth to his servants who truly "slay themselves all the day long" for him, according to the word of the psalm (Ps. 43:22). I began to waver within myself and to think along these lines.

On the one hand, if the Jews had lost the way, Christians might be running in the path of the Lord's commands. If observance of the legal rites still pleased him, he would not have so deprived the Jews, who observed those rites, of the aid of his grace that he would have dispersed them, proscribed from all goods and homeland, far and wide through all the nations of the earth. On the other hand, if he cursed the sect of the Christian religion, he would not have suffered it to spread and prosper so greatly throughout the earth.

Hoisted on this two-horned doubt, I was uncertain where to turn or to what path I should chiefly trust. I had absolutely no idea what could come of these uncertainties. Thus beset, I endured in my heart the greatest battles of thoughts fighting among themselves. I remembered things that

I had once heard about the conversion of St. Paul, from Christian clergy as well as laity: namely, how, called by God's wonderful clemency to the catholic faith, he was established preacher and protagonist of the Church, which earlier he persecuted with a tyrant's cruelty. Abruptly, I converted to God with all contrition, and I prayed to him with tears that if he were the author of the Christian religion, he would reveal that to me through secret inspiration, or through the vision of a dream, or, surely, which I judged most effective, through some visible sign, and that he who drew the Apostle Paul to the flock of his Church, even when he was kicking in pride against the pricks, would also draw to that flock me, a man most humbly obedient to his commands.

MGH, 93

God, who always piously hears a righteous petition, long deferred but did not reject my desire. Later he not only fulfilled it but deigned to heap even fuller gifts of his grace upon it, as the sequel of these matters will prove.

Chapter 7. *How, when he returned to his parents, his Jewish guardian, accusing him of familiarity with Christians, was instantly smitten by divine vengeance.*
After these things the Easter festival came and went. The bishop repaid his debt to me, and together with the Jew who was attending me, I returned to the metropolis of Cologne, where I was living [late spring 1128 or 1129]. He did what he had once threatened to do, greatly weakening the affection of my parents and friends toward me by accusations that contrary to what was allowed, I had consorted with Christians in such an eager and familiar way that I could now be thought, not a Jew, but a Christian. The only reservation was that with simulated piety I had continued, simply out of habit, practicing my ancestral religion.

God, the Lord of vengeance [cf. Ps. 93:1], soon worthily repaid him for this malign accusation; for, according to the prophet's word, he ground him down with double grinding [cf. Jer. 17:18].[27] Suddenly seized with a severe, painful fever, he died within fifteen days and, in misery, passed from the anguish of this world into the eternal torments of hell. Thus, "the just Judge" [cf. 2 Tim. 4:8] in one and the same act showed mercy and truth: truth, on the one hand, by repaying him with punishments rightly due him and mercy, on the other, by freeing me from his assaults and accusations.

MGH, 94

Chapter 8. *How, for the sake of his enlightenment, he afflicted himself with a three-day fast.*
I trusted in God's piety all the more because I had experienced it in this vengeance upon my accuser. I began again to implore him, as I had earlier

with continual prayers, to deign to reveal to me "the way of truth" by a night vision as [he once revealed] to holy Daniel mysteries of dreams.[28] I followed the example of that same Daniel by dedicating a three-day fast to God for obtaining this, my most ardent desire [summer 1128 or 1129].

I knew that Jews and Christians did not keep the same rule of fasting, since Christians eat on fast days at the ninth hour, abstaining from flesh, while Jews, continuing until evening, are allowed to eat flesh and anything else. But I did not know which of these pleased God the more. I decided to keep both without distinction. And so, according to the rite of Christianity, I abstained from flesh, and extending the fast until evening in the fashion of Jews, I remained content with a little bread and water.

Because of the exceeding great avidity of my desire, I gave myself to sleep earlier than usual, hoping that divine consolation would be forthcoming, according to the order with which I had sought it. But in vain. For such was the measure of my sins that that night flowed away to no avail. Wherefore, I grieved deeply but did not fall headlong into impatience. To the contrary, because of this delay, my desire increased. Thinking that the self-denial of the previous day had been too meager, given what I was asking, I decided to eat nothing at all that day.

Going into my chamber early, as before, I awaited with unspeakable desire the aid of a divine visitation. However, that night also passed away in vain, and while it took its shadows with it, it left me, in my wretchedness, shrouded in a hideous darkness of unbelief. Even so, I did not despair of God's consolation. Again pouring tear-filled prayers before his pious eyes, I begged him to end the suspense of my ardent desire with possession of its object.

At length, exhausted by extreme abstinence from food, for it was summer, my whole body languished. I was not able to keep the vow of fasting until evening. About midday, an intolerable weakness of the flesh forced me to take a little water. And so, the third night was at hand, on which [according to the precedent of Daniel] the supreme expectation of my visitation was pinned. Nevertheless, it, too, passed without result.

Having wakened early, and seeing the darkness of night reddened by the sun, I was wracked with groans and grieved beyond what can be said or believed because I had not been worthy, measured by the example of Daniel, to be enlightened by Christ, the true "sun of justice" [cf. Mal. 4:2].

The Jews saw me, contrary to usual practice, tortured by abstinence. They suspected that among the Christians I had admitted some crime, and at the same time the accusation of that Jew [Baruch], already mentioned, gave credence to this kind of condemnation.

When I learned their suspicion, it was the cause of further distress and so increased the burden of grief for my heart. I had always lived among the Jews in a well-pleasing fashion and without contention, and I could not bear this ill repute [*infamia*] among them without disquiet. However, I considered that God is merciful and more disposed to give human beings great things after testing their perseverence in prayer and their patience under delay.

Amid this weakness I regained constancy of mind. I began again to knock ceaselessly with tears and prayers at the door of divine goodness, seeking to obtain the outcome of my desire. With the prophet, I said to him, "Show me your ways, O Lord, and teach me your paths; direct me in your truth" [Ps. 24:41].

Chapter 9. *That, to inquire into catholic truth, he spent time in assiduous disputations with teachers of the Church.*
Again, as I thought things out regarding the studies to which I was applying myself for knowledge of truth, it seemed good to look for men of the Church who were most skilled in the Old Testament and to confer with them about the contradictory religious ways of Christians and Jews. If they could show me the authority of their sect from manifest testimonies of the Law and Prophets and affirm in a probable fashion that entrance to the Kingdom of Heaven was open to their sect alone (as they said), I would yield to reason. I would take counsel for my salvation, and setting aside the ancestral tradition which I followed, I would freely embrace what had been approved as truth to me.

And so, launching forth opportunely inopportunely, I did not cease day after day to beat with my questions upon religious teachers of the Church and most of all, as I said, those skilled in the Old Testament. Seeing that I did this, not intending to stir up contention, but out of zeal for knowing truth, they toiled by their disputations and admonitions to separate me from "the Synagogue of Satan"[29] and to incorporate me into the bowels of holy Church.

They brought forth for me many testimonies from the Law and the Prophets concerning Christ's advent. Most stubbornly supporting myself on the letter alone, I either contended that the passages in question had nothing to do with Christ, or if I could not deny the connection, I perverted them with some sinister interpretation. If, caught by plain argument, I could do neither, at the very least, by a crafty sleight of hand, using verbal ambiguities, I evasively worked around to another question that I had to solve.

For since I was judged by my people a "scribe learned" in the Law, I was dumbfounded to be overcome or left no escape by assertions of the Christians that the Jews despised as old wives' tales. Wretched man that I was, I did not consider that this confusion, by which I was confounded out of my own error, pleased God and that it brought, not shame, but rather glory upon me. Therefore, by an appetite for vainglory, I locked the door of truth to myself, as if by some bolt, so that I could not believe, just as in the Gospel the Lord says to the Jews: "How," he says, "can you believe, who receive glory from one another and do not seek the glory that is from God alone?" [John 5:44].

Although I seemed in words to rebut the assertions of the clergy, still whatever things they had proven to me by plain reason and manifest authority I received with a grateful mind, and I most diligently stored up in the treasure chest of my heart the very beautiful allegories that they drew forth from the Old Testament.

MGH, 98   Chapter 10. *How he was forced to marry against his will and purpose and, through his love, remained entangled in his old error.*
The Devil, the author of envy, still held me ensnared in the bonds of unbelief. He saw me daily hurrying to church and most avidly hearing the word of God, by which I was fortified against the ambushes of all his tyranny. Consumed with mighty envy of the progress that I made in these ways, he sallied forth against me with the weapons of his ancient fraud. He administered the draft of death to the first parent [Adam] by a woman's hands and reserved for most holy Job only his wife, among all goods, not to console, but to subvert him.[30]

And so, to my ruin, he coupled a woman to me in marriage. Now, a certain Jew named Alexander came to me. I had been betrothed to his daughter, a virgin. Alexander began to insist strongly that I set the date for the wedding. He admonished; he exhorted; he urged. However, I was still uncertain whether I should persevere in Judaism or turn to Christianity. Prudently foreseeing that if I were bound to a wife, I would have to spend my days in care of the household, rather than in disputations, as I had grown used to doing, I decided for the time being to put the marriage off as long as possible until I was worthy, through God's mercy, to know by some sure sign what I had to do to heal my soul.

Thus, with a deliberate plan in view, I answered that I received his advice with a grateful mind, as though it descended from charity itself. But, for the moment, I would not be able to heed it, since I had decided to go to

France for the sake of my studies, before marrying.

Alexander often tried to bend my mind to assent, but he foresaw that he was going to make absolutely no headway. He turned from prayers and blandishments to threats and terrors in the fashion of a scorpion,[31] brandishing its tail. Constrained to go before the Jews' council, he pleaded that I had been so depraved by the pestilential tales of the Christians that neither the pious counsel of my parents and friends nor, what was more serious, legal authority could ever incline me to consent to marriage.

Asked by the Jews whether this were so, I did not entirely decline marriage. I wished to put it off for the time being on grounds of expense, and I presented the same reason for delay to them as to my father-in-law. Hearing that I wanted to go to France and suspecting that this reason was not sincerely set forth (as indeed it was not), they all opposed me with one accord, shouting with raucous voices that this was a sign of apostasy, that it had nothing to do with my intent to study, as I said, but that it was motivated rather by love of inquiring into Christian superstition.

What more? When they saw the constancy of my mind in this resolve, they proposed that I choose one of two alternatives: to wit, either, without any excuse, to agree to consummate the marriage, according to the precepts of the Law, or, if some other course of action took my fancy, to leave their synagogue.

Lest anyone perhaps consider this a light matter among them, he should know that, among Jews, to be outside the synagogue is the same as, among Christians, to be cast out of the Church by excommunication. But, as Scripture says, "Where there is no fence, possession lapses" [Eccles. 36:27]. Unhappy man that I was, since according to the deserts of my unbelief, I was not fenced about by divine protection, I had lost to the Devil's theft all the little possession that I had gained by my early devotion to seeking out the way of truth. Moreover, at the first warning of the Jews, I was smitten rigid with immense fear, as if no recourse to any further remedy would have been open to me once I was excluded from their synagogue.

But if there were some approach to salvation outside the synagogue, nevertheless (since I did not know it, nor, as I had proven, was I able by any efforts to come to its perfect enclosure) I thought it would be safer for me to persevere to the end in that tradition which I had suckled once from my mother's breasts[32] than ill-advisedly to aspire to any new religion that persuaded me by no evidence of signs or reasons, especially since even erring, perhaps, through unavoidable ignorance, I could secure an easy forgiveness from a pious judge.

I wasted time in this most demented way of thinking, "and my foolish heart was darkened" [cf. Rom. 1:21]. All the earlier purpose was laid aside. The most ardent desire with which I had burned earlier for hunting down truth was discarded. I gave perfect joy to the Devil, who was raging against me, and gave myself over entirely to destruction, according to the words with which the Lord reproaches some through the prophet, "an alliance with death and a pact [of false security] with hell" [Isa. 28:15].

Without any further reconsideration, obeying the unanimous will of the Jews, I designated a day for them when the nuptial bed would be occupied. My marriage caused them such great exultation, and the good will of all toward me rose to such a pitch, that the common enthusiasm shown by them all exhilarated me by as much as terror had earlier repelled me.

When the day of the marriage feast was at hand, many gathered together there, not only Jews but also my Christian friends. The Jews, indeed, delighted in my false happiness. The Christians, however, grieving with Christian affection over my deadly misfortunes, prayed that some mitigation of piety would come for them from above.

"How, they said, poor Judah, did you fall so quickly and easily from your good intention to such a depth of perdition? Why did you so quickly look back when you had laid your hand to the plow? We were always giving you admonitions of salvation to which we hoped you were sometime going to assent, believing in Christ, the author of our salvation. And yet, see, contrary to our hope, you have chosen instead to follow your lusts. Having despaired of salvation, you have given yourself over entirely to perdition. Alas, unhappy wretch. You have deceived us, and you were yourself wretchedly deceived. 'O that you knew and understood and foresaw the last days!' [cf. Deut. 32:29]. Then you could know what torments await you, what fires of blazing hell will receive you if you remain in this superstition.

"Wherefore, let the saving counsel of our charity please you now, and while the gate of penitence is still open, take care with all urgency for your salvation; for if you are unwilling to do this while you can, you will not be able then, when you begin to have the will to change, too late. But if you have embraced the faith of Christ with all your heart and have been regenerated by his saving bath, you will obtain from him entire forgiveness of your errors and a perfect knowledge of the whole truth that you had begun to study.

"For although, as he says, he 'will cast out no one who comes to him' [John 6:37], he bestows grace most abundantly on those turning again to him by faith. He says that he was sent by God the Father solely for the sake of recalling them from their error, saying, 'I am not sent' he says, 'except to the lost sheep of the house of Israel' [Matt. 15:24]. He who first came to look for you will easily give himself to you to be found if you seek him with upright faith and a pure heart."

By the plowshare of this exhortation of theirs, the Christians strove to break through the iron hardness of my heart and to soften it to the grace of compunction. I, however, did not hear their most wholesome admonitions. I was as one deaf, not having ears of the heart, the ears of understanding, which the Lord in his gospel requires, saying, "He who has ears to hear, let him hear" [Matt. 13:9, 43]. And since I lacked spiritual hearing, I despised what I perceived with the corporal ear alone.[33] Thus, Scripture was fulfilled concerning me: "When the sinner comes into the depth of evil, he despises" [Prov. 18:3].

Straightway, I experienced the corruption of the flesh. Deceitful pleasure and feeling for the wife joined to me so blinded my mind that I could not feel the most heavy languor of my soul.[34] Such lack of feeling is usually a sign of extreme despair. I had overcome none of the assaults of temptations, as before, but I was as one entirely defeated and rendered powerless by them. I thought myself blessed in this false peace of vices. I began to vaunt myself under the circumstances on the supreme pleasure of the flesh, by which I had earlier feared to be cast down.

As the Apostle wrote concerning married persons: "A man who has a wife cares for the things that are of the world, how he may please his wife, and he is distracted" [1 Cor. 7:33]. I began to be lost through various cares of the world and to seek none of those things that are God's. I chose to attend only to those things with which I could be well pleasing in the eyes of my wife.

Chapter 11. *How, after he had been bound to a wife, a visitation of divine grace rekindled his mind with devotion for inquiring into the way of its Truth.*
After three months had run their course, during which I had begun to labor under this lethargic sickness of my soul, by the mercy of God I returned to my heart. As though waking from the heavy sleep of earlier ignorance, I began to consider from what point I had fallen through negligence and into what a whirlpool of wretched delight I had come. And since, as we read, "He who seeks after knowledge also seeks grief" [cf. Eccles. 13:18], I began to suffer terrible pain as I considered my pitiable state. I beat my breast with my fist, and amid continual moans, I poured forth floods of

tears. I admitted that I was wretched and unhappy because, for the slight pleasure of the flesh, I had cast myself down into the vast whirling maw of perdition.

Through the renewed grace of this compunction, I began little by little, with confidence in God's great piety, to cut off the superfluous cares of the world from my mind and to restrain the lusts of the flesh with the bridle of continence. As I had shown my [bodily] members to be weapons of iniquity for sin, so in every way I toiled to show the same members to be weapons of righteousness for God.

And yet, still retaining the earlier doubt about the mutually contrary belief of Jews and Christians and knowing that "without faith it is impossible to please God" [Heb. 11:6] and that everything "that is not of faith is sin" [Rom. 14:23], I began once more to strive for some way (God favoring the effort) in which I could cast the dark cloud of this ambiguity from my heart and find the light of true belief.

As before, I diligently sought out the most skilled teachers of the Church and demanded from them an explanation [ratio] of their faith and religion. They supplied me most copiously with many witnesses from Scripture and various figures of the Old Testament. But, pursuing things in an inverted order, I wished to supersede faith with understanding. Thus, I was never able to attain that understanding which is rightly coupled to faith according to the word of the prophet who said, "Unless you believe, you will not understand" [Isa. 7:9].³⁵

One day, however, I happened to enter into debate with a certain master, whom I have already mentioned. When, after a long protracted discourse, no assent could be twisted out of me to the things that he was quite aptly saying, one of the clergy assisting him, discerning the hardness of my heart, said, "Why, O Master, why are you striving in vain? Why are you flinging words into the wind? Why cast seeds of sand? You certainly know, as the Apostle says, that 'until the present day, when Moses is read to the Jews, a veil is laid over their heart' " [2 Cor. 3:15].

Hearing this, and understanding (as I was extremely well trained in the Old Testament) the circumstance that called for this remark, I was smitten with fear. I considered that just as once the children of Israel were not able without a veil between them to look upon the face of Moses, when it was made to shine with great brightness on the mountain, so I would never be able to attain, on the bright peak of my mind, the mystical understanding of the Law of Moses without the interposed shadows of some kind of carnal figures.³⁶

Thus, I began again to seethe with anxiety. I did not know what to do or how to remove this veil from my heart so that I could grasp the bright light of Truth with the uncovered eye of the mind. I fled to the "Father of lights" with a contrite and humbled heart. I cast down tearful prayers in the sight of his goodness, exclaiming with the psalmist, "Uncover my eyes, and I shall consider the wonders of your Law. Give me understanding, and I shall consider your Law, and I shall guard it in my whole heart" [Ps. 118:18, 34].

Since, through the teachings of Christians, I recognized that the power of the holy cross was great, I frequently signed my heart with the sign of the same cross, hoping that its aid would be most effective in removing the veil of disbelief from me.[37]

What could that most savage Enemy, with his thousand arts, do when he saw me (whom he still held captive under the sway of his tyranny through the snares of disbelief) armed against him by such a defense? Or when would he suffer his bondsman, whom he held by just laws, to go away from him, when he never ceased with impious and wrongful cruelty to pursue and capture even the very servants of his own Lord, namely some of the faithful? Therefore, to seduce me more easily when I was off guard, he transfigured himself into an angel of light, assailing me, not with a bold frontal assault, but with subtle fraud.[38]

To be exact, he began to recall mandates of the Law to my memory.[39] Among them was the precept of the Jews that in no regard whatever were the impure rites of the Gentiles, execrable to God, to be imitated, lest those whom God had elected for himself from among all nations to be his peculiar people be seen to partake of those superstitions in some way or to be like [the Gentiles].

I believe that that most cunning Enemy acted in this way so that he could deflect my intention from its purpose the more easily; for through this tactic he showed me to be a prevaricator of the Law. The thing was done as follows. By a diabolic inspiration, my own conscience began to rebuke itself harshly as a transgressor of the divine Law in this regard; and (as I thought) to secure forgiveness of this enormity, it castigated me with a strict penance of tears and fasts.[40]

Later, returning to my mind after this madness and perceiving that this penance was one of offense, rather than of propitiation, I began again to bewail the error of my ignorance. With the same frequency as before, I defended myself, in hearty devotion, with the sign of the cross.[41] But alas! I was unworthy to feel the healing remedy of the cross, since I did not yet acknowledge that I had been redeemed by its living price from the curse of the Law.

What was I to do?

Hope for all counsel and aid had fled from my mind. Again, therefore, tears flowed in rivers; again, wrenching sobs began to break forth from the depths of my heart. I said against myself: "Woe is me, pitiable wretch that I am! What am I to do? Where am I to flee? What hope of salvation can there be for me anymore, since I am neither perfectly a Jew nor a Christian? If, 'coming swiftly as a thief in the night,' the last day of my life finds me such as I now am, where shall I go? I shall perish utterly."

So great was the bitterness of my heart that even when the tongue was silent, my thin and unkempt face displayed a better sign of it [than words]. For all those who had known that I was born of great forebears and that I abounded in knowledge of the Law and in possessions, seeing me so suddenly haggard by unaccustomed weakness, were all the more thunderstruck, for they had never seen me beset by any need.

Chapter 12. *How he was enlightened through prayers of women religious.*

MGH, 107

With all confidence I fled to God, who alone "regards toil and sorrow," as to a "tower of strength." I "poured out my prayer in his sight" and "set forth the tribulation of my heart before him." I beseeched him with tearful prayer that, according to the multitude of my griefs in my heart, his consolations might make my soul glad and he might deign to stretch forth the right hand of his majesty to lead me out of "the darkness and shadow of death" [cf. Luke 1:79; Ps. 106:10].

He saw that I was utterly perishing of my own weakness. Therefore, what I faithfully asked of him, I was worthy to receive effectually. By his inward inspiration, I began prudently to consider how, if a person of servile estate has lost his lord's favor, he cannot regain it unless friends of the same lord intercede for him. Thus, unless I was supported by intercessions of the holy Church, I could not obtain the grace of Christ.

And so, as I thought about whose prayers I could commend myself to in order to obtain more than great merit before God, I recalled two sisters who led the celibate life together in Cologne, enclosed for God next to the monastery of St. Maurice.[42] Their names were Bertha and Glismut. Their holy way of life had spread the odor of good repute through the whole extent of that city. Hoping that their patronage could greatly assist me before God, I hurried with all speed to them. With many tears, I opened to them the spurs of temptations with which I was being goaded, and I humbly begged them to see fit to direct their prayers to God for my enlightenment.

With bowels full of all piety and compassion, they gushed forth abundant tears over my great miseries, and they promised that they would pour untiring supplications out to God for me, as long as it took for me to be worthy to receive the hoped-for consolation of heavenly grace.

O how true is that statement of the Apostle James: "The constant prayer of the righteous avails much" [James 5:16]! Not at all much later, by their merits and prayers, so great a brightness of Christian faith suddenly shone in my heart that it entirely put to flight from it the shadows of all former doubt and ignorance.

It was indeed an appropriate about-face for women to raise up by their prayers a man who had fallen because of a woman. O you devout and holy women, therefore, whoever may read these words or hear them read, receive the outstanding and imitable example of prayer in these blessed women. Know that the quieter your prayers are, the more sincere they are, and so the more effective before God for obtaining whatever things are sought.[43]

Look at me. Neither the explanation [*ratio*] given by many concerning the faith of Christ nor the disputation of great clerics could convert me to the faith of Christ, but the devout prayer of simple women did.

Chapter 13. *How, after his enlightenment, he frequented churches and advanced in the faith.*

Having found, by God's grace, the precious pearl of catholic faith, I began, after the example of that merchant in the gospel [Matt. 13:46], to despise all temporal things for love of it, so that I might be worthy to be enriched by so very joyful and salubrious a possession. Unburdening myself, as far as I could, of all cares, I became impatient of every delay. I scarcely took food at home. I began to frequent the basilicas of the saints with great devotion. Listening to the word of God, I assimilated in delight what I heard both with the hearing of the heart and with that of the body.

I did this secretly, since, still weak and tender in faith, like Nicodemus, who came to Jesus by night, I feared persecution by the Jews.[44] With that same Nicodemus, I heard the Lord dreadfully thundering in his gospel, "Except a man be reborn of water and the Spirit, he cannot enter into the kingdom of God" [cf. John 3:5], and I began to desire the washing of this regeneration all the more ardently, since, without its healing remedy, according to this statement of the Lord, I should never be able to enter the heavenly kingdom.

Chapter 14. *How he also strove to withdraw a child, his own brother, from Judaism and gain him for Christ, and what traps and persecutions by the Jews he endured.*

The Lord commanded that the children of Israel not go out of Egypt empty-handed, but that they despoil Egypt as they left. Knowing this command and taught by such an example, I did not want to go out of Egypt—i.e., the darkness of Jewish unbelief—empty-handed, but to take away, not plunder of gold and silver, or any precious raiment, but plunder of a rational being which would not only adorn the temple of the supreme King but would also be worthy to be his temple, as the Apostle Paul says, "the temple of God, which you are, is holy" [1 Cor. 3:17].[45]

I had a seven-year-old brother in Mainz, by my father, not by my mother. With the most ardent desire, I wished him to be a coheir with me of divine grace through the regenerative washing [of baptism]. Thus, although we did not have the same mother by birth in the flesh, we might, at the same time, have the Church as our mother, by rebirth in the spirit.

However, the Jews saw that I no longer habitually went among them in their synagogue, although, as can be known from the preceding, I had greatly feared to be absent from their gathering. They perceived that the circumstances of this quite unwelcome change were not frivolous. Therefore, laying traps for me, they began to watch with particular care all my ways and acts. They caught me doing almost nothing daily but spending time in disciplines of the Church. Their zeal flared up against me so fiercely that, if they had had a chance to do the crime, they would not have shrunk from stoning me with their own hands.

They were blinded by the darkness of their perfidy and malignity. To the increase of their damnation, they strove to involve others in the crime of murder, which they were not able to perpetrate by themselves. But they were to procure none of the fruits of crime other than hurling themselves into the guilt of wishing it.

Having found out that I had decided to go to Mainz, "they met together against me," thinking up, as is written, "plans that could not be made firm" [cf. Ps. 2:2; Ps. 20:12]. For, without my knowledge, they sent letters written in Hebrew to the Jews of Mainz, through the agency of Wolkwin, a chaplain to Queen Richenza. The sum of those letters was that they had discovered me to be an unbeliever and an apostate and, according to the rigor of legal condemnation, they had imposed the appropriate penalties.[46]

But, as the Apostle says, "If God be for us, who can be against us?" [Rom. 8:31]. He who "scatters the plans of the Gentiles and condemns the plans of princes" [Ps. 32:10] scattered their plan with a simple nod of the head. Not only did he powerfully free me from their snare, but he also mercifully achieved the pious desire that I had conceived for securing my brother.

Chapter 15. *How, in an amazing way, he came into possession of the letters that the Jews wrote against him, and consigned them to the flames.*
God so disposed things that I happened to fall into company with the cleric just mentioned as he went along the way to discharge his mission in Mainz. Neither of us knew the business of the other. We chatted about many things as we went along together. He mentioned by name some of my kinsmen who lived in Mainz, not knowing that they were related to me. He said that he had some secret message to deliver to them.

When I heard this, being still entirely ignorant of the Jews' plot against me, I nevertheless began to suspect that the Jews had engineered a great evil for me through his mission, which was the case. And so, when I spoke to the cleric about this, I said that he should carry the Jews' letters with the greatest regard for his own soul.

He had been asked to conceal the matter and denied that he was carrying any letters. But I entirely disbelieved his denial. I firmly insisted that the matter was as I had said, adding that a heavy weight of divine vengeance was hanging over him, if against my advice he presumed to deliver to the Jews of Mainz the letters that he had received, since a seedbed of great evil lay hidden in them.

With many urgent prayers and threats, I finally extorted a confession of the truth from him. He confessed to me that everything was as I had said, and he asked that I disclose to him the business with which the letters were concerned. Then—amazing but, as God is witness, most true to tell—I declared their sense and sum to him, only from the conjecture of my heart, as though I had read them or learned about them from some informant.

This happened, not by chance, but by the inspiration and providence of God, who so disposed events as to snatch me from the most malign "expectation of the people of the Jews" and to bring the holy business that I had in hand to a glorious outcome. He produced the letters for me. Taking them, I unfolded and read them through. I found, as I had conjectured, the most malign accusations of the Jews against me written in them. And, with the greatest exultation, giving thanks to God for my deliverance, I burned those pestiferous texts [*apices*] in the fire.

Chapter 16. *That, when he came to Worms, he faithfully preached Christ in the synagogue of the Jews.*
Then, therefore, I sang with the unspeakable victory dance of the psalmist: "Our soul has been snatched as a sparrow from the snare of the hunters. The snare is smashed, and we are freed" [Ps. 123:7]. I began to burn so powerfully in love of the catholic faith and religion that charity cast out every fear that sprang from my faintheartedness.

I dared not only to believe that "Christ was the power of God and the wisdom of God" for justification and to confess the same "with my mouth for salvation" but also constantly and freely to preach to his enemies, the Jews.

Coming to Worms, where I had a brother-german named Samuel, I entered the synagogue of the Jews on the day when they usually go there. I heard them reading the superstitious comments of their Gamaliel on the Old Testament. Soon, ignited by divine fervor and with great confidence and grace of speech, I entered into a debate over prophecy with them. I opportunely demonstrated there whose faith I belonged to and how much I had profited from many disputations of Christians with me concerning the orthodox faith. Against the stupid old wives' tales which that same Gamaliel had pieced together from written texts, I uttered for them the honey-sweetness of spiritual allegories. With many and valid authorities of divine preaching, I shut up their mouth which, in their blind pride and proud blindness, they had presumed to raise against heaven, blaspheming Christ and derogating from his holy Church.[47]

Can you imagine how great a stupor of amazement then seized all the Jews who were present when they saw me, the strongest assailant of their paternal traditions, while they had hoped that I, as a Jew of the Jews, would be their defender? Taking up single-handed combat of debate also against the president of the synagogue, named David, and the brother whom I mentioned before, I took a long time reviewing, in opposition to them, the pages of the Law and the Prophets. Defending and proving the Christian faith by the all-satisfying testimonies of these pages, I shut off every access they had to calumny against Christ and his holy Church.

Seeing that I favored Christians with such stubborn zeal, they began to call me "semi-Christian."⁴⁸ They reproached me with this name as though I had been badly circumvented by their crafty opinions.

Finally, however, while they were arguing whether mind and tongue agreed in all the things that I had set forth against them for defense of the Christian faith, I took fright. I feared that if I confessed the bare truth to them, I should somehow be confined, being abducted either by my brother or by their traps. And so I tempered my response. I neither denied that I was a Christian, nor did I openly declare it. I said the following: "Since I frequently dispute with Christians, I have learned, for the greatest part, their subtle arguments against the Jews. I wanted to transfigure myself into their persona, [to play their role,] so that, instructed by this dress rehearsal of my assertions, you would seem the better informed to them when push came to shove."⁴⁹

They gratefully accepted this response.

Chapter 17. *How, arriving at Mainz, he secretly kidnapped his brother.*
After these events, I came to Mainz; furtively, I kidnapped the boy from his mother. Because of fear of the Jews, I wanted to take him in secret outside the city to a certain place where I had ordered a servant to wait for us with horses. But understanding that this flight had been perpetrated, not by his, but by divine instigation, and that it belonged, not to his, but to God's lot, the most cruel Enemy of human salvation toiled by the malignant art of his deceit to block my way.

For although the route across the city was very well known to me, my eyes were so blinded by diabolic illusion—which is amazing to say—that from the first to the sixth hour of the day, meandering through all the squares of that city, I could not find the exit. The boy was weary and weeping for weariness. Taking pity on him, I put him on my shoulders to carry. Many Christians seeing this derided me as a fool.

In great confusion of my countenance and unbelievable anguish of heart, I humbly implored the only refuge open to me: divine assistance. Secretly, I marked my forehead with the sign of the cross.⁵⁰ An astonishing thing! Though I had turned and returned again and again, I had in no way been able to find the gate of the city. Suddenly, when I armed myself with the sign of the cross, the diabolic illusion that had blinded me failed. In joy, I saw and recognized the gate; and when I went out, I found the servant furnished with horses where I had ordered him to be.

A little time, then, after we had left the city, Jews of Cologne arrived by boat. Whatever things they had perceived about me hostile to their confession they divulged to the Jews of that city: to wit, how at Cologne I had secretly deposited books and money with Christians, inasmuch as I had stubbornly decided to go over to their sect.[51]

Having heard these reports, the mother of the boy, most deeply troubled and terrified, had me searched for high and low. When I was nowhere to be found, the extremity of her grief made her as one mad. She ran to the leading men of the city with a most bitter cry, proclaiming with a voice of sorrow that her son had been furtively taken from her. They at once sent messengers to apprehend me.

But as one should never resist the ordinance of God, so they could not apprehend me, for I was serving that ordinance. Therefore, a fugitive with the boy, I set out on a journey to the monastery which is called Welanheim {i.e., Flonheim}. I arrived there at evening.

When they knew the pious desire of my heart, the brethren received me with great joy and charity. While we were still eating, lo, a messenger sent to look for us stood at the gate. He asked the porter whether a Jew taking a boy with him had gone in.

The porter was a simple man, suspecting no danger in the messenger. He gave him the simple truth. To keep the brethren from sustaining any harm on my account, I commended the boy to them so that they might imbue him with sacred letters, and then I secretly fled from there to a monastery called Ravengiersburg. There, I was kept by the brethren with great exultation and catechized on the third of the Calends of November.

Chapter 18. *Concerning a vision that he saw before baptism.*
After about three weeks had rolled on, and after I had been made a catechumen, on the fourth day before the Sunday when I was to be baptized, I saw a dream that was very sweet to see and to recount {21 November 1128 or 20 November 1129}.[52]

Toward the east, I saw the sky open. The structure that was imaged forth, which appeared to me through sight, was adorned throughout with purest gold. There, I saw the Lord Jesus sitting on the highest of all thrones with all power and honor and in the majesty of the Father. He held, in place of a scepter, the triumphal sign of his cross upon his right shoulder. I seemed to myself to be sitting together with his most excellent friends.

I was delighting beyond measure in the unutterable sweetness of contemplating him when, behold, two sons of my aunt, the one named Nathan, the other, Isaac, passed behind me, ceaselessly pacing to and fro.[53] From this pacing of theirs it was evidently given to those who paid attention to understand that this blessedness had been shown to them, not for solace, but for torment, so that they might be tortured inwardly in the mind by that very fact that they did not deserve to enjoy the glory of the saints which they were seeing.

I turned around and spoke to them in this way: "O wretched and unhappy men, does not that sign of the cross which you see above Christ's shoulder recall to your mind Isaiah's prophecy, 'whose empire is upon his shoulder' [Isa. 9:6]? You once spurned belief that this prophecy alluded to Christ, when I admonished you. Now you see yourselves perpetually confounded by its fulfillment."

Overwhelmed by utter fear, they were scarcely able to answer me with low and stifled voice, saying: "O kinsman, the things that you remember have been proven true, but, alas, all too late for us. The span allowed for penance that brings salvation has been lost. We have been consigned to eternal hell, without hope of following after salvation." Hardly had they finished these words when they were suddenly removed from the midst. Scripture was fulfilled in them, which says, "Let the impious be removed, that he may not see the glory of God" [cf. Isa. 26:10].

And so, awakened, I recalled with what great prayers and tears and frequency of fasts I had sometimes striven to obtain such a vision from heaven for my enlightenment. I began to overflow with spiritual gladness in these things that I had seen and to repay God the thanks that I owed for so sweet a vision, through which I was worthy to be confirmed in his faith.

MGH, 118

Chapter 19. *How he was baptized, and what tricks of the Devil he endured in that baptism.*
The Sunday came on which I was to put off "the old man with his deeds" [cf. Col. 3:9¹] and to put on the new through the washing of rebirth. And so all the clergy of the city of Cologne convened, with festal exultation, at the basilica of St. Peter, prince of the Apostles, where the font had been prepared to celebrate the saving mystery. About the third hour, when the font had been consecrated and made fecund for the regeneration of souls through invocation of the Holy Spirit, I confessed with my whole heart the faith of the holy Trinity and stepped into the font with great devotion and contrition of heart.

But alas! Hard as it is to say, the Enemy's deception did not stop its assaults against me even at the moment of baptism. For, just as, according to the Evangelist's witness, the epileptic boy being freed from possession of demons by the mercy of the Lord fell down in a more grievous seizure at the very instant when [Christ] compelled the evil spirit to come out [Luke 9], so indeed the ancient Foe made even heavier attacks against me then, at the very moment when he saw that I was being snatched from his tyranny by the divinely instituted sacrament of salvation.

Although I had been sufficiently imbued, according to my capacity, with other matters concerning orthodox faith, one thing only I had not been taught: that baptism entailed threefold immersion in the name of the holy Trinity. I had not been taught this through negligence on the part of the ministers, or rather by the deceptiveness of the Enemy who was laying traps for me.

I stepped into the waves of the life-giving font. Immersed in it once, toward the east, I believed that that one immersion sufficed for the renewal of the ancient state. But the clerics standing around the baptistry shouted that I ought to be immersed more times. Having already just left the font, I could not hear their voices distinctly, nor, since water was running down the hairs of my head, could I see clearly the gestures that they were making to me. Therefore, wiping the water from my face with my hands, I heard what they wanted, but, stiff with the bitter cold of the font,[54] I at first did not willingly yield to their wish; but, bent by the gentle admonition of my baptizer, I did what had to be done for salvation. And so, considering that I had satisfied the divine mysteries by the second dipping, I began to want to get out of the font. I was almost frozen rigid by its extreme cold. But again the clergy clamored with loud shouts that to complete the sacrament I had humbly to submit to be immersed to the south in the saving waves. Overcome therefore by diabolical fraud, I suspected that they were making a laughingstock of me.[55]

Consequently, as Naaman the Syrian once indignantly began to depart when he received the Prophet Elisha's command to dip himself seven times in the Jordan, so with equal madness, inflamed with a great fury of mind and impatient of all delay, I also wanted to jump out of the baptistry. But thanks be to God that, while the Enemy rose up, he did not prevail against me. For, in the same way as that man, Naaman, yielded to the prophet's salutary counsel, bent by the admonition of his companions, so, too, the gentle exhortation of religious clerics who were present strengthened my faintheartedness in the faith.[56] The contagion of suspecting evil, that I had conceived, was cast out of my mind.

Therefore, to compare new things in detail with old, Naaman, washed in the waves of the Jordan seven times, was visibly cured of leprosy of the flesh. I, [washed] in baptism by seven-form grace of the Holy Spirit, was invisibly cured of leprosy of the soul. His flesh, with the stains of leprosy washed off, took on the purity of an infant. The Church, a virgin mother, gave birth to me in a new infancy; through the washing of regeneration, I was stripped of the skin of the old existence. Indeed, just as I changed the order of my former life in this washing, so also I changed the name that belonged to me. I, who was called Judah, now took the name Herman.

With what great outcries of praises, with what great joys in common did not only the clergy but also the whole people celebrate this glorious "change of the right hand of the Most High" [cf. Ps. 76:11], this return of the lost sheep carried on the shoulder of the pious Shepherd back to the holy Church's flock! Nor was this out of order. For how should the Christian people not rejoice over the penitence of a converted sinner, for whom, as the Lord bears witness, the hosts of angels rejoice more than over ninety and nine just persons?

But the Jews, who have zeal of the Law, "but not according to knowledge" [Rom. 10:2], inconsolably bewailed me, with a most bitter sorrow, as one perfidious and lost.

Chapter 20. *How, after baptism, he renounced the world and bound himself to divine service under the order of canons regular.*
And so, the impure spirit was expelled from the house of my heart by the washing of regeneration. I was afraid, indeed trembling with fear, lest that spirit returning should find the same house, although purified by the saving bath and adorned with the sacraments of Christ, empty of the practice of spiritual discipline. I feared that it would then enter and occupy it with a plague seven times worse than before, such that my latter states should be worse than the former ones.

I toiled with sleepless care to make the habitation closed tight to the malign intruder but worthy of the kind Christ. And so, heeding the gospel precept, "If you wish to be perfect, go and sell all that you have and give it to the poor and come, follow me" [Matt. 19:21], and again, unless a man "renounce all that he possesses, he cannot be my disciple" [Luke 14:33], I happily began to despise all goods that I seemed to have temporally, in hope and desire of eternal ones, to the end that, released from the toilsome burden of the world, I might tread quickly and freely along the narrow way that leads to life.

Learning also, as the psalmist says, that "it is a good and joyful thing for brethren to live in unity" [Ps. 132:1], I passed over to the famous canonry of Cappenberg, which I recalled above, a place where the religious life existed in its full extent, as to some safe harbor from shipwreck on this world's sea. There, I went to fight naked with the naked Enemy.⁵⁷ There, I changed my life with my way of dress, according to the rule of St. Augustine, to await the end of the present life and the promise of the one to come.

I also took upon myself the yoke of learning the Latin language and became so proficient within five years, by God's gift, that the charity of the brethren judged me apt to undertake holy orders and kindly drew me into them. I humbly and justly felt that I was unworthy of this advancement and protested that I was less than deserving; I modestly refused as much as I dared and as much as was fitting.

But "God, who always gives grace to the humble" [1 Pet. 5:5], seeing me choose the lowest place among those at his feast, saw fit to say to me, "Friend, go up higher" [Luke 14:10]. Exulting, not with swagger but with trembling (as is written), in his vocation, I ascended step by step through the canonical orders until I reached the office of priestly excellence.⁵⁸

Then, for the first time, I understood the dream that I had seen before my conversion and that I inserted at the beginning of this little work. As I promised above, I shall explain the interpretation of it—what it foretold would happen to me.

Chapter 21. *That he then understood the first dream that he saw in childhood concerning the grace of Christ that was going to come to him, and how he interpreted it.*

This is the interpretation of the vision. That worldly emperor who appeared to me signifies the heavenly King, of whom the psalmist says, "the Lord of virtues, he is the king of glory" [Ps. 23:10]. He had a certain great prince, i.e., that angel whom, at the beginning of his creation, he made more noble than all other angelic spirits and placed above all other orders of angels. That angel was truly dead from the time when, rising in his pride against God, he was stripped of the glory of his dignity and, from being archangel, was made devil.

And so, the King of kings deigned, through his grace, to visit me with these [signs]. He gave me a white horse when he granted the grace of holy baptism, by which I was "bleached whiter than snow." He also gave me a belt, when he bestowed on me virtue to restrain the torrential desires of the flesh. In the seven pennies of heavy coinage are rightly understood the gifts of the seven-form Spirit which complete anyone, adorning [the recipient] with moral gravity. When, through the gifts of this holy Spirit, purity of life begins to glitter, as assayed silver, the person who receives them also begins to tinkle sweetly to others, concerning the love of God and eternal life, which the sound of silver well signifies.

Lest they be easily lost, however, these seven pennies were contained in a purse. I hope that this signified that I would not wantonly lose the spiritual gifts [*charismata*] of the Holy Spirit, mercifully conferred upon me, but that they would remain with me to the end, to overcome all assaults of temptations and to attain the heavenly kingdom.

Further, the princes were indignant at my achieving so happy a success because malign spirits, whom the Apostle calls "rulers of the world" [Eph. 6:12], and Jews, who, on account of the Law received from God, took for themselves first place among all other nations, envied me for having been worthy to receive Christ's grace, of which they themselves were unworthy.

But, girded with that glittering belt—that is, the strength of continence—I sat upon the royal horse because the grace of baptism "was not vain in me." The use of the horse indicates that grace is always to be perfected by spiritual exercise with God's help, and I labored to turn it to good use. I also followed Christ the King, despising the world and things that are in the world. I rejected not only all things that were mine but also myself for love of him, doing the work that he claimed for himself when he said, "I came not to do my will, but that of him who sent me," the Father [John 6:38]. And, well-seated on the snow-white horse, I accompanied the King, since no one will be worthy to follow Christ's footsteps without following upon the grace of baptism, which, as we said before, is figuratively represented by the white horse.

Moreover, I think that the palace, into which I followed him, designates the place of my conversion.[59] For by it, indeed, what is implied except so many palaces of the supreme King: namely, the monastic houses of clerics and other religious living according to rule throughout the world? In these, at any rate, Christ is believed to dwell, by grace, as a king in his palace, at home after a fashion and among his own, on account of chastity of life and a religious way of behavior.

Further, I approached the table of the King to make merry, when, although unworthy, I undertook the sacrosanct mystery of the altar. To sit at table is humbly to approach the altar of Christ. But words cannot worthily unfold of what sort the banquet of this heavenly table is, or how sweet its delights. Only those know who have been worthy to experience it through God's grace. Of what sort, I say, the banquet of the faithful soul is, no one understands, as I said, unless he experiences it. To understand, one must approach the reverend table of the altar with singleness of faith, with true humility and contrition of heart, and with sincere devotion of mind. Thus, one may be fattened at that table on the flesh-meats of the immaculate Lamb, Jesus Christ, and be inebriated with the cup of his sacrosanct blood.[60]

Continuing with the allegory, the salad that I seemed to myself to eat at the royal table, I think designates the gospel of Christ. For just as that salad was made up of various kinds of herbs, so the gospel of Christ is composed of various precepts pertaining to eternal life. To eat a salad at the royal banquet, therefore, is for the priest assisting at the Lord's altar to consider carefully and subtly the precepts of the gospel. It is for him to do this as though chewing the cud in the mouth of the heart, which is to say, weighing how humble, devout, radiant with chastity, and fervid with charity he should be who wishes to celebrate the mystery of so great a sacrament in a decent fashion, acceptable to God.

Christ the King feasts with us because he feeds on the sweetness of our spiritual progress. Indeed, in the Apocalypse he himself bears witness that there is sweet refreshment for him in the heart that is pious and bound over to divine services. He said, "Lo, I stand at the door and knock. If anyone open the door to me, I shall go in to him and dine with him, and he with me" [Rev. 3:20].

I think that it was not beside the point that I seemed to see myself eating from the same vessel with the King. The one vessel signifies the unity of the catholic faith. He eats salad from one dish with Christ, therefore, who, with collaboration of grace, keeps the precepts of the holy gospel in the unity of the catholic faith.

Now, therefore, I abide, by God's grace, in that unity, as was once shown to me by the presentiment of this most happy vision. I serve him, as has been written, "with fear, and I exult with trembling" [Ps. 2:11]. I exult, I say, with trembling, because I owe it to his grace, by which I am now faithful, to rejoice. There remains that which I should fear in the abyss of his—for me hitherto—most profound and unsearchable judgments. I know not whether, according to them, I am worthy of love or hatred.[61]

What mortal, however just, however holy, does not dread that terrible sentence of our Savior, which says, "Many are called, but few are chosen" [Matt. 20:16]? However, I trust in the Lord Jesus that he who began a good work in me will perfect it to the end. Indeed, the magnitude of former benefits promises me the greatest hope of future ones.

For behold, the merciful Lord, the bestower of mercies, has raised up "the pauper from the dung heap and seated him with the princes of his people" [Ps. 112:7–8]. This he did when, pious and merciful, he deigned not only to join me to his faithful through the unity of the catholic faith (mercifully snatched as I had been from the most filthy and impious sect of Jewish supersition) but also to gather me to the glorious banquet of his table, through the grace of the priestly office.

Who, O Lord, can worthily weigh these bowels of your piety toward me, unworthy as I am? Who can worthily gauge such immense riches of your goodness? I hope, Lord, and, faithfully presuming on such great kindness, I believe that "your mercy will follow me all the days of my life"; for you have already deigned to give me in advance such great pledges of graces, for which, as is worthy, I do not cease immolating praises and sacrifices of jubilation to you, my most pious illuminator.

You also, whoever read or hear this account, rejoice and be glad with me, for I was dead, and I live again; I was lost and have been found [cf. Luke 15:6, 9]. With me, therefore, magnify the Lord, who lives and reigns unto the ages of ages. Amen.

CASE 3

The *Dialogues* of Constantine Tsatsos

From Theology to Existentialism

The accounts by Augustine and Herman-Judah purport to be records of historical fact. Yet there is no independent corroborating evidence for either. The existence of Herman-Judah has been questioned, as well as the veracity of the account attributed to him; and one can well imagine that a record of Augustine's spiritual quest written by his mother or by the brother so slightingly treated in the *Confessions* would not conform in every detail with the bishop of Hippo's. Between us and the experience configured in the text stands the impenetrable screen of the author's fictive imagination. Need any historical event stand behind it?

With Constantine Tsatsos's *Dialogues in a Monastery*, we cross the border from the fictive to the fictional. Still, it is as true a witness to paradigms of conversion as the other two texts; and because it does not cloud the hermeneutic issue by purporting to record actual events, it brings us to recognize more starkly than others the distance between experience and text. Tsatsos is as authentic a witness to norms of conversion that he considered authentic as Augustine and Herman-Judah were to what served as authenticating norms for them. All that we can see in any of the three cases is a stylized representation, a screen patterned by methods of understanding.

To be sure, we also enter a historical epoch at least as unlike twelfth-century Germany in degree as Herman-Judah's world was from north Africa under the late Roman Empire. Throughout *Understanding Conversion*, I emphasized that Christian ideas about conversion broke with classical tradition. Christian and classical traditions shared the proposition that beauty was a principle of thought—indeed, an attribute of God, pure thought. But ideals of beauty in the tradition that I was examining were no more those of pre-Christian Antiquity than were the styles that assimilated ancient models and recast them into something entirely new. I was also concerned to identify some ways in which the Christian repertory of paradigms of conversion have continued, even in recent times, to shape ideas about human nature.

My last case study is chosen to underscore a second break in tradition, comparable with the one that occurred in the Age of the Church Fathers: the rejection of theological norms by modern secularist ways of understanding. It also illustrates how opposites can be made to coincide when, through a distinctive intellectual alchemy, a twentieth-century writer imaginatively blends fragments of Christian doctrine with teachings of a cherished pre-Christian Antiquity.

But it is clear that the tension between formal signs of conversion—defined by acceptance of a creed and submission to institutions that guarded it—and supernatural conversion no longer vexed Tsatsos as it had Augustine and Herman-Judah. With Tsatsos, we enter a realm in which what was called conversion was entirely different from the related but diverse subjects that Augustine and Herman-Judah called by that name. Tsatsos retained metaphysical speculation about natural being but renounced the supernatural. Even more, what he called conversion did not transcend nature or, indeed, have much to do with nature; it was rooted in the circumstances of existence. The stylized norms of conversion that informed his imagination were quite different from those that directed the fictive narratives of Augustine and Herman-Judah.

The adjectives *mystical* and *humane* are seldom appropriate to one and the same text, least of all to one by a secular head of state. But such were terms that the eminent writer Pandelis Prevelakis applied to *Dialogues in a Monastery*, by Constantine Tsatsos. Prevelakis recognized that this book, with its multiplicity of themes and its combination of Platonic (and Neoplatonic) philosophy with skepticism, was hard to absorb. For, he noted, Tsatsos had drawn from streams that in earlier times had refreshed the human spirit—living waters of myth, philosophy, esthetics, and religion—but that in the spiritual aridity of the present day had become inaccessible to many. The appearance of an English version of so exceptional a landmark in literary and political history invites further explorations through its corridors of thought.[1]

In 1975, after a coup d'état had restored democratic government to Greece, Constantine Tsatsos (1899–1987) was installed as first president of the Hellenic Republic. Tsatsos had chaired the committee that drafted the new constitution (1974–75), but that was only one chapter in a varied career. At first he was a practicing attorney, then a professor of the philosophy of law, and, intermittently after 1946, a member of the Greek Parliament and a minister of state. Through the distractions of public life, he published works in the fields of history, belles lettres, and philosophy, including, notably, esthetics. Issued just before his presidency began, *Dialogues in a Monastery* (1974) is a lens that Tsatsos used to focus his humanistic pursuits under despotism, one growth, to use his own phrase, in "the rotten soil" of dictatorship (p. 42). Yet, there is an astonishing and ironic contrast between Tsatsos the restorer of democracy and Tsatsos the philosopher.[2]

As a work composed in momentary eclipse from power by a man who soon after became head of state, Tsatsos's *Dialogues* has one distant counterpart: Cardinal Lotario dei Segni's *On the Misery of the Human Condition*. The cardinal intended to write a corresponding treatise on the dignity of human nature, but that project was forestalled by his election as Pope Innocent III (reigned 1198–1216).

Apart from the purely external analogy between their authors' circumstances, Tsatsos's treatise shares with Lotario's the theme of conversion (*metanoia*), implicit in all discourses on the formation of the mind. Yet even this correspondence in theme is slender. Lotario meant to induce his readers to repentance, to a change of life, by pressing terror of the Last Judgment upon them. By contrast, praising love but mistrusting dominance of emotion, Tsatsos portrayed conversion in the oldest philosophical sense: a turning of the mind—which is to say, reason—toward wisdom (e.g., pp. 75, 76). Tsatsos cast his treatise in a dramatic form and set the action in a religious house dedicated to divine Wisdom in a particular aspect, the monastery of the Transfiguration.

Certainly, Tsatsos recognized that conversion as the turning of the mind toward wisdom could produce a formal change of life, as it had done, long before the fictional *Dialogues* began, when the abbot Synesios, the instigator and helmsman of the dialogues, and his spiritual son, Sophronios, embraced monasticism. He did not envision a further transformation of the soul from its own nature into another, a divinization. But even the formal change of life was not the outcome for the other participants in the conversations. For them—two philosophers, a classicist, and a historian—the road of conversion did not end in the monastery of the Transfiguration.

It led back to the worlds from which they had come, without any evident change of heart and without foreseeable goal.[3] Indeed, even Synesios's monastic conversion made him more plainly what he already was and was becoming, and his turning continues through the monastery toward a later, and by no means nominal, transfiguration.[4]

Metaphysics did not lead beyond nature to the supernatural; in some contexts, it hardly led beyond experience to nature; it was existential. Whether with or without a change of heart, conversion as portrayed by Tsatsos is not an event but a way of experiencing "the tragic character of life" (p. 89).[5]

There is another great difference between Lotario's prescript for conversion and Tsatsos's. For Tsatsos almost entirely set doctrinal Christianity aside. Indeed, his portrayal of conversion has scarcely greater Christian content than do those of Plato and Plotinus. To be sure, there are allusions to Scripture (Matt. 23:37, p. 176 [hen and chicks]; Matt. 4:19, p. 37 ["fishers of men"]; John 20 [the apparition of Christ to Thomas]). But neither these figures of speech, nor the discussion of sin (pp. 87ff., 93), nor the statement of Nicene belief concerning the Incarnation (p. 63) stands anywhere near the center of Tsatsos's interpretive enterprise. He wrote convinced that "the dogma of Christianity [was] antithetical to its essence" (p. 67), that, far from bearing on God's relation to human beings, Christ's teachings pertained to "man's worldly destiny," elucidating love as "a new rule in the relations among men, a new way of human progress" (pp. 19–20). It is not surprising to find that Abbot Synesios was a unique "dissonance" whose existence would be disbelieved by "other Orthodox clerics" and laymen (p. 127). Like Augustine of Hippo, Synesios found his spiritual guide, the Neoplatonist Plotinus, relatively late in life. Unlike Augustine, Synesios thought it necessary to complete Plotinus's teachings, not with scriptural teachings on Christ as the propitiation for sin, as mediator and advocate, but with Gregory of Nyssa's mystic apprehensions of divine essence, the Being of beings (pp. 174–75; cf. Augustine's *Confessions* 9.21). Tsatsos expresses antipathy to St. Paul, one of Augustine's main authorities concerning Christ's redemptive work, for the Apostle's hatred of the body and his character as lawgiver. In both regards, Tsatsos held, Paul was hostile to the love taught and exemplified by Christ (p. 31). There is no *consensus fidelium* to guide Tsatsos's conversion. All seek redemption; none agree on the redemptive word (p. 92).

Conversion according to Tsatsos has greater affinities to the lonely esthetic conversion of James Joyce to art than to the moral change of heart that Lotario demanded.[6] Different as it is from paradigms of dogmatic Christianity, conversion according to Tsatsos by no means recapitulates the paradigms of pre-Christian Antiquity. The *Dialogues* bears the marks of its times. My task is to trace the pattern of understanding embodied in the words of the *Dialogues*. The categories of analysis that I shall use are drawn from Martin Heidegger, who appears in the *Dialogues* as the spokesman of "pure and simple existentialism" (p. 144).

A word of explanation may be helpful. Heidegger drew a fundamental distinction between what is said and the saying of it. The participants in the *Dialogues* consider what is said abstractly, as the "universal affirmation of Being in its universality" (pp. 157–62). This affirmation, drawn from existentialist philosophy (and, more particularly, the author explains, from that of Heidegger), is presented as an antidote to the despair which Tsatsos portrays as pervading the fragmented world of knowledge. The affirmation of Being is also an affirmation of the meaning in human existence (p. 159), grounded in the Logos, the principle of freedom. The symbolic form of the suprarational Logos is the absurd (pp. 16, 160).

Existential in ideology, Goethean (or Faustian) in inspiration, the yes that is said to Being also harbors a dynamic element inherited from Platonism. The *Dialogues* begins and ends with testimonies to the Platonic concept of participation. At the outset Tsatsos asserts that material things participate in corresponding abstract ideas and that through this participation human actions gain meaning because they become not only actual in their own existences but also symbolic by participation in ideas (p. 14). At the conclusion he asserts the participation of human beings in God (as Being). "You too are an element of God whether or not you are conscious of it" (p. 180). But this is a particular extension of the argument for the "sacred nature of all things" (p. 168). As an epitome of the yes that is said, Tsatsos employs the conventional misquotation of an absurd "Greekling" created by the Roman comedian Terence: "Homo sum et nihil humanum a me alienum puto" ("I am a human being, and I think nothing human alien to me").[7]

One must be struck by the non-Hellenic character of what is said, underscored by Tsatsos's historically correct acknowledgment that Cicero, and not a writer of ancient Greece, was the first humanist (p. 52).[8] What is said is an artifact of conversion; the saying is the act of conversion itself. What is true of the artifact may not apply to the transformation that produced it. Between artifact and conversion there is an intervening element: the work of thought and writing that digested the experience of conversion into a text.

Thus, whether the text is Augustine's *Confessions*, Herman-Judah's *Short Account*, James Joyce's *A Portrait of the Artist*, or Tsatsos's *Dialogues*, to discuss conversion is to consider three separate but interlocking subjects. The task is partly a venture in literary criticism (the portrayal of understanding deliberately set forth in the text), partly one in hermeneutics (the unspoken processes of thought by which the text was composed), and partly one in religious phenomenology (the actual experience of conversion filtered, first, through the author's mind and, second, through the text).

Tsatsos himself described the event of conversion—both conversion to monastic life and saying yes to Being—as a leap (pp. 153, 157-59, 174). This is no broad jump in one plane, but rather, like Kierkegaard's leap of faith, a jump into the depths. Thus, I come back to categories provided by Heidegger, Tsatsos's archetypal existentialist.

Two of them—the origin of the saying and the saying of what is said (the yes)—concern the leaper's point of departure, and these will disclose the ways of understanding set forth in the text. Thus, beginning at the outer edge of the problem, I find that the origin of the saying illuminates the circumstances under which the *Dialogues* was written—the social circle to which Tsatsos belonged and Tsatsos's own preoccupations. It also illuminates the point, within the *Dialogues* as a composition, from which all lines of argument depart: namely, the view of human existence as essentially defined by pain.

Two further categories—the content of the event that is called "saying" and the unsaid in the yes—concern the impulses propelling the leap. These will lay open the unspoken processes of understanding by which the text was composed. How does the yes come to be said? The saying that is conversion is not to be found in static forms (of words, for example), but rather in the emotions as they say, or bring forth, those forms. Tsatsos made the entire structure of the *Dialogues* an example of how to retrace the process of saying the said; the entire work is a regressive passage from words to meanings to the affective silence in which meanings begin. Here, one first confronts the gap between experiencing conversion and talking about it, the disability of thought to grasp, and of language to express, the experience of conversion; a gap that few are able to detect and that must be bridged, if at all, in solitude.

The final Heideggerian category—the translation of the saying—brings the reader to the goal of the leap inward, the experience of conversion itself. The preceding categories describe circumstances of conversion. Translation is the act by which the mind is changed. As a principle of composition, according to Tsatsos, the category of translation underlies various discourses on verbal translation, poetry, and the deliberate construction of life as poetry. As an access to the theme of conversion, it discloses the anguish with which the poetic act translates the artist into the work of art.

These categories are generally useful, but they possess a distinctive cast in Tsatsos's *Dialogues* due to a bifurcation in Greek literature. It must strike any reader as ironic that a primary architect of democratic government should espouse the adamantly antidemocratic propositions of the *Dialogues*. This tension was grounded in historical experiences. I shall not here explore the yet deeper basis in the collective experience of Greece expressed and nurtured in the Greek language itself. I refer to the distinction between literary Greek (*katharevousa*), an academically "purified" version of the classical language, and demotic, which is still regarded by some as a semibarbarous dialect, a compound of Greek with additives from alien tongues, including those of the many foreign powers which have occupied Greece in its long history. The linguistic tension between *katharevousa* and demotic was, and is, both a real linguistic division and a paramount symbol of social and political distinctions. One need only remember the astonishment of Ioanna Tsatsou that her father, who normally wrote either in French or in "flawless" *katharevousa,* once composed a poem in demotic.[9] Something of this profound linguistic touchstone of association was at work when political enemies denounced as authoritarian and reactionary the democratic constitution over whose writing Tsatsos presided, notably for the wide powers assigned the president of the Republic.

The Origin of the Saying

The writings of others have already invited us behind the doors of the house on Kydathineon Street, in Athens, where this book was written, that street at the foot of the Acropolis, running between the National Gardens and the theater of Dionysus. We have followed the building of the house (1932–33) for the patriarchy of Stylianos Seferiades, all lawyers and poets, and the gradual departures from it, by Stylianos himself, when, abruptly retired from the University of Athens during the regime of Metaxas, he made his home in Paris (1938–51), doubly parted from his children by distance and remarriage; by one son, Angelos, who emigrated to the United States in the anguish of civil war and died there (1946–50); intermittently by his elder son, George Seferis, in his diplomatic and literary careers, and, finally, in death (1971). Now, his son-in-law Tsatsos has withdrawn from the stage; and only Seferiades' daughter, Ioanna Tsatsou, like the others a jurist and poet, is left on Kydathineon Street.

We know something about the experiences in that house, where Tsatsos was arrested and sent into internal exile under Metaxas (1939), where the streets filled with students to acclaim him for defying the occupying powers at the cost of his professorship (1941), and whence he fled to escape arrest by the Germans (1944).[10]

We have also been taken into the circle of writers in which the inhabitants of Kydathineon 9 moved—Palamas, a near neighbor in Plaka; Sikelianos, who became a good friend of Seferis; and Myrivilis, who was often a guest of the Tsatsoi and a frequent correspondent of Ioanna Tsatsou, a man to whom "Costakis . . . gave lots of ideas."[11] The name of Kazantzakis is conspicuously missing.

Broadly, the origins of the saying lay in this circle and in the experiences of its members during the turbulent and sanguinary career of their people during the first half of the twentieth century. Of course, the origins were more exactly the reflections of one man, the author. We know that there was something in the texture of his thought that set him apart from those among whom he lived. So devoted was he to his studies that when blackouts of war forbade open light, he read far into the night behind shuttered windows even in the suffocating heat of summer (1943).[12] A "dark imagination" ran through his philosophy, drawn, as it was, from the font of German Romanticism. He was Costakis the pessimist, rebuked at least once by Seferis for bringing philosophical morbidity too close to life; and he also crossed swords with Seferis in a celebrated literary debate (1938). "It is certainly remarkable," one observer said, "that one lives on one floor and the other on another floor in the same building, but they carry on their discussion in writing." And still, "Costakis loved George. If he had not, life would not have been livable."[13]

Such are not the origins identified in the *Dialogues*. One acknowledged there recurs throughout the many variations on the theme of tragic existence: that origin is suffering. The doctrines that art is rooted in suffering and that art, and indeed all creative effort, is an escape from the pain of existence are well known in Greek literary criticism.[14] "No matter where you touch a Jew," says one of Kazantzakis's characters, "you find a wound."[15]

But, in the *Dialogues*, Tsatsos denied a similarity between the historical position of Jews, elevated to power as far as the Diaspora scattered them and numerous, and the Greeks, few, "powerless [and] alone" in their tragic circumstances, devouring "each other like starving dogs" (p. 69; Tsatsos's comments on World War II include no reference to Jews).

Tsatsos locates the origin of his saying in wounds, some of them specific to individual actors in the *Dialogues*, while others are endemic to the human condition, and yet others, characteristic of his own culture and time. "The pain of an incurable wound" became "the secret law of [Synesios's] life" (pp. 127–28), an analogy, perhaps ironic, to the "thorn in the flesh, the messenger of Satan," given to keep the Apostle Paul from vainglory (2 Cor. 12:7). The occasion of the *Dialogues* was Ipliksis's mental distress, evidently the wound to which Synesios refers (pp. 2, 5). Individual suffering could disseminate itself. Synesios left the world for the monastery because he had been touched by the "gravely wounded soul" of Nouty, his beloved yet "a broken creature" (pp. 105, 109). "The power of suffering," Synesios recalled, "made me a Christian; it made me a Christian mystic" (p. 117).

The pain of individuals was part of the general "tragedy of existence"; and the participants in Tsatsos's *Dialogues* identify a number of ways in which human existence, in general and in their own day, inflicted wounds. Much discussion concerns the rule of love, supposedly antithetic to the rule of law, in Christianity. Whatever may be said about its ramifications, the discourse on love throws into high relief the fact that all the discussants are male and, indeed, that they are advanced in years, though plainly not stricken by age. It is possible to deduce that at the time of the *Dialogues*, Synesios and Ipliksis were more than sixty years old (p. 4). Basset, having taken up studies in Germany not long after 1927 (p. 144; the year when Heidegger's *Sein und Zeit* was published) appears to belong to the same generation. Manhorst can only have studied with Jaeger at Berlin (pp. 4–5) before Jaeger was forced into exile in 1936. One hardly knows how to estimate the age of the monk, Sophronios, who studied in Berlin when "Jaeger's predecessor, Wilamowitz, was in his prime," presumably well before Wilamowitz died at the age of eighty-three (1848–1931), and possibly before Jaeger assumed his professorship in Berlin (1921). "Who can forget imminent death," asks Harrer, one's own or that of the cosmos? The despair of our times, he adds, "comes chiefly from fear of death" (p. 143). Toward the beginning of the *Dialogues*, Synesios said: "It is a chilly business, personally and alone, every day, to contemplate the ages, because death is always there in the midst" (p. 22).

The wounds of decades and awareness that death is imminent in each moment are fresh in the minds of the aging discussants, but other wounds are evident in the exclusion of women from among them. It would be too facile to explain the location of the *Dialogues* in a setting devoid of women as expressing norms of a patriarchal culture which still makes the New Year's wish for "male children and female lambs."[16] But the effects of tradition are apparent.

Ioanna Tsatsou herself witnessed to the weight of this culture when, remembering the numerical predominance of males over females in her generation of law students (1924–27, in Athens), she wrote: "The male mind suited me, not lost in trivialities. The jealousy and hypocrisy of the female sex surprised me, humiliated me." Recording the fortitude of Lela Karayannis, arrested and executed by the Germans (1944), she also commented: "She has a masculine mind, as Solomos says, a strong mind and the instincts of the most perfect woman." With her masculine mind and female instincts, in the last moments, "covered with wounds, she asked to lead the dance—like the heroines of the Greek Revolution—so as to give courage to the others about to die."[17] Perhaps in silent deference to Ioanna Tsatsou, the author gave the leader of the dialogues the name of Synesios of Ptolemais (c.370–414), a disciple of another woman celebrated for her masculine intellect, the Alexandrine Neoplatonist Hypatia.[18]

The constitution written under Tsatsos's chairmanship granted equal rights and obligations to men and women in an effort to relieve women of the illiteracy and domestic bondage to which tradition had confined them. As president, he was threatened with excommunication if he signed a bill permitting abortions.[19] Yet the portrayal of women in the *Dialogues* indicates little sense of equity between genders.

In Tsatsos's scheme of understanding, women serve as symbolic devices to elucidate the wounds of love. Eros, the lowest form of love, acts in the driven sexual foraging with which the future abbot Synesios sought comfort after Nouty's death (p. 116) and in the dalliances of his friend Ipliksis (p. 151). The philosopher transmuted the "cry of the physical orgasm" into perception of spiritual beauty (pp. 123–24). This fusion of flesh and spirit eluded the great majority who "remain[ed] animals, or who from time to time bec[a]me animals under the mask of men." Necessary as the ascent from orgasm to spiritual ecstasy was for seekers of true beauty, for them "physical union with a beautiful female form is an agonizing act. The main thing is the form; the flesh is merely a necessary means." The complex of pain was even wider. Changing the gender referent, Tsatsos wrote that one man did not love another for his beauty, worthiness, or ideality but for the common fate that was tormenting lover and beloved and grinding them both to dust. The love that impelled the lover required, not union with the beloved (for sexual passion is incompatible with friendship), but self-annihilation, sacrifice, for humanity (pp. 27–29, 34). It is not clear what is meant when Ipliksis insists that the erotic principles enunciated by him as a man apply *"mutatis mutandis* to a woman" (p. 32). Certainly, he posits a difference between male and female mentalities, the familiar difference between intellect and instinct: "The young woman will understand it, not as aesthetic theory, but in the act of love, as passion" (p. 12).[20]

Thus, the womanless company portrayed by Tsatsos employs women as interpretive devices in the *Dialogues*, no less instruments in the service of logic than women had been in the service of their own vagrant sensuality (e.g., p. 5; no families are mentioned). The ageless and endlessly repeated wounds of eros are only the first rungs by which mystics ascend the "terrible ladder that is lost in the heights" (p. 33).

The ascent of discourse also moves well beyond sexuality to the enduring misery of the human condition, ever bearing its mortality within itself. But, in Tsatsos's view, the tragic character of human existence has now received a particular modulation, an "ideological void" that had endured for a century and that has precipitated the decline of European civilization (pp. 44, 46). An abyss gapes before the soul, no less fearful than the emptiness in the soul. Contemporary life inculcates universal bitterness; for in an age of atrocities the meaning of human existence has come to depend on the slender thread of belief in the absurd, all other grounds having dissolved in futility and meaninglessness (pp. 40–41, 73, 89).

As humanists, the participants in the *Dialogues* seek to escape from their predicament through Hellenism; but the career of Hellenism itself in the last century is an index of the calamity. Jaeger, the imputed teacher of some of the discussants, was able to write of ancient Greece: "The Greek mind owes its superior strength to the fact that it was deeply rooted in the life of the community."[21] But the Hellenism represented in the *Dialogues* is by no means indigenous to Greek culture of the twentieth century. It is the creation and the legacy of foreign scholarship, beginning with Cicero, "the first humanist" (p. 52), and even the Greek participants trace their intellectual descent to cultures other than their own, chiefly to the German academic world. Tsatsos asserts "the anaemia of the true Greek logos" (p. 41). His Hellenic actors represent "the fortunate few" in Greek society, "the families of wealth who have been able to afford foreign education."[22]

The pages of the *Dialogues* contain many references to scholarly and literary writings. Yet if the books cited were actually assembled, modern Greek literature would be represented (I believe) by only four authors, and those are poets.[23] There would be no works by modern Greek philosophers, theologians, historians, or philologists. It is remarkable that Tsatsos never represents his gathering of scholars adjourning to the monastic library to consult archives or manuscripts, though at the end Synesios limply alleges, "I have the holy books and other texts of secular learning" (p. 181)—as remarkable, indeed, as the fact that despite extensive talk about beauty and the beautiful, none of the participants goes off to see whether there are any mosaics or murals in the chapel.

Even granting a continuity of ethos that encompasses Plato, Aristotle, Plotinus, Gregory of Nyssa, and writers in the present day, it is clear that "the works of the logos . . . [and] custodians of the mysteries" (p. 39) in the *Dialogues* were strangers in the communities in which they lived. The French and German participants were outsiders because of the exoticism of their studies; the Greeks, by virtue of the derived and alien sources of their learning. Each in some measure had "exchanged his own culture for another," with the consequence that a disjuncture appeared between the native matrix and the alien grafting.[24]

The common pain of eros and the contemporary anguish of alienation combine in Tsatsos's story of Nouty, which appears almost as a diversion at midpoint in the narrative structure of the *Dialogues* but actually serves as a parable of Greeks regarding themselves in German culture.

There is no need here to consider in detail the elaborate symbolism of this account. Tsatsos explains how, in the aftermath of World War II but before his conversion to the monastic life, Synesios returned to Germany in search of two friends who had endured persecution by the Nazis. Breaking his journey at Graz, he met and fell in love with Nouty, an Austrian aristocrat in reduced circumstances. Nouty had been abandoned by her German fiancé, a bitter man inwardly destroyed by the war. She cherished a great love for him, and she fled to his arms when he reappeared at the very moment when Nouty and Synesios were to have been married. She and her husband abandoned Europe for the United States. Yet within three years Nouty committed suicide, tortured by the man to whom she had been faithful. Experiencing a protracted emotional death by stages, Synesios entered the monastery sometime after Nouty's "martyrdom."

In the unity of love, Synesios said: "I was myself. I was she" (p. 105).[25] About the time when the *Dialogues* was published, Tsatsos is reported to have written to an unknown woman, "I wish I could be worthy of you, young, strong, free, carefree, to flog you and make you mine, to tame you . . . to make you the book that I shall write."[26] The parable of Nouty is a tale of tragedy, the entwining pain of two blighted existences, the erotic wounds of sexuality common to mankind, the sufferings of Greeks who received from Germany both Hellenism and despair, and the sufferings of women transfigured into the books of men.

The Saying of the Said

Among the wounds that gave rise to the saying of yes to Being were divisions among scholars.[27] Those divisions began in mutually exclusive propositions and ended in mutual unintelligibility. The *Dialogues* presents an array of abstract methods of discourse which seldom intersect. Conversion does not produce a change of mind any more than it does a change of heart. For this reason, Tsatsos leads the participants to a conclusion that places all their analytic and expository skills in question.

If the origin of the saying was the enactment of the tragedy of existence, the saying itself was, paradoxically, in silence. The saying is not in the words uttered, for words are symbols. The plight of the contemporary word is that "the word is no longer a transmissible idea, no longer a link in a chain" of signification (p. 132). For the key to the unspoken and unspeakable language of symbolic communication has been lost in multiplicity. To cure the wound of learned culture, subconscious meaning must be reanimated and given "the form of language" (p. 79).

Accordingly, Ipliksis asserts, "I am not an Asiatic. I am a European, and I want evolving forms," not a chaos, such as contemporary thought is said to present, but "motion guided by reason" (p. 74). Yet Synesios eventually affirms: "Time does not exist. Space does not exist. Perhaps even reason does not exist. Only a silence searching for the infinite" (p. 152). While they might appear to define antitheses, these statements in fact define two points in the movement of the *Dialogues* itself. For that movement is the saying, or evolving of forms, by which silence that is there from the origin of the saying is by the end brought to the surface and made the culmination of discourse.

Tsatsos's portrayal of conversion in both its forms points toward the absolute in the saying rather than toward the relative in the said. His model of intellectual asceticism was the monk's continual discipline of conversion, the "silent struggles" of the hesychast against himself (p. 78). The monk knew, as the philosopher discovered, that in the encounter with the absolute his soul must keep silent (p. 119). To advance in his implacable conflicts, the monk practiced emptying the conscious of himself and sought to learn not to learn in order to learn the unlearnable things unknown by him (p. 18). Scholars were to imitate monks in being "still and try[ing] to hear what a familiar voice is saying to [them] in an unknown language" (p. 9), a speech that is consciousness without words (cf. p. 132). The *Dialogues* culminates as the participants gather for the last time, a "silent chorus . . . of kindred souls" (p. 181).

Such was the prototype of intellectual anchoritism. Even among philosophers, disciplined to precise verbal discourse, the meanings of words continually change (p. 53). And this is one reason why, in their relentless destruction of old norms (or "idols"), practitioners of logical truth move aimlessly in "universal futility," sometimes fiddling "again with crumbling idols because nothing new has been put in their place" (pp. 40–41). The mutual repugnance of existentialist philosophies is one instance of this Babel of scholars who "live among strangers, speaking strange tongues[, and] debase the holiness of earthly life by making it into an endless chain of futile daily events" (pp. 78, 94). Knowledge was never complete; there was only the continual approach toward the ever inaccessible. Indeed, the meaning of human existence was vindicated by the freedom of this endless struggle, a net without escape, a movement whose affirmation of Being demanded continual negation of what was (pp. 147–49). This was a struggle of solitude, if need be of silence, in which the "true man" spoke "his own language, a language spoken by very few, sometimes by no one else" (p. 78).

The wordless turnings of monastic and philosophical conversion alike return to the erotic element in the origin of the saying: that is, to the union of "two human beings . . . soul and body, at the supreme movement of their union [who] live something, understand something unutterable, incommunicable. . . . And the meaning which they understand, if by chance they can grasp it, is wisdom, identical with the wisdom of the philosophers" (p. 12). In the persona of Ipliksis, Tsatsos continues to affirm that the experience of understanding can be relived by symbols. But he has constructed the *Dialogues* on the premise that the event of saying, prior to that of understanding, is approached, not by the multiplication of symbols, but by the elimination both of words and of the logic informing words and rational understanding. As an unfolding of forms, saying is a sequence of eliminations, ending in self-emptying silence.

Early in the *Dialogues*, Synesios defines this process of mystic intellection, which is also renunciation. It is, he asserts, the "austere consciousness" by which he has advanced, leaving at length "only the communication with God" in his hands. Ipliksis responds that the same process is known also to the moral norms of secular learning. Goethe frequently invoked "this merciless discipline" of concentration on a single objective without which no virtue could be attained. It "is a basic law of life; it is the law of the self-determination of conscience" (pp. 22–23), which is also the freedom to say yes or no to Being (pp. 157–62). This hesychastic process of saying is the structure of the *Dialogues*, as I shall now briefly explain.

Tsatsos's concept of struggle could have left him with the existentialist doctrine of continual crisis: that is, a doctrine that existence and freedom are real only in action—specifically in the act of choice—and, therefore, that the exercise of choice must be continually repeated.[28] Every instant of decision becomes a crisis, a turning point, in which Being is encountered and, by choice, disclosed or negated.

But what is said—the yes to Being—is categorical. It excludes the need for ever-repeated crises, just as it counteracts the "anguish and despair" in which, Tsatsos judged, existentialism left contemporary human beings (p. 141). "How," he said, "shall we master the crisis which plagues the inner man?" (p. 49). If the crisis of despair were to be "passed through" (p. 45) and not continually repeated, the coordinates of crisis, time and space, had to be reduced to silence.

Thus, the *Dialogues* begins with a preliminary discussion of the need for a way of understanding that encompasses both logical and esthetic thought. The disabilities of words, in and of themselves, to serve suprarational faculties of mind or to express suprarational meanings demanded that they (and other modes of expression) comprise a language of symbols, corresponding with authentic thought, as well as a language of reason, and that symbols participate by likeness in the realities expressed by them.

After stating his program in this essentially Platonic way, Tsatsos went on to consider the obstacles that it encountered in a hostile and uncomprehending world. Looking first to historical causes, he took note of the disequilibrium introduced into civilization by the imperfect fusion of Christianity with its ethos of love and hatred of the body and Hellenism with its graduated ascent from carnal eroticism upward to union with God. The discussants then review the failure of the contemporary world, "the age of the technician, of the machine" (p. 39), to find a spiritual direction or the happiness of the soul distinct from "the happiness attached to material goods" (p. 45).

Since the dimensions of world history prove too elusive to serve the needs of the discussants, they turn, in detail, to Greece and Hellenism. Their conversations reveal that this ethnic tradition, extending over many centuries, provided no surer guidance than Christian doctrine or world history to redress "the emptiness in the contemporary soul" (p. 73). Even the sage advice that "the spiritual man" must practice self-denial, an anchoritic withdrawal, to achieve the authenticity of judgment by which he could "reanimate meaning and give it the form of life" is no conclusion (p. 79).

For the anchorite's struggle to reach the absolute was endless, a movement explained in one way by the theology of original sin and in another, by the existentialist doctrine of anxiety. Perhaps what was called God, or the absolute, was the collective accumulation of human struggles, just as every soul was the history constituted by its individual agonies (cf. p. 89).

At this point in the *Dialogues*, the said—the yes to Being—has not yet been uttered; but the saying has passed through elimination of language and ethos (including ethnic tradition) as means toward the absolute. By introducing the parable of Nouty here, Tsatsos summarizes what has been achieved in the process of eliminating language and ethos and anticipates the stage yet to come.[29] Synesios's flight to the monastic life introduces the third, and last, means toward the absolute to be reviewed in the *Dialogues*: namely, spirit.

Discussions before the parable of Nouty turned chiefly on historical subjects. Those after it concern subjects of learned ignorance on levels of increasing abstraction. The discussants consider beauty, as expressed (or deformed) in poetry. They then take up the subject of reason. They are plagued by the discrepancy between the absolute, which is their goal, and the historical relativism of all intellectual efforts. There is no escape from their dilemma. But they conclude that the absolute resides, not in knowledge, but in freedom and that the fate of imminent death in historical relativism can be mitigated by uttering the existential yes in freedom. Thus, truth can be approached with "a less relative relativism" of knowledge and a freedom that is absolute.

But the problem of historical relativism has not yet been laid to rest. At this stage, near the end of their spiritual eliminations, they recognize that their own ways of thinking are the legacy of previous generations. This legacy was formed by the fewest of the few, men whose writings have been regarded as miracles through the centuries; but they, especially those who exposed and quickened the powers of the soul beyond logic, were fashioned by God and manifested his word. Whether God were understood as existing or as eternally created by human beings in their struggles (and thus, in some sense identical with the created world), this assertion of divine authorship eliminates the separateness of authors and prepares for Synesios's climactic affirmation of the coincidence of opposites (p. 175). Finally, all else having been eliminated, the *Dialogues* is reduced to the "silent chorus of friends," divided by words and propositions, but one, by virtue of participation in God, existing or eternally created.

Discourse on spirit, following the parable of Nouty, retreats from the vast array of the collective works of human spirit to the narrow powers of the individual soul, and finally to one small point: the divine spark in each soul.

The saying of the said permits only one further reductive step: the elimination of eliminations. The participants depart.

The structure of the *Dialogues* is part of its message. At the moment when author's saying and reader's reading coincide, the experience of the saying as elimination can be relived in its role as a principle of composition. "In the old days," Picasso remembered, "pictures went forward toward completion by stages. . . . A picture used to be a sum of additions. In my case, a picture is a sum of destructions."[30]

The Content of the Saying

The saying of the yes is not the word, yes, that is said or the fixed arrangement of spoken words that comprise a text. The saying is the process of eliminations moving toward silence. Synesios characterizes every act of choice in that process as a "sacred office" that one always performs alone, not the fixed form of a liturgy, but rather a movement, a "passage to what comes after death" (p. 94).

The content of such a saying cannot be propositions, methods, and conclusions. Rather, it must be the impelling force that informs the movement. Tsatsos identifies a twofold force: faith and love. The participants find these virtues lacking in the world around them; the degree to which they themselves possess, or are possessed by, faith and love is unclear. Yet by now one distinction must be evident between conversion as portrayed in the *Dialogues* and conversion in the doctrinal tradition of Christianity. As a turning of the mind toward self-emptying and silence, this conversion lacks zeal, most notably missionary zeal.[31]

St. Paul insisted that spiritual gifts be rendered intelligible for "the edifying of the Church." "He that speaketh in an unknown tongue speaketh not unto men, but unto God; for no man understandeth him, howbeit in the Spirit he speaketh mysteries. . . . Except ye utter by the tongue words easy to be understood, how shall it be known what is spoken? For ye speak into the air" (1 Cor. 14:2, 4, 9).

As unwilling witnesses to the anguish of despair, the participants in the *Dialogues* lack the virtue of hope, which, according to Paul, gave direction to faith, and charity, the perfection of love toward God and neighbor. It was for charity's sake, Paul wrote, that believers should follow after spiritual gifts, cautious of knowledge, which "puffeth up," desirous of "charity [which] edifieth" (1 Cor. 14:1; 8:1). But even as he left collective faith (the *consensus fidelium*) unmentioned, so Tsatsos also acknowledged his aversion to Paul for his intrusion of legalism into the doctrines of Jesus, the great teacher of humane love (pp. 31, 47, 61).

"What is spoken," Heidegger wrote, "is never and in no language, what is said."[32] Tsatsos illuminates the saying of faith and love in an exchange between two discussants about Synesios. Manhorst idealizes the abbot's entire openness in "reveal[ing] his whole soul and offer[ing] his thought in all its purity, as if on a tray." This illusion, Ipliksis responds, is mistaken. For Synesios displays only "what can be of interest to others. He does not reveal what is hidden beneath this offering, the pain of an incurable wound which became the secret law of his life" (pp. 127–28). Thus, the saying that is faith and love and that informs the choice to say yes to Being is in hiddenness and pain.

It occurs at the point where "human thought [is] linked to human imagination" (p. 121). Unenlarged by charity, thought and imagination restricted the meaning that Tsatsos intended when he affirmed, with Terence, that nothing human was alien to him. Without reaching forth to God or neighbor, the saying was a private event for the sayer, edifying himself.

Much concerning the nature of faith can be deduced from its object. Carnal love, or eros, is a bridge to the Good, and the "great lovers" are those who pass up the ladder, or chain, of being to God, the "supreme idea" (pp. 33, 174). The highest intensity of carnal pleasure is reached when it is projected into the metaphysical dimension and man, the flesh "as an undivided unity" with spirit, "unites with the object of his passion" (p. 32). But Synesios has assured his companions from the beginning that no one achieves union with God (p. 1; cf. p. 27), and there is no indication that the object of faith is a God who loves and is loved, or who, indeed, is love.

The abstractness with which God is characterized as Being, or as the entity "eternally constructed" by human experience, cools the affective content of the saying as much, indeed, as the pantheisms of Spinoza and

Goethe which form the background of positions set forth in the *Dialogues* (p. 168). The cooling effects are immediately apparent in Tsatsos's treatment of fear.

In traditions of moral theology, fear of God, which was caused by faith and manifested both in servile and in filial modes, was the beginning of true wisdom. Such fear was capable of extreme statements, including Kazantzakis's characterization of God as "the ravenous beast of the celestial jungle . . . the Invisible, the Insatiable, the simple-hearted Father who devours His children and whose lips, beard, and nails drip with blood."[33] Nothing could be further from the abstractions that Tsatsos calls God.

Correspondingly, fear is diminished; it has no place in conversion. Tsatsos adverts to fear in two regards. The first is the fear and hatred of the body which entered Hellenistic thought and pervaded Christianity and, which, in both, produced "flight from passions begotten of the body" (p. 65). The second is the existential dread taught by contemporary philosophy in the form of " 'anxiety' about life and the agony of death" (pp. 93, 141). Moral theology taught the cultivation of fear. Tsatsos advocates a catharsis casting out pity and fear (p. 117). His aim is purity of thought and exaltation of feeling (p. 79), an "Epicurean calm" that springs from and enhances "the inner harmony and tranquility of the cultivated soul" (pp. 45, 83). Within the soul thus disciplined to calmness stands an impregnable fortress, from which the wise can securely gaze upon those tossed on the churning sea below (cf. p. 150).

Under the aspect of faith, conversion, the saying, is "the leap which we must attempt in order to approach [the yes, the 'affirmation of the Logos']" (pp. 153, 157, 158–59).[34] The leap must be ever repeated as a habit of soul. In the *Dialogues* the leaps convey one beyond the confines of words and logic. But since even God is encompassed by the great chain of Being, the "suprarational" is by no means the "supernatural." Ipliksis knows no theological dogma in which he can believe; he admires (rather than believing in) Christ. And yet he explains the cause of "emptiness in the contemporary soul" as the "lack of faith," by which is meant an unshakable affirmation of some first principle, whatever it may be.

"When no metaphysical faith exists," Harrer adds, "and, at the same time, there is a lack of faith in human reason, then chance replaces reason and the electronic brain replaces the human mind" (p. 75). Midway between knowledge and opinion, faith gave certainty to the believer, but not necessarily to others. Those who believed in revealed truth mistakenly transposed the mythic forms of religion into the dimension of time (p. 2).

Given the dogmatic indifference of Ipliksis and others, what assurance was there that monks correctly believed that they had attained the truth (p. 5)? The fideism of the discussants is also precarious. Despite their personal ingenuity, long intellectual pedigrees, and staunchness in an alien world, they encounter the risk that their adversaries who believe "that truth is nothing" are correct and that human endeavors "will never be able to rise from the bottomless abyss of Nothing" (p. 158).[35] Since articles of faith cannot be demonstrated by logic, there is even the chance that the "vulgar mob" are correct in their unbelief, in their lack of spirituality (pp. 2, 45, 78); at the least, belief in Nothing is a kind of faith.

One measure of the distance between the impregnable calm of faith according to Tsatsos and the fearful faith of moral theology is his insistence that the soul must experience evil in order to nourish good (p. 80). Another is the contrast between the sterility of Tsatsos's eros, crowned by the encounter of solitary soul and abstract God, and Augustine of Hippo's portrayal, in his *Confessions*, of the spiritual fecundity of the Church through conversion.[36] Nothing in Tsatsos's *Dialogues* contradicts the statement that Thomas Aquinas extracted from Aristotle's doctrines: "Knowledge is perfected by the known being in the knower; whereas love is perfected by the lover being drawn into the beloved."[37] However, lacking the doctrine of charity shared by Augustine and Thomas, Tsatsos was not able to argue that the nature of the good was through love to communicate itself and that of absolute good, to communicate itself absolutely. Withdrawal into the impregnable fortress of the soul, the monastery, or Epicurus's garden left the many to be regarded, from afar, as spectacles by the "noble few," "the few true ones," "the custodians of the mysteries" (pp. 32, 39, 40, 45, 126, 180).[38] Perhaps the mob itself was the surging menace (p. 45).

The arc excluding the many lies close to the stronghold. The great line of exclusion lay between the few and the many, whose souls are like the primal cosmos "before the land was separated from the waters" (pp. 1, 2, 24, 48, 74, 124, 162). But I have already indicated distinctions between the noble few and women, the Jews, and "Asiatics." The distinctive character of the Hellenic-Christian ethos, with humanity as its center, also excludes ancient peoples in China and India and the Aztecs. It dismisses most elements of the contemporary world, including the American "mentality" and "way of life" and a small people in the Far East "endowed with a genius for mimicking the technical achievements of the West." The peoples of Africa also live beyond the pale.

The xenophobia of those within the stronghold extends also to many who live in geographical Europe, but who, lacking correct understanding, are "not truly Western European[s]" (p. 51), those who practice asceticism without the happiness belonging to "the inner harmony and tranquility of the cultivated soul," poets who have fallen prey to the bankruptcy of reason taught by existentialism, existentialists viewed as "pseudo-despairers . . . monkeys of despair [who] are amusing, but hardly worth discussing," academic technicians discounted as "barbarians of positivism," and above all the "vulgar mob" intent on defiling and destroying God's creation (pp. 1–2, 43–44, 46, 47, 51, 53, 58, 69, 74–76, 83, 131, 139, 143). Most disastrously for continuity, and for the central humanistic function of teaching, Tsatsos dismisses the young, who, "with their still innocent gaze," see the ugly void around them and "want to destroy all that exists . . . without knowing the art of living" (p. 41; see above, n. 2).

But the informing content of the *Dialogues* was declared from the beginning. It was, not charity, but "disgust with men's affectations," a wish to withdraw "far from the mob of the many," the ignorant masses "around us" (pp. 1–2, 40, 45). Tsatsos repeatedly draws the contrast between the converted few and the unconverted many, whose convictions need not detain the wise. On the one hand, he portrays the wise soul, in solitude, contemplating the storm-tossed world from its serene and passionless heights; on the other, "the souls of most men . . . like starving bats, flying around in the darkness" (pp. 48, 180).

Are there young monks in the monastery of the Transfiguration? Even the custodian is old (p. 3). Do the aging participants in the *Dialogues*, all teachers, have students and successors? If so, are they among the young destroyers? As he portrays the informing force of faith and love, Tsatsos reveals a cause for the death of humanism.

What is Unsaid in the Said

The conversion of the "noble few," as set forth in the *Dialogues*, was neither intellectual nor moral but esthetic. It occurred at the juncture of thought and imagination; it was informed by faith and love; it advanced by symbols in which, for those of spiritual discernment, "the imagined and visionary unite[d] with the perceptible and the real" (p. 14). The search for the unsaid in the said was a familiar part of esthetic analysis. The technical structure of Bach's compositions was not the music in the notes. Homer deliberately abstained from describing Helen, thus "making us see in Helen what was not described or stated" (pp. 9–10). But there was a distinction between esthetic criticism in formal analysis and esthetic assimilation in conversion. Conversion required the willing suspension of disbelief, the synonymity of "aesthetic" and "mystical" (p. 126).

Tsatsos exercised both ways of saying the unsaid in the *Dialogues*. For example, formal analysis of narrative, with its theme of death, is enriched by the unsaid in his choice of the name Synesios for the leader of the conversations and of the monastery of the Transfiguration for the setting.

There are resonances between Tsatsos's Synesios and his namesake, Synesios of Ptolemais. Educated in Neoplatonic philosophy, the historical Synesios represented the confrontation of Hellenism and Christianity. His own conversion to Christianity did not remove his pre-Christian propositions or ways of thinking; but neither doctrinal variations nor marriage impeded his consecration as bishop. Social and political decay elicited literary declamations from him, including the *Katastasis*. He died defending his see against barbarian incursions. Given Tsatsos's decision to locate the fictional monastery in Arcady, the historical Synesios's claim to descent from kings of Sparta may have been an added consideration.

The allegorical reasons for placing the *Dialogues* in a monastery dedicated to the Transfiguration are perhaps more evident than those for locating the monastery in Arcady, a depopulated and austere region, parts of which are still roamed by wolves. But just as the monastery represents institutions whose days appear to be numbered,[39] so, too, Arcady in the cryptic words "Et in Arcadia ego" became a figurative allusion to death. It was a signature of the German Romantic tradition, which Tsatsos affirms as his own (pp. 41, 171) and which he followed in his highly idealized picture of the Arcadian landscape. For the German Romantics, Arcady was a symbol of nostalgia for life that was irretrievably lost.[40] In the *Dialogues* it is reminiscent of the failed efforts of George Gemistos Plethon to restore Hellenism in the ill-fated Byzantine outpost at Mystra (cf. p. 56) and of the sequence of vanished powers that passed through the gates of Monemvasia. "Here," Kazantzakis wrote of the Peloponnesus, "are the famished, bloodstained roots."[41]

Even the names of three great teachers invoked by discussants have a place in the formal code of humanistic and cultural decay. Both Jaeger and Jaspers (pp. 4–5, 144, 176–77) were excluded from their professorships by the government of Adolf Hitler; but Martin Heidegger flourished in those years and, after a momentary eclipse in the wake of World War II, returned to the full rights, duties, and prerogatives of his position.

Such instances of the allegorical unsaid as these are common in works of historical fiction. But Tsatsos went beyond employing the unsaid as a formal device of narrative. He was preoccupied with it as the space in which imagination intersected with thought, the point of esthetic assimilation.

Synesios's statement that "those of us who have come here for this reunion, excepting only Basset, are all of German culture" (p. 171) is one instance in which the unsaid functions both as formal narrative technique and as subject. In this sentence Tsatsos identifies the two principal foreign influences in modern Greek thought and life, the German and the French. He also alludes to a distinction between his own German education and the French acculturalization of the Seferiades patriarchy, including, of course, Ioanna Tsatsou, who as a child in Paris immersed herself in French Romantic poetry.[42]

Tsatsos makes his own affinity to German culture evident in Synesios's dismissive reference to Teilhard de Chardin, the only Frenchman counted among his intellectual guides, in the assertion that Gallicanism and Calvinism obstructed "the development of free metaphysical thought" (seconded by Sophronios's objection to "the Catholicism of the French"), and in the identification of France as the source of what Tsatsos regards as impoverished and deformed poetics that had spread to all countries, including Greece (pp. 130–31, 170, 174, 177).

By the unsaid in the sentence "we . . . are all of German culture," Tsatsos gratifies the need expressed when Ipliksis affirmed that he was not an Asiatic but a European. But he also testifies to the foreignness of ideas set forth in the *Dialogues* and to the extremely complex workings of the German presence in Greece. Beginning with "the alien character of the monarchy," one need but refer to the atrocities during the Italo-German occupation of 1941–44 and to the "unhappy notoriety" that many Greeks educated in Germany achieved during the humiliation and fratricidal conflict of those years.[43]

Synesios's calm affirmation of his intellectual antecedents encases the quite different assertion made by Dr. Christos Karvounis, executed by the Nazis in 1943. Karvounis had vainly offered himself as a substitute victim to avert the simultaneous execution of four sons from the same family. " 'You are a barbarous people,' he said to the official in perfect German. 'I am ashamed to have wasted eight years in your country. Eight years gone, lost.' "[44]

The unsaid in the yes that is said to Being includes such wounds as these, not least because the ideas of an alien culture made it thinkable, and the words of an alien tongue first made it speakable. Of course, the unsaid in the yes includes things given by that heritage that cannot be said, "something which is not expressed in words," and the essence of the unutterable (pp. 18, 126), things that need the yes as their symbol, just as "religion needs art, not to beautify the mystery of the liturgy, but to express it" (p. 7).

Yet, as I have shown, the saying of the said, even that of the yes, may not enable the spiritual anchorite—monk or philosopher—to communicate with others, for "he speaks his own language" (p. 78). Another barrier to communication is that even for the anchorite, the yes that is said is reached not only by recollection but also by forgetting. There is a striking contrast between Plato's doctrine of anamnesis, wisdom achieved by recollection of truths beheld in a previous and higher existence, and the doctrine of amnesty at the heart of Tsatsos's yes. Plato's conversion is one of surprised discovery; Tsatsos's, of calm release.

The monastic discipline of self-forgetting and self-emptying is his paradigm.[45] The parable of Nouty sets forth the deliberately forgotten wound at the core of Synesios's yes (pp. 118, 127–28). The probing of an old wound prompted the yes that Ipliksis uttered in his analysis of poetry and in his secret writings. These works, he said, were not poems but might eventually seem poems "to some future beings, or to some beings who will never be born, or to some woman who will half understand my poems" (p. 136). Self-forgetting is part of the esthetic experience through which music, for example, can raise its hearer "beyond heaven itself" (p. 121).[46] But it also builds a pearllike structure around the wound at the heart of the yes, the word whose saying enables the noble few, each alone, "to forget, or better, to rise above the tragedy of [their] existence," and, like Synesios, to reject all temporal things and stand "quietly waiting at the gates of Eternity" (pp. 33, 128).

The simandron in Tsatsos's monastery of the Transfiguration echoes a forgotten Arcadian simandron that sounded over the dead at Kalavryta.[47]

Translation of the Saying

Thus far I have identified some characteristics of conversion, a turning of the mind toward truth, as characterized by Tsatsos. In each instance, Tsatsos remained true to Plato's assertion that "the true philosophers are always occupied in the practice of dying" (*Phaedo*, 67). Spiritual progress is a movement of elimination and self-emptying toward silence. It is limited to a few, who neither can nor should speak for the edification of the many.

The core of the quest for truth is unsaid and incompletely accessible, if at all, in what is said. The dynamic of conversion is faith and love, which latter is passionless purity and exaltation. I have yet to consider the particular kind of event by which, in Tsatsos's interpretive order, transfiguration of soul occurred.

Varied as accounts of conversion to Christianity are, they generally include components that are absent from Tsatsos's reflections both on monastic and on philosophical conversion. Among them, charity is most conspicuous by its absence. As I turn, finally, to the event of conversion itself, it is important to identify one result of charity's absence. Patterned on the Old Testament model of election, Christian teachings posited conversion as a response to vocation. What instigates conversion in Tsatsos's *Dialogues* is not a call from within authoritative texts but a presence sensed and understood through a code of symbols: not a supernatural call but a natural, if superrational, *aistheton,* accessible also to the mystic who "has a kind of intellection when he claims, by this method, to arrive at understanding" (pp. 120–21).[48]

"If then I know not the power of the voice," wrote St. Paul, "I shall be to him, to whom I speak, a barbarian, and he that speaketh, a barbarian to me" (1 Cor. 14:11). The critical element for Tsatsos was not "the power in the voice," as a personal vocation, but the abstract "poetic word."

The impersonal *aistheton* follows from Tsatsos's characterization of God as Being and the apex of the Plotinian chain of Being. Among the diverse conceptions of God set forth in the *Dialogues,* none repeats the personal God of Scripture who calls. The assertions that each person is "an element of God" and that each carries in his humanity a "spark from God's Light" derive from the conception of God as, in some way, identical with the whole of material creation and history. Correspondingly, neither the personal existence of God nor personal immortality of believers is sustained by the doctrine that, after death, human souls "merge" with God (pp. 180, 182). A greater possibility of personal separateness exists in the assertion that "the hand of God has tossed us [into the world] only to test us and to see whether we deserve eternity or death" (p. 87). But this point of view excludes the action of grace, operating through vocation, as clearly as the other.

To be sure, there are some references, implicit and explicit, to divine inspiration and grace (pp. 1, 173–75), but these are hardly more than rhetorical turns of phrase. Synesios's statement that poetry is a divine gift certainly does not imply theological grace, as he indicates by his subsequent reference to the poet's sacrifices to the Muses (p. 136).

Allusions such as these must be read in the light of the assumption, evidently shared by all participants, that they have the freedom to choose among the many roads that lead to God (p. 179). "Only one thing," Ipliksis says, "you do not give; it is what God has entrusted to you and you owe it to Him: the height where you have established yourself, the inviolable distance between the transitory and the eternal" (p. 180). In its spiritual asceticism, the soul may also make history a road leading to the absolute; indeed, "progress to God is the supreme obligation of humanity" (pp. 87, 99), a duty that does not require the vocation of grace to fulfill.

Without the supernatural, charity, and vocation, the event of conversion is set forth, in literary terms, as translation. It is no accident that translation is synonymous with conversion and transfiguration, the dominant motifs of the *Dialogues*. From all that has been said, however, it should be apparent that the *aistheton* to be translated, or transfigured, in the conversion of the wise is not what is said but the saying; not the static form, yes, that is uttered but the esthetic content conveyed in the faith and love that are its saying.

Tsatsos provides examples of this focal point. The *aistheton* in poetry is the moving rhythms that in their passage create a discourse, a "musical fabric," a "fabric of meaning" (p. 133). The *aistheton* in music is the "silent vision" that it conveys in its performance (p. 120). In any art, it is the *poiesis* of the maker's moving hand, a gesture continually vibrating in the work (p. 122).

The *aistheton* is a transforming act in process, and Tsatsos readily applies this paradigm to individual existence. Synesios "cultivates no art; his own life is a work of art" (p. 128). Is Ipliksis a poet or not? "It doesn't matter," Synesios assures him, "whether others understand your poetry. What matters is to understand to the very end the poetry of life, and to force yourself to give the form of a poem to your own life" (p. 136). As noted earlier, this creative effort occurs in the crises of choice, the "sacred office" performed by each human being every moment, alone, an office that is a rite of passage "to what comes after death" (p. 94).

Ipliksis's short discourse on translating poetry illuminates, by analogy, the conditions and limits of translating, or transfiguring, the *aistheton* in art or nature into the poem of one's life. The object, he says, is not the meaning and imagery of the words, which careful translation can reproduce, but "the poetic element of poetic utterance." The rate of success in translating the latter, "the poetic word," is minuscule. Indeed, the formal components of a poem—the words, meanings, rhythms, and patterns of sounds, not to mention the "ethos" of the language itself—are obstacles that rarely can be surmounted. Translation of the "aesthetic feeling which is the essence of a poem" depends upon structural affinities between the two languages, psychic affinities between author and translator, the "suitability of the poem for translation into the designated language," relentless toil no less than that in original composition, and, finally, good luck. Adhering to the argument that sense, not words, should be translated, Ipliksis concluded that with its greater linguistic freedom, the paraphrase perhaps conveyed "the poetic word" better than literal translation (pp. 128–31).

In this brief discourse Ipliksis epitomizes in miniature the broad understanding of conversion that I have reviewed, not least the insistence on the fewness of the noble and true, the practice of spiritual asceticism by them, the location of authentic meaning beyond words in the realm of symbolic thought, and, above all, the disabilities of language. Indeed, Ipliksis continues the discourse by affirming that the difficulties encountered in translation are the same as those encountered when esthetic feeling is rendered, as it must be, into logical sequence, "sealed and enclosed in little iron cages" of words (p. 129). This, in turn, is an analogue of the transfiguring "comprehension which is not knowledge like that of the sciences, but . . . aesthetic, mystical" (p. 126).

Love can give the illusion that an *aistheton* and its transfigured likeness are identical. Synesios expressed such an illusion when he recalled his love for Nouty: "I was myself. I was she" (p. 105). It was also present, with implications of the power of a creator over his material, in the thought that a lover could write to his beloved, "I wish . . . to make you the book that I shall write,"[49] even as the god Pan made pipes from the reeds into which Syrinx had been transformed to save her from his ravishment. An author may play variations on the theme of this illusion, presenting diversity where there is a single *aistheton,* multiply perceived. For in drama as in these *Dialogues*, the author himself may be all the characters, assuming various personae in his search for hidden truth (cf. p. 22).

But the division between the poetic word felt in the saying and the poetic word expressed in the said remains. The power of belief demands utterance, even when the artist speaks for himself alone "so that he can discover and gain possession of his own self." It demands utterance even in the discipline of self-forgetting. To withdraw from public utterance is not to avert the inclination of what "begin as symbols [to] end as dogmas. Thus, even [in religious discourse], every initial expression of feeling is already the beginning of an alienation. It is the destiny and, in a sense, the immanent tragedy, of every spiritual form that it can never overcome this inner tension; to extinguish it is to extinguish the life of the spirit. For the life of spirit consists in this very act of severing what is whole in order that what has been severed may be even more securely united."[50]

Quite naturally, the participants in these dialogues labor not only under the wounds caused by the segmentation of the world of knowledge but also under the yet more inward fragmentation in which "the soul of the scientist and generally of every scholar is being chopped to bits" (pp. 24, 141) by the translation of feeling into words to which they have devoted their lives.

Tsatsos's portrayal leaves no escape from the conclusion that conversion itself inflicts these wounds and, more precisely, that it inflicts them precisely in the act of translating the *aistheton,* the vibrant poetic word. The pain of saying the yes that is said is heightened when the translator encounters an *aistheton* of beauty that refuses to be transfigured. Tsatsos must often have encountered this difficulty as he attempted to assimilate into Greek philosophical arguments that are difficult to penetrate in their original German texts. Indeed, rare and important testimony to the multiple anguish of translating, or transfiguring, the *aistheton* comes from within his own family. As a young man, George Seferis wrote much, and at times all, of his poetry in French. "The French expression suited him with its clarity, its infinitely original nuances as they appear in the great masterpieces. Only this expression could serve the Greek sense of measure which he carried inside him." By contrast, the Greek language tormented him.[51]

The pain of artistic creation in the service of art as a forgetting of, or withdrawal from, the pain of existence is by no means a theme original to Tsatsos. For it is always true that "the change demanded of us by the passage from one civilization to another is tantamount to a genuine conversion."[52] But the fact that he unfolded this theme as an intellectual émigré in his own country gives his dramatic representation unusual importance, beyond what his text would inevitably possess as evidence of a great statesman's intellectual commitments at a decisive moment in the history of his country.

The loneliness in conversion according to Tsatsos resembles that in James Joyce's esthetic conversion to art, though Joyce was able to express his in analogues drawn from sacramental theology, while Tsatsos largely abandoned both the language and content of doctrinal Christianity. Joyce's portrayal of esthetic conversion also differs from Tsatsos's in its acknowledgment of the tragic wounds caused by having no way to express his transfiguration other than in the language, and according to the intellectual norms, of foreigners, the conquerors of his homeland. But the two portrayals are at one in representing the isolation of the artist, alien in thought and esthetic capacity from his own people.

In their effort to characterize the transfiguring event of conversion, writers in the Christian tradition frequently employed analogues of play. For in the theater or in athletic contests, play was a means by which an actor could take on another persona and spectators could be transformed by empathy into actors.[33]

But play is not a conspicuous motif in the *Dialogues*. "Sophronios," Abbot Synesios said to his elderly brother monk, "You must learn to make a joke and take a joke. . . . The joke indicates a kind and serene soul" (p. 166). Did Tsatsos himself receive such advice in the perilous autumn of 1942, when "even the pessimistic Costakis [was] mak[ing] jokes"?[54] At that moment, he must have been acutely aware of his mixed debt to German culture. His pursuit of poetry marked an alien acculturation of a different kind, one that characterizes the *Dialogues*. "You know very well," Stylianos Seferiades said to his daughter, "that in Greece a poet is not considered a serious person." Were not "all these poets, good or bad, useless people"?[55] Perhaps a correct response was that the Greeks themselves were "not a serious people" and that very few of them had a fundamental consciousness of the tradition that united the past of their own people with its future.[56] Perhaps this was Palamas's meaning when he told the two young poets Seferis and Tsatsos that "in the long run, poetry is a game."[57]

Occasionally, translations suggest symbolism unanticipated in the original. Innovation of this sort occurs in the English version of the *Dialogues*, which locates the "Monastery of the Transfiguration, on a mountain in Arcadia, not far from the Gulf of Myrto" (p. xiii). The original specifies the coast of the Myrtoan Sea.[58] But "the Gulf of Myrto" introduces an appropriate, if unintended, symbolism into Tsatsos's discourses on Christianity and Hellenism and into the interplay of mysticism and humanism that characterizes them, an interplay evolved through the ages by the diffusion of culture in Antiquity from Greece to the Latin West and its refraction in recent times from Germany again to Greece.

From the house on Kydathineon Street, it is a short walk to the Parthenon, "the sacred rock with the cave of Pan. For me," Ioanna Tsatsou wrote, "this cave was a symbol of ourselves."[59] The Athenians extended the honor of cult to Pan for assisting them repulse the Persians at Marathon; but his homeland was Arcady, the setting of the *Dialogues*. By chance, the only gulf, or bay, of Myrto that I can identify is farther north, near the waters where long centuries ago was heard the ghostly wail, "Great Pan is dead."[60] The death of Athens was transformed at Marathon into victory over alien despotism. Longer and more mysterious transfigurations befell Pan, the stranger in the cave. For the passage of faith into faith converted the part of him that could be translated into another alien, the Pantocrator beyond the dome of heaven, like him a "Shepherd of bright stars."[61] But death and transfiguration did not cease; for, according to Tsatsos's refracted philosophy, the Pantocrator, with its residue of Pan, proved to be chaff, burst and cast aside by the living kernel of religion (p. 179). Only the depths of the cave were constant.

Summary

These inquiries have had a simple purpose: to distinguish between the experience known as conversion and texts about it. It would not have been possible to demonstrate the same point three times without drawing a few perhaps less evident conclusions from the effort.

I have proposed that the experience of conversion is inaccessible through the screen of the text and, indeed, that there is, interpretatively speaking, little to distinguish a fictive reconstruction of an actual event from the fictional invention of one that never happened. The result is not to dismiss the entire literature of conversion as without historical reliability. It is to establish the study of conversion as a venture in poetics, for texts witness to processes of composition and to habits of thought at work in them more than to the dramatic events that the texts portray. Processes and habits are historical, too.

When one asks, "What is called 'conversion'?" interrogation of a text has already begun. The words of the text become witnesses to their own careers as historical artifacts and to the choices by which authors decided to use them, rather than others, and to use exactly those words in specific ways. Despite their very great differences, the three books that I have considered confirm that critics must seek the guidelines of an author's poetics between the lines as well as in the words on the page. As Heidegger observed, "What is spoken is never and in no language what is said."[1]

To be sure, the analytical categories proposed by Heidegger and applied here in discussing Tsatsos's *Dialogues in a Monastery* open one way to explore the spaces between the lines and to recover at least part of what is unsaid in the said. They could be applied with profit to any text.

Summary   145

My ambition in these studies has not been to define the experience of conversion. Experience is messy, paroxysmal, arrhythmic. The vibrant rhythms of temperament, intellect, and tradition that bring them to life for a given person and make them recognizable as conversion resemble the rhythms of music. Souvenirs of such rhythms may survive in a text about conversion, like the invisible design and the static lines and patterns in a painting, waiting to be roused into illusory movement by viewers' imaginations.

I abandoned the possibility of recovering the experience of conversion itself, as known by any author. But it is something to have found that, for each of the three authors, the experience of play was crucial at one level in detecting the complex rhythms in what was called conversion, at another in being absorbed into them by the play of one's own mind, and, finally, in making a fiction (a text) about the experience. It was up to readers, individually, to know whether, or in what degree of dissonance or harmony, the rhythms kept like pressed flowers in any text resonated for them.

This is not the kind of play that can be dismissed as a frivolous pastime, "child's play." It is closer to the kind of play by which children train themselves to enact the social roles that they expect to perform as adults. It is closest of all to great rituals of high culture, drama or music, which exist only in performance. A tragedy or song never exists on a printed page, but only when it is actually being played. No performance—no actor's or musician's interpretation—is the same as any other. Here, the analogy between play as ritual in conversion and play ritualized in art is applied in yet another way, for no performance grips the mind and heart of every member of the audience. Only some are, as they say, "inspired" by it and feel that the performance is for them, that its complex rhythms resonate in and with those of their own minds and hearts, each perhaps in a distinctive way.

Recognizing the fictive nature of texts about conversion raises the question of how individual persons were able to take certain experiences to heart and, even while reducing what had happened to logical order, to feel themselves so entirely swept up into the performance known as conversion as to be changed to the marrow of their bones.

How can anyone convey to another the exhilaration of being caught up in the music, lifted through all its sonorities to a higher existence, and, at least for an instance, transfigured? I come again to the unsaid and unsayable in the said of these texts.

Some of the static lines in three texts have been detected. By exploring the unsaid in the said—reading the spaces between the lines—I have located some dynamic rhythms in the minds and hearts of three authors that rendered experience into order for them and made it resonate as conversion.

Augustine, Herman-Judah, and Tsatsos were moved by quite different personal rhythms. Empathy, so vital for Augustine and Herman-Judah, was all but denied by Tsatsos. But rhythms ingrained by tradition appear in their equation of conversion with the quest for truth, in their doctrines on the fewness of the wise, in the austere asceticism entailed by enlightenment, in the estrangement of the wise from the great mass of humanity and the resulting dangers and struggles, and, finally, in the predominance of men among the wise. Tradition, too, prepared them all to accept faith as a mode of knowledge and, most striking of all, to believe that human beings, as they came into the world, contained the potential for humanity—a buried treasure—that only the inspired few could know to seek, find, and perfect. The poetics in a text betray what its author considered essential to that greater enterprise, the poetics of realizing potential humanity.

Most of the different prescriptions for how to pursue this quest, given by philosophies and religions, have been modulations or offshoots of teachings inherited from classical Antiquity. Augustine, Herman-Judah, and Tsatsos are three examples of quite different—in some regards, mutually incompatible—doctrines that claim descent through the same learned tradition and that are intelligible only in the context of that tradition.

Augustine, Herman-Judah, and Tsatsos followed one another in the sequence of years, but their ways of thinking could flourish at the same time, as, in fact, they do in the present day. A complete history of ideas of conversion in Western culture would trace, not the linear development of one paradigm through the ages, but a luxuriant ramification of many paradigms, each setting forth a different understanding of what was called conversion and the whole presenting a repertory of choices to people in any given age.

Coming from so many different schools and beliefs, this widely shared demand for personal and collective transformation into a higher, perhaps nobler, existence has given Western culture its characteristic restless, questing nature. If I am right in assuming that Arabic and the languages of Buddhism lack the exact word *conversion* and the idea of a mystic, personal union defining that word, such as Christianity teaches, the singularity of Western ideas about how to realize potential humanity stands out all the more sharply. In Faust, the West has epitomized its restless, discontented quest for a better life, militantly advocated in calls for continual reform and revolution, calls that conflict over what that conversion is to be.

One result of these case studies is certainly to warrant proposing that even quite a small text, such as the single word *conversion,* can have as many layers of meaning as a pearl and, like a pearl, can owe its beauty to an original irritant, still to be found when the process of formation is over, at its core.

Many conversion accounts can be studied in this way, moving from what is called conversion to traces of rhythms left in the text, and from these to the actual rhythms that made experiences live and move as "conversion," sometimes in sharp dissonance, sometimes in sweetest harmony, for some person.

John Henry Newman's *Apologia pro Vita Sua* is a particularly fascinating example because, unlike Augustine's *Confessions,* and Herman-Judah's *Short Account* for that matter, materials exist from which the context of the book can be reconstituted in some detail. Like Augustine's *Confessions,* Newman's *Apologia* (1864) was written many years after the events described, and the spiritual turning point portrayed was bafflingly intricate and drawn out over a considerable space of time (1839–45). Another similarity is that the two books were not simply apologetic but blatantly polemical and that they were written against declared enemies by men who were both able and adept controversialists, masters of rhetoric, virtuosi in the deployment of overstatement, startling metaphors, and, to be sure, sarcasm, in order to ensnare their readers. And so, while Newman wrote the *Apologia,* above all, to defend his honesty and truthfulness, the account is fictive.

The spaces between the lines begin to appear when one looks for the main figure, the convert, John Henry Newman. For, as he wrote, the *Apologia* is not an autobiography. It is a history of his ideas, abstract and detached, and at many points a variation on the theme of Newman's own theory of the historical development of doctrine. The links in the chain are logical, consecutive, and intact; the development is impersonal.

The still traceries of Newman's "silver-veined prose"[2] veil the quickening rhythms that the text betrays in the spaces between the lines and that the context demonstrates. There one finds the concealed but glowing fervor with which he wrote the *Apologia,* working against the pressure of deadlines as the book was published section by section, serialized in weekly installments. One regains the "extreme pain" of mind and body that Newman endured writing sometimes twenty hours a day through periods of heartrending spiritual anguish and tears, always driven by his ingrained, haunted sense of impending death.

The rhythms in Newman's mind and heart that resonated as conversion in 1864 may not have been exactly the same as the ones that he felt in 1839–45. With its classic detachment and control, the stillness of his silver-veined prose edited out the causes of conversion with the dark and rushing vortex of what was personal. The irritant at the center of the pearl is scarcely detectable.

But traces accumulate as the reader passes through the events and relationships of his childhood and takes account of the many and consistent disappointments in later life, including the duplicity with which he was dealt by cardinals and Curia. By 1864 he was haunted with sadness. He had begun much, he thought, but accomplished little and completed nothing that mattered. He suffered recurrent depression. But these appraisals expressed an attitude toward himself, an abiding discontent, that was present from his early life onwards and that characterized his anxious and excitable temperament, the suppressed passion that he displayed so mordantly as a controversialist and so affectingly as a poet.

The stormy needs of Newman's heart felt that the rhythms of history resonated harshly for him when, in 1839, he concluded that he was himself teaching doctrines that heretics, centuries before, had taught and that the papacy alone had remained firm to the faith of Christ at every stage as the interpretation of those original doctrines unfolded their content and implications through the ages. Newman the poet sensed varieties of truth inaccessible to Charles Kingsley, the Regius Professor of Modern History at Cambridge, whose attack provoked the *Apologia*. And apart from the dissonant concord of historical and poetic truth, other harmonies and rhythms cultivated by his ear for the life-quickening powers of music and his skill as a violinist worked upon him in 1839 as in 1864. The meter of words evoked the rhythms of music for Newman as it had for Augustine. And these resonated with the inaudible harmony of all worlds and times. Such ritualizations of play built up the beauty of the word *conversion* for him, like Augustine, a guardian of sacred rites. As he reflected on his anguished self-recognition in 1839 (writing *Certain Difficulties Felt by Anglicans in Catholic Teaching*), he used a singular and telling phrase when he wrote that the "musical words" of Pope Leo I, refuting heretical pronouncements, were constantly in Newman's own ears and on his tongue.

ABBREVIATIONS

NOTES

INDEX

Abbreviations

Conf.	Augustine of Hippo, *Confessions*
Corp. Christ., ser. lat.	*Corpus Christianorum, series latina*
CSEL	*Corpus Scriptorum Ecclesiasticorum Latinorum*
En. in Ps.	Augustine of Hippo, *Enarrationes in Psalmos*
Ep.	*Epistola*
MGH	*Monumenta Germaniae Historica*
Epp. K.A.	*Epistolae Karolini Aevi*
Ldl	*Libelli de Lite*
SS	*Scriptores*
SSrrG	*Scriptores Rerum Germanicarum in Usum Scholarum*
Migne *PL*	J. P. Migne, *Patrologiae Cursus Completus, series latina*

Notes

Preface

1. In these comments, I gratefully rely on the index to Augustine's *Confessions* published by CETEDOC in the series Instrumenta Lexicologica Latina. (Brepols: Turnhout, 1983). Readers should consult the microfiche in that volume for a complete key to the locations of *convert, conversion,* and similar words.

2. The only exception, for which no reason is evident, is in a passing reference to Evodius, one of those with whom Augustine proposed to follow an ascetic life after his baptism (9.8.3).

3. E.g., R. S. Pine-Coffin, *Saint Augustine: Confessions* (Harmondsworth: Penguin, 1961), 192, 194, 196. See also Pine-Coffin's reading of *Conf.*, 8.4.9 (ibid., 163).

4. On Augustine's analogy between the *Confessions* and the category of the Psalms called "songs of degrees," see below, case 1, at n. 205.

5. See below, case 2, translation, *MGH*, 69, 91, 92, 124.

Case 1. Augustine of Hippo's *Confessions*

1. Reported by Henry Crabb Robinson, in Alexander Gilchrist, *Life of William Blake*, ed. Ruthven Todd (New York: Dutton, 1945), 335. For a further discussion of Augustine's concept of meaning, see the chapter "Rhetoric Swallowed Up in Hermeneutic: The Case of Augustine," in Karl F. Morrison, *"I Am You": The Hermeneutics of Empathy in Western Literature, Theology, and Art* (Princeton, N.J.: Princeton Univ. Press, 1988), 172–90.

2. See the excellent comparison by Paula Fredriksen, "Paul and Augustine:

Conversion Narratives, Orthodox Traditions, and the Retrospective Self," *Journal of Theological Studies*, n.s., 37 (1986): 3–34.

3. W. J. Sparrow Simpson, *Augustine's Conversion* (London: SPCK, 1930), 11–13; Robert McMahon, *Augustine's Prayerful Ascent: An Essay on the Literary Form of the Confessions* (Athens: Univ. of Georgia Press, 1989), xix, 2, 139 (on the "latency" of Augustine's "narrative pattern").

4. Fredricksen, "Paul and Augustine," 4.

5. Arguments for a plurality of conversion are set forth by Jean-Marie Le Blond, *Les conversions de saint Augustin* (Paris: Aubier, 1960). Pierre Courcelle judged that Augustine experienced four conversions, to philosophy (on reading Cicero's *Hortensius*), to Manichaeism, to Neoplatonism, and, finally, to Christianity (Courcelle, *Recherches sur les Confessions de Saint Augustin*, 2d ed. [Paris: E. de Boccard, 1968], 49, 60, 258). Leo C. Ferrari identified three turning points (reading the *Hortensius*, joining the Manichaeans, and converting to Christianity) that added up to one progression (Ferrari, *The Conversions of Saint Augustine*, Saint Augustine Lecture Series, 1983 [Villanova, Pa.: Villanova Univ. Press, 1984], x). Antoine Reymond held to the view that the crisis at Milan was Augustine's one and only conversion (Reymond, "Saint Augustin et la conversion," *Augustinian Studies* 13 [1982]: 100). The same position was taken by Jean-Pierre Belche, "Die Bekehrung zum Christentum nach Augustins Büchlein *De Catechizandis Rudibus*," *Augustiniana* 27 (1977): 358–59. See also the critical review by E. Ann Matter, "Conversion(s) in the *Confessiones*," in Joseph C. Schnaubelt and Frederick Van Fleteren, eds., *Collectanea Augustiniana: Augustine, "Second Founder of the Faith"* (New York: Peter Lang, 1990), 21–28.

6. *Conf.*, 11.9.11 (*Corp. Christ.*, ser. lat. 27:199–200). Hereafter, I shall refer to the *Corpus Christianorum* edition only by the page(s) cited.

7. Ibid., 7.10.16 (p. 103). See also ibid., 7.21.27 (p. 112): "et consideraveram opera tua et expaveram."

8. The two passages occur in *A Vision of the Last Judgment* and in the "Auguries of Innocence," at the end.

9. *Conf.*, 10.8.14 (p. 162).

10. Ibid., 10.35.54 (p. 184).

11. Quintilian, *Institutes*, 9.2.40, 43.

12. *Conf.*, 7.21.27 (p. 110). See also ibid., 7.21.27 (p. 111): "non habent [the Neoplatonists] illae paginae vultum pietatis huius," and 9.3.4 (p. 136): "Quaesivi vultum tuum, vultum tuum, domine, requiram."

13. Ibid., 8.7.16 (p. 123).

14. *En. in Ps.* 123, 1, 3 (*Corp. Christ.*, ser. lat. 40:1825–26).

15. Ferrari, *The Conversions of Saint Augustine*, 59.

16. Ibid., 84.

17. References to deaths occur at *Conf.*, 9.3.5–6 (pp. 135–36) (Verecundus and Nebridius), 9.6.14 (p. 141) (Adeodatus, Augustine's son), and 9.11.28 (pp.

149–50) (Monica). The death of Patricius, Augustine's father, is recorded at ibid., 3.4.7 (p. 30). For a dating of the composition of the *Confessions*, it is important that the death of Ambrose (397) is not recorded.

18. On Augustine's use of calculated hermeneutic strategies, see Calogero Riggi, "S. Agostino perenne maestro di ermeneutica," *Salesianum* 44 (1982): 71–101, and Goulven Madec, "Diagramme augustinien," *Augustinianum* 15 (1985): 78–94. For a general review of the demands of narrative coherence and historical accuracy in the *Confessions*, see Matter, "Conversion(s) in the *Confessiones*," esp. 23–25.

19. E.g., *Conf.*, 10.1.1 (p. 155).
20. Ibid., 10.2.2 (p. 155).
21. Ibid., 10.23.33 (p. 173).
22. Ibid., 4.14.22 (p. 51).
23. Ibid., 5.1.1, 10.2.2 (pp. 57, 155).
24. Ibid., 2.3.5 (pp. 19–20). See McMahon, *Augustine's Prayerful Ascent*, 1.
25. *Conf.*, 2.3.5, 10.3.3 (pp. 19, 156).
26. Ibid., 7.3.5 (p. 95).
27. Ibid., 1.9.14 (p. 8).
28. Ibid., 6.6.9, 3.10.18 (pp. 79, 37). Cf. ibid., 6.14.24 (p. 90).
29. Ibid., 1.6.9, 11.15.18 (pp. 5, 203).
30. Ibid., 7.3.5 (p. 95).
31. Ibid., 9.1.1 (p. 133).
32. On the fictional contrivances in Augustine's description of how he received the spiritual gift of continence, see Ferrari, *The Conversions of Saint Augustine*, 63.
33. *Conf.*, 8.1.1, 9.1.1, 10.34.53, 12.24.33 (pp. 113, 133, 183, 234). Cf. ibid., 5.1.1 (p. 57).
34. Ibid., 9.13.36–37, 10.4.5 (pp. 153–54, 157).
35. Ibid., 2.3.5, 8.1.1 (pp. 19–20, 112). On Augustine's failure to give one precise definition of *conversion* and on the multiple senses in which he used the word, see Belche, "Die Bekehrung zum Christentum nach Augustins Büchlein *De Catechizandis Rudibus*," 356–63.
36. *Conf.*, 11.2.3 (p. 195).
37. Ibid., 8.4.9, 9.2.2–3 (pp. 119, 133–34).
38. Ibid., 10.3.3–10.4.6, 13.26.41 (pp. 156–58, 267).
39. Ibid., 12.14.17 (p. 224).
40. Ibid., 9.4.10 (p. 139).
41. Ibid., 10.35.57 (pp. 185–86).
42. Possidius, *Vita Augustini*, chaps. 9, 12 (Migne *PL* 32:41, 43). The violence of the Circumcellions may be referred to at *Conf.*, 7.21.27 (pp. 111–12), where Augustine writes of keeping a road guarded: "Cura caelestis imperatoris munitam, ubi non latrocinantur qui caelestem militiam deseruerunt; vitant enim eam sicut supplicium."

43. *Conf.*, 10.4.6 (pp. 157–58); Paulinus, *Vita Ambrosii*, chaps. 12, 20 (Migne *PL* 14:33, 36).

44. *Ep.* 29, 11 (Migne *PL* 33:119–20). The contrast was beautiful for the same reason as an artist places white beside black. The church was confiscated by Augustine's faction in 405/6 but soon returned to the Donatists, who purified it by washing the walls.

45. On Augustine's self-justification by drawing analogies between his conversion and the Apostle Paul's, see Fredricksen, "Paul and Augustine," 25; it was a tactic which, as Fredricksen noted, Augustine used again much later in the Pelagian dispute. See also Ferrari, *The Conversions of Saint Augustine*, 66–67.

46. See above, n. 38.

47. Cf. *Conf.*, 11.2.2 (p. 194).

48. Rebuttals to these charges are scattered throughout *Contra Cresconium* and *Contra Litteras Petiliani* (*CSEL* 52:3–227, 325–582). See Vernon J. Bourke, *Joy in Augustine's Ethics*, Saint Augustine Lecture, 1978 (Villanova, Pa.: Villanova Univ. Press, 1979), 11.

49. *Conf.*, 5.13.23 (p. 70): "rhetoricae magister."

50. *Conf.*, 9.2.4 (p. 135): "cathedra mendacii."

51. Cf. Possidius, *Vita Augustini*, chap. 8 (Migne *PL* 32:39–40).

52. Quintilian, *Institutes*, 9.2.65–66.

53. *Conf.*, 1.11.17 (p. 10). Cf. ibid., 9.12.33 (p. 152): God is "pater omnium fratrum Christi."

54. Ibid., 9.7.16, 10.2.2, 10.5.7, 11.1.1, 12.6.6, 13.25.38 (pp. 142, 155, 158, 194, 218, 264). McMahon, *Augustine's Prayerful Ascent*, 27–28, stresses Augustine's assertion of his own divine inspiration, without relating it to the bishop's own political dangers.

55. *Conf.*, 10.43.70 (p. 193).

56. Ibid., 5.9.17 (p. 67). See also ibid., 13.34.49 (p. 271): The body of the Church existed in God's Word by predestination before all time. See also ibid., 5.9.17 (p. 67).

57. Ibid., 8.2.3–8.3.8, 8.6.15 (pp. 116–18, 122–23). See also ibid., 13.23.33–34 (pp. 261–62), and below after n. 116.

58. E.g., ibid., 7.21.27 (p. 112).

59. Ibid., 8.3.6 (p. 117). Augustine also applied the parable of the prodigal son to himself in discussing his time among the Manichees. Ibid., 3.6.11 (p. 32).

60. Ibid., 6.1.11 (p. 32); Luke 7:12–15.

61. On failure of memory, see *Conf.*, 1.7.12, 9.7.16 (pp. 7, 142). On pacing the narrative, see ibid., 9.8.17 (p. 143). On omission of some visions confided to Monica, see ibid., 5.9.17 (p. 67). In general, see John A. Mourant, *Saint Augustine on Memory*, Saint Augustine Lecture, 1979 (Villanova, Pa.: Villanova Univ. Press, 1980), esp. 61–70.

62. On omissions, intentional and inadvertent, see Courcelle, *Recherches sur les Confessions de Saint Augustin*, 41–43, 188–201 (the scene in the garden at Milan, "fiction littéraire et réalité"). See also Alfred Warren Matthews, *The Development of St. Augustine from Neoplatonism to Christianity, 386–391 A.D.* (Washington, D.C.: Univ. Press of America, 1980), 8–9.

63. *Conf.*, 9.4.7 (p. 137).

64. Ibid., 6.1.1, 9.10.26 (pp. 73, 148). See ibid., 9.9.22 (p. 146): "Nutrierat filios totiens eos parturiens, quotiens abs te deviare cernebat."

65. Ibid., 9.9.21 (p. 146).

66. Possidius, *Vita Augustini*, chap. 26 (Migne *PL* 32:55).

67. *Conf.*, 10.32.48 (p. 181), quoting Job 7:1. See also *En. in Ps. 144*, 4 (*Corp. Christ., ser. lat.* 40:2090): "Etenim ne accidat aliquid quod ferre non potestis, ipse facit. Ideo cum timore debes esse, quando tibi bene est; neque te ad hoc parare, quasi ut numquam tenteris. Si enim numquam tentaris, numquam probaris. Nonne melius est tentari et probari, quam non tentatum reprobari?" On the special character of the idea of conversion in North Africa, by virtue of its stress on penance and incorporation in and through the sacramental structure of the Church, and on the effects that this tradition had on Augustine's thought, see Belche, "Die Bekehrung zum Christentum nach Augustins Büchlein *De Catechizandis Rudibus*," 353–63.

68. *Conf.*, 10.30.42 (p. 177).

69. Ibid., 8.4.9 (pp. 118–19).

70. Ibid., 1.10.16 (p. 9). See also ibid., 13.14.15 (p. 250); "Quis enim nos discernit nisi tu?"

71. See above, n. 38. For another approach to the idea of conversion as a gradual process, see Geoffrey Galt Harpham, "Conversion and the Language of Autobiography," in James Olney, ed., *Studies in Autobiography* (Oxford: Oxford Univ. Press, 1988), 48: "Conversion is a constant, ceaseless process capable of absorbing any value, any thematization. It is the unchanging condition of our existence." Harpham, however, does not attribute this idea to Augustine as a conscious, architectonic premise in the *Confessions*. Professor Ann Matter kindly drew my attention to Harpham's article.

72. *Conf.*, 10.29.40, 10.31.45, 10.37.60 (pp. 176, 179, 187–88). See also ibid., 10.30.41 (p. 176). Cf. ibid., 8.7.17 (p. 124), Augustine's prayer that God would give him chastity and continence, "but not now."

73. Ibid., 3.8.16 (pp. 35–36).

74. Ibid., 10.35.55 (p. 185).

75. Ibid., 1.13.21 (p. 11).

76. Ibid., 3.2.2–4 (pp. 27–29).

77. Ibid., 4.5.10 (p. 44).

78. Ibid., 1.6.8 (p. 4).

79. Ibid., 3.1.1 (p. 27).
80. Cf. ibid., 3.2.3 (p. 28).
81. Ibid., 10.3.3–4 (pp. 156–57).
82. Ibid., 2.2.4 (p. 19). Augustine's insistence that his conversion was due, not to his own, but to God's action raised serious theodical problems (Reymond, "Saint Augustin et la conversion," 99). Yet Augustine contented himself with repeating theodical conventions derived from Stoic and Neoplatonic sources. They generally turned on the esthetics of order, as in Augustine's figure of the world as a painting, or a song, in which God, the composer, added contrasting elements for the beauty of the whole. See Josef Kopperschmidt, "Rhetorik und Theodizee: Studie zur hermeneutischen Funktionalität der Rhetorik bei Augustin," *Keryma und Dogma* 17 (1971): esp. 284–86, 289. On incarnational theodicy in broad terms, see Kenneth Surin, "Theodicy?" *Harvard Theological Review* 76 (1983): 225, 247 (the doctrine of the Incarnation is necessary to any theodicy).
83. *Conf.*, 1.14.23, 3.1.1, 3.3.5, 5.3.4, 6.6.9, 7.7.11–7.8.12, 9.4.12 (pp. 13, 27, 29, 59, 80, 99–101, 140). Augustine experienced sickness or some other debility at every major turning point in his conversion. The most dramatic occurred at the crisis of conversion itself, when he experienced difficult breathing and chest pains which impaired his professional activity as a rhetorician. It was also significant that he, who lived by eloquence, was afflicted with a toothache at that time, so painful that he could not speak. He had, he recalled, not known such pains since infancy (ibid., 9.2.4, 9.4.12, 9.5.13 [pp. 134, 140]). Augustine described the conversion crisis in medical terms at ibid., 6.1.1 (p. 74) and God as a physician at ibid., 6.4.6, 7.7.11, 7.8.12, 10.28.39 (pp. 77, 100, 101, 175).
84. Ibid., 9.13.35 (p. 153).
85. Stephen D. Benin, "Sacrifice as Education in Augustine and Chrysostom," *Church History* 52 (1983): esp. 11; Michael Grant, *Saint Paul* (Glasgow: Fount, 1978), 126.
86. *Conf.*, 6.6.26 (p. 90).
87. See above, nn. 25–31; *Conf.*, 7.3.5 (p. 95).
88. *Conf.*, 7.3.5 (p. 95).
89. Ibid., 2.3.8, 3.3.5 (pp. 21, 29).
90. Ibid., 6.12.21 (p. 88).
91. Ibid., 2.3.8 (p. 21).
92. Ibid., 6.11.19 (p. 87).
93. Possidius, *Vita Augustini*, chaps. 26, 27 (Migne *PL* 32:55–57). See Augustine's references to his maternal and paternal grandmothers (*Conf.*, 9.8.17, 9.9.20 [pp. 143, 145–46]), his two mistresses (ibid., 4.2.2, 6.15.25 [pp. 40–41, 90]), his betrothed (ibid., 6.13.23 [p. 89]), and the wife of Verecundus (ibid., 9.3.5 [p. 135]), apart from his nurses in infancy.
94. *Conf.*, 13.23.33, 13.32.47, 13.34.49 (pp. 261, 270, 272).
95. Ibid., 1.11.17, 9.9.19 (pp. 10, 145). Cf. Augustine's statement that God

beat him and so wounded his face that his eyes were swollen shut (ibid., 7.7.11–7.8.12 [pp. 99–101]).

96. *De Beata Vita*, 2.10, 2.16, 3.20 (*Corp. Christ., ser. lat.* 29:71, 74, 76); *Conf.*, 1.18.29 (p. 16).

97. *Conf.*, 2.2.4 (p. 19).

98. Ibid., 5.8.15, 6.2.2 (pp. 65, 74–75).

99. Ibid., 9.4.8 (p. 137).

100. See James McEvoy, "Anima una et cor unum: Friendship and Spiritual Unity in Augustine," *Recherches de théologie ancienne et médiévale* 53 (1986): 40–92, 80–91 (on monastic friendship).

101. *Conf.*, 4.4.7 (p. 43). This passage was one of the two in the *Confessions* about which Augustine had second thoughts; see *Retractations*, chap. 32 (*CSEL* 36:138).

102. *Conf.*, 3.8.15 (p. 35). Compare Augustine's comment on his male friend—"nihil quaerens ex eius corpore praeter indicia benevolentiae" (ibid., 4.9.14 [p. 47]—with his comment on sexual delights in Carthage—"amare et amari dulce mihi erat magis, si et amantis corpore fruerer" (ibid., 3.1.1 [p. 27]).

103. Ibid., 4.4.7, 4.12.18 (pp. 43, 49). On the love of God and neighbor as a divine gift, see Jean-Pierre Belche, "Die Bekehrung zum Christentum nach Augustins Büchlein *De Catechizandis Rudibus*," *Augustiniana* 32 (1982): 301.

104. *Conf.*, 11.29.39, 13.8.9 (pp. 214–15, 246). See also ibid., 10.6.8 (p. 159). See Jean-Pierre Belche, "Die Bekehrung zum Christentum nach Augustins Büchlein *De Catechizandis Rudibus*," *Augustiniana* 29 (1979): 269.

105. *Conf.*, 9.2.2 (p. 134). On Jesus as the bread eaten by the faithful, see ibid., 7.10.16 (pp. 103–4): Christ the bread will not be changed into the flesh of those who eat the bread; they will be changed into him.

106. Ibid., 4.1.1 (p. 40). Cf. ibid., 13.22.32 (p. 260): Through the Gospel, the Apostle Paul gave birth to sons, whom he nourished with milk and fostered as a nurse.

107. Ibid., 4.12.19 (p. 50).

108. Ibid., 7.18.24 (p. 108).

109. Ibid., 11.29.39, 13.8.9 (pp. 215, 246). Cf. ibid., 10.6.8, 10.27.38 (pp. 159, 175).

110. Ibid., 13.13.14 (p. 249).

111. Ibid., 8.11.27 (p. 130).

112. Ibid., 4.2.2 (p. 41).

113. See *Sermo 119*, 4.4 (Migne *PL* 38:674): "vulva matris, aqua baptismatis"; *Sermo 121*, 4 (Migne *PL* 38:679–80).

114. *Conf.*, 8.12.30 (p. 132).

115. Ibid., 13.21.30, 13.25.38 (pp. 258–59, 264–65).

116. Ibid., 13.23.33 (p. 261).

117. Ibid., 12.10.10 (p. 221).

118. Cf. Augustine on Tyconius (*Contra Epistulam Parmeniani*, 1.1.1 [*CSEL* 51:19–20]), Donatus, Parmenianus, and Cresconius (*Contra Cresconium*, 1.2.3 [*CSEL* 52:327]).

119. On the fictional character of Book 8, especially of the scene in the garden at Milan, see Ferrari, *The Conversions of Saint Augustine*, 51–55, developing arguments earlier expressed by Courcelle, *Recherches sur les Confessions de Saint Augustin*. See also McMahon, *Augustine's Prayerful Ascent*, 2–6, 10.

120. *Conf.*, 2.3.6, 9.12.32 (pp. 20, 151).

121. Ibid., 3.10.18, 8.12.28 (pp. 37, 130); Ferrari, *The Conversions of Saint Augustine*, 58. Cf. Matthew 24:32; John 1:47–50.

122. See above, n. 20.

123. *Conf.*, 13.23.34 (p. 262). On convention, cf. ibid., 1.13.20 (p. 11), an idea more fully developed in the *De Doctrina Christiana*.

124. *De Civitate Dei*, 22.29 (*Corp. Christ., ser. lat.* 48:861–62); *Conf.*, 13.21.29 (p. 258), quoting 1 Cor. 14:22. On the disutility of the Gospels in the world to come, see below, n. 138.

125. See David Chidester, "The Symbolism of Learning in St. Augustine," *Harvard Theological Review* 76 (1983): 76, on the analogy between learning and the creative act.

126. *Conf.*, 12.1.1, 12.32.43 (pp. 217, 241).

127. Ibid., 13.14.17 (p. 224). See also n. 128.

128. Ibid., 1.16.26, 5.6.10, 9.2.2, 9.5.13 (pp. 14, 62, 134, 140). On multiple interpretations of Moses, see ibid., 12.16.23–12.21.30, 12.23.32, 12.30.41–12.32.43 (pp. 231–32, 233, 240–41). On people as vessels, see also ibid., 1.3.3 (p. 2): all things are vessels full of God, but when they are broken, God is not spilled out.

129. Ibid., 3.6.10, 4.15.27 (pp. 31, 54).

130. Ibid., 5.9.1 (p. 66). On Augustine's assumption of a "symbolic synesthesia" in which all the senses (notably sight and hearing) converged, see Chidester, "The Symbolism of Learning in St. Augustine," 83–85. Cf. the argument of Paul J. Archambault regarding the interplay of language and memory, which does not, however, dispense with the importance in Augustine's epistemology of images drawn from memory as the precondition of words (Archambault, "Augustine, Memory, and the Development of Autobiography," *Augustinian Studies* 13 [1982]: 23–30).

131. *En. in Ps.* 95, 4 (*Corp. Christ., ser. lat.* 39:1345–46).

132. *Conf.*, 13.10.12 (p. 247).

133. Ibid., 3.5.9, 5.14.24, 6.3.3, 6.5.8, 6.11.18, 7.21.27, 8.2.3 (pp. 31, 71, 78, 86, 110–11, 114); *De Doctrina Christiana*, 1.6.6, 2.6.7–8, 3.37.56 (*Corp. Christ., ser. lat.* 32:9–10, 35–36, 115–16).

134. *Conf.*, 4.13.20, 6.4.6 (pp. 50–51, 77).

135. Ibid., 8.8.19 (p. 125).

136. Ibid., 10.3.3–4, 11.2.2–11.3.5 (pp. 156–57, 194–97).
137. Ibid., 11.3.5, 11.6.8, 12.32.43 (pp. 196–97, 198, 241).
138. *Tractatus in Evangelium Iohannis*, 35.9 (*Corp. Christ., ser. lat.* 36:322–23).
139. See above, n. 22.
140. *De Trinitate*, 15.23–24 (*Corp. Christ., ser. lat.* 50A:522).
141. *Tractatus in Evangelium Iohannis*, 23.11, 35.3 (*Corp. Christ., ser. lat.* 36:240, 319).
142. *De Trinitate*, 8.6.9, 11.7.11, 15.15.25 (*Corp. Christ., ser. lat.* 50:280–84, 347–48, 50A:498–99).
143. *Conf.*, 10.6.10 (p. 160).
144. Cf. ibid., 4.15.25 (p. 53).
145. Ibid., 11.5.7 (pp. 197–98).
146. Ibid., 10.9.16–10.11.18 (pp. 163–64).
147. Ibid., 10.20.29, 10.22.32, 10.24.35–10.26.37 (pp. 170–71, 172, 174–75).
148. Ibid., 10.15.23 (p. 167). Cf. *De Musica*, 6.11.32 (*Bibliothèque augustinienne*, ser. 1, 4:428): "Sed cum sibi isti motus occursant, et tanquam diversis et repugnantibus intentionis flatibus aestuant, alios ex aliis motus pariunt; non jam eos qui tenentur ex occursionibus passionum corporis impressi de sensibus, similes tamen tanquam imaginum imagines, quae phantasmata dici placuit. Aliter enim cognito patrem meum quem saepe vidi, aliter avum quem nunquam vidi. Horum primum phantasia est, alterum phantasma. Illud in memoria invenio, hoc in eo motu animi, qui ex iis ortus est quos habet memoria."
149. *De Trinitate*, 8.6.9, 11.7.11, 15.15.25 (*Corp. Christ., ser. lat.* 50:280–84, 347–48, 50A:498–99).
150. *Conf.*, 1.8.13 (p. 7).
151. Ibid., 1.13.20–1.14.23, 1.17.27, 4.4.7, 4.8.13–4.9.14 (pp. 11–13, 15, 43, 46–47).
152. Ibid., 1.8.13 (pp. 7–8).
153. Ibid., 5.5.8 (p. 60): "Ecce pietas est sapientia," quoting Job 28:28.
154. *Conf.*, 1.10.16, 1.14.23, 3.3.5, 10.35.55–57 (pp. 9, 12–13, 29, 185–86).
155. Ibid., 5.3.3–5, 10.35.55–57 (pp. 58–59, 185–86).
156. Ibid., 5.4.7 (p. 60).
157. See above, n. 20.
158. *Conf.*, 5.5.8–9, 12.5.5 (pp. 60–61, 218).
159. Ibid., 11.31.41, 13.38.53 (pp. 215–16, 273).
160. Ibid., 12.6.6 (pp. 218–19).
161. Ibid., 11.29.39 (p. 214).
162. Ibid., 9.3.6 (p. 136).
163. Ibid., 3.7.12–14, 4.3.5, 5.3.3–6, 5.5.8–9, 10.11.18, 10.23.33, 10.32.48–10.35.57, 10.37.60, 10.42.67, 12.14.17–12.15.22, 12.18.27,

12.24.33–12.26.36, 12.32.43, 13.13.14, 13.21.29–31 (pp. 33–34, 42, 58–61, 164, 173, 180–86, 187–88, 191–92, 224–26, 229–30, 233–36, 241, 249, 257–59).

164. Ibid., 10.25.36, 10.40.65 (pp. 174, 190–91). The hierarchic movement of perception from awareness of physical existence, to perception of the soul through the body, and finally to the inward power of the soul occurs in ibid., 7.17.23 (p. 107). See also ibid., 3.6.10 (pp. 31–32), the contrast of sense of the flesh with understanding of the mind.

165. Ibid., 9.10.23–26 (pp. 147–48).
166. Ibid., 7.10.16 (pp. 103–4). Cf. ibid., 7.17.23 (p. 107).
167. Ibid., 11.9.11 (pp. 199–200).
168. Ibid., 8.12.29 (p. 131).
169. Ibid., 9.1.1, 13.23.33 (pp. 133, 262). See ibid., 8.1.2 (p. 113), on the sweetness of God and the beauty of his house. On sweetness of the world, ibid., 2.1.1, 8.5.12 (pp. 18, 120). On redemptive sweetness, ibid., 4.5.10, 5.13.23, 7.20.26, 9.6.14–9.7.15 (pp. 44, 70, 110, 140–42).
170. Ibid., 10.31.43 (pp. 177–78). Possidius, *Vita Augustini*, chap. 22 (Migne *PL* 32:51–52): as bishop, Augustine always supplied wine at dinner.
171. *Conf.*, 2.3.6, 6.2.2, 9.8.17–18 (pp. 20, 74–75, 142–45).
172. Ibid., 8.3.7, 10.31.45 (pp. 117, 179). See also ibid., 5.13.23 (p. 709): Ambrose's words administered the fatness of God's grain, the gladness of oil, and the sober drunkenness of wine to God's people.
173. Ibid., 6.6.9–10 (pp. 79–80).
174. Ibid., 1.6.7, 16.26, 3.4.8, 5.6.10, 7.20.26, 9.6.14 (pp. 4, 14–15, 30, 61, 110, 141).
175. Ibid., 1.5.5 (p. 3).
176. See Augustine's statement that God alone cured him "a libidine vindicandi" (ibid., 10.36.58 [*Corp. Christ.*, ser. lat. 27:186]). In general, see Anne Marie La Bonnardière, "Le dol et le jeu d'après Saint Augustin," in Terenzio Alimonti et al., eds., *Forma Futuri: Studi in Onore del Cardinale Michele Pellegrino* (Turin: Bottega d'Erasmo, 1975), esp. 873, 876–81. La Bonnardière, however, has no specific discussion of play. See also W. Weismann, *Kirche und Schauspiele: Die Schauspiele im Urteil der lateinischen Kirchenväter unter besonderer Berücksichtigung von Augustin*, Cassiciacum, 27 (Würzburg: Augustinus-Verlag, 1972). "We all remember," Bourke noted, "how Monica was scandalized when Licentius sang (while seated in an outdoor privy): 'O God of hosts, convert us, and show thy face, and we shall be saved (Psalm 79:8)'" (Bourke, *Joy in Augustine's Ethics*, 26, citing *De Ordine*, 1.8.22).
177. *Conf.*, 9.8.18 (p. 144).
178. Ibid., 1.10.16, 1.19.30 (pp. 9, 16–17).
179. Ibid., 1.9.15, 1.10.16, 1.19.30 (pp. 9, 16, 17). Cf. the statement by Helen Suzman, the twentieth-century advocate of civil rights in South Africa,

concerning her education in a convent school: "The canings we got when we lost in sports taught me a crucial lesson for my political career. . . . How to be a terrible loser!" (*Christian Science Monitor*, 12 Aug. 1986, p. 10).

180. *Conf.*, 1.9.15 (p. 8).
181. Ibid., 4.1.1, 11.29.39 (pp. 40, 214). Cf. ibid., 4.3.5 (p. 42).
182. See above, n. 154.
183. *Conf.*, 6.8.13 (p. 83). Cf. ibid., 1.16.26 (pp. 14–15), on Terence's portrayal of a character who was transformed by the impression made on him by a picture of Jupiter, in the guise of a rain of gold, ravishing Danae.
184. Ibid., 2.4.9, 2.9.17, 4.4.7, 4.8.13 (pp. 22, 26, 43, 46–47).
185. Ibid., 1.6.9, 3.10.18, 6.6.9, 6.14.24, 11.15.18 (pp. 5, 37, 79, 90, 203).
186. Ibid., 4.3.5–6 (pp. 42–43).
187. Ibid., 8.6.14, 8.12.29 (pp. 121, 131). For a view of this account as a study in cumulative precedents, rather than a sudden, emotional cataclysm, see Matter, "Conversion(s) in the *Confessiones*," 23–25.
188. Ibid., 13.14.15 (p. 250), quoting Song of Sol. 2:17.
189. Ibid., 8.6.14, 8.12.29–30 (pp. 121, 131). See *Tractatus in Evangelium Iohannis*, 53.7.9 (*Corp. Christ.*, ser. lat. 36:322–34): "Proferimus codices a Iudaeis"; "codex Isaiae proferatur a Iudais"; "non aperietur codex apostoli"; "depositurus sum et ego codicem istum [the text of the Gospel of John]."
190. On the *Retractations*, see Possidius, *Vita Augustini*, chap. 28 (Migne *PL* 32:57). On *De Pulchro et Apto*, see *Conf.*, 4.15.27 (pp. 53–54). On the *City of God*, see Theodor Birt, *Das antike Buchwesen in seinem Verhältniss zur Litteratur* (Berlin: Hertz, 1882; rept. 1959), 147. See also *De Musica*, 6.13.44 (*Bibliothèque augustinienne*, ser. 1, 4:450): "Quid me putas hinc diutius debere dicere, cum divinae Scripturae tot voluminibus et tanta auctoritate et sanctitate praeditis, nihil nobiscum aliud agant, nisi ut diligamus Deum et Dominum nostrum ex toto corde, ex tota anima, et ex tota mente; et diligamus proximum nostrum tanquam nosmetipsos?"
191. *Conf.*, 6.3.3 (p. 75).
192. E.g., ibid., 4.10.15 (p. 48): "glutine amoris."
193. Ibid., 4.4.7 (p. 43): "agglutinas."
194. See Birt, *Buchwesen*, 14–17, 228–29, 255. See also Augustine's reference to Ambrose perusing columns (*paginas*) on the scrolls, not pages (*Conf.*, 6.3.3 [p. 75]) and his further mention of singing "de paginis poetae cuiuspiam" (ibid., 4.3.5 [p. 42]). The "paginae" of the "libri genethliacorum" did not have the "vultum pietatis huius" (ibid., 7.21.27 [p. 111]). See also Augustine's equation of the "libri Platonicorum" with "volumina" (ibid., 7.20.26 [pp. 109–10]) and his reference to the "volumina" of poets and of the Manichaean sect read by Faustus (ibid., 5.6.11 [p. 62]).
195. *Conf.*, 13.5.16 (pp. 250–51). See also ibid., 13.18.22, 13.34.49 (pp. 253, 271): "firmamentum scripturae tuae," or "firmamentum libri tui."

196. Ambrose, *Exameron*, 1.6.21 (*CSEL* 32, pt. 1:17–18). On the existence, and the disadvantage (weight), of leather scrolls, see Theodor Birt, *Die Buchrolle in der Kunst: Archäologisch-antiquarische Untersuchungen zum antiken Buchwesen* (Leipzig: Teubner, 1907), 24.

197. Birt, *Buchwesen*, 237.

198. *Conf.*, 11.11.13 (p. 201), 11.15.16 (p. 203), 11.15.20 (p. 204), 11.16.26 (p. 204), 11.21.27 (p. 207), 11.23.30 (p. 209), 11.28.37–38 (pp. 213–14), 11.31.41 (p. 216).

199. Birt, *Buchwesen*, 375.

200. Kurt Weitzmann, *Illustrations in Roll and Codex: A Study of the Origin and Method of Text Illustration*, 2d ed. (Princeton, N.J.: Princeton Univ. Press, 1970), 89.

201. *Conf.*, 2.3.7 (p. 20).

202. Ibid., 10.6.9 (p. 159).

203. Ibid., 10.6.8 (p. 159).

204. *De Trinitate*, 12.14.23 (*Corp. Christ.*, *ser. lat.* 50, pt. 1:376-77). Cf. the ode "Portlandia," written by Ronald Talney, a Portland attorney, on the occasion of the unveiling of the monumental statue, *Portlandia*, in Portland, Oregon (1983):

> She kneels down,
> And from the quietness
> of copper
> reaches out.
>
> We take that stillness
> into ourselves,
> and somewhere
> deep in the earth
> our breath
> becomes her city.

I am obliged to Mr. Talney for his generous permission to reproduce these stanzas.

Augustine's view was that the "rays of the eyes" reached out to the object of vision (extramission, rather than intromission, as suggested in Talney's verse; *Conf.*, 10.6.9 [p. 159]). However, both texts posit the absorption of the object of vision by the seeing subject.

205. Possidius, *Vita Augustini*, chap. 31 (Migne *PL* 32:63).

206. *En. in Ps. 132*, 6 (*Corp. Christ.*, *ser. lat.* 40:1930).

207. *Retractations*, chap. 19 (*CSEL* 36:96). See *Conf.*, 9.4.8 (p. 137).

208. *Conf.*, 9.4.8 (p. 137).

209. Cf. Psalm 95:4: "Magnus Dominus et laudabilis nimis," instead of "valde," as in the other two instances.

210. *Conf.*, 1.7.12, 9.3.6, 12.6.6 (pp. 6–7, 136, 219).

211. Ibid., 11.28.38 (p. 214). Cf. ibid., 11.31.41 (pp. 215–16).

212. Ibid., 13.9.10 (pp. 246–47).

213. Ibid., 9.4.8, 9.6.14, 9.7.15–16, 10.33.49 (pp. 137, 141–42, 181). See the quotations of Ambrose's *Deus Creator Omnium*, ibid., 9.12.32 (pp. 151–52), and the citation in ibid., 10.34.51 (p. 183). Ambrose's poem is a recurrent point of reference in Augustine's writings. See also *De Musica*, 6.9.23, 6.17.57 (*Bibliothèque augustinienne*, ser. 1, 4:410, 472), and *De Beata Vita*, 4. 35 (*Corp. Christ., ser. lat.* 29:85).

214. E.g., *En. in Ps. 119*; 1 (*Corp. Christ., ser. lat.* 40:1776).

215. *En. in Ps. 123*; 1–2 (ibid., 1825).

216. *Conf.*, 8.1.1, 9.2.2, 10.4.5–6, 11.1.1 (pp. 113, 134, 157–58, 194). Obviously, the character of the *Confessions* as a psalm does not exclude its other characters as prayer and drama. McMahon, *Augustine's Prayerful Ascent*, 1, 3–7.

217. *En. in Ps. 111*, 2 (*Corp. Christ., ser. lat.* 40:1802).

218. See above, nn. 136, 137. *Conf.*, 12.26.36 (p. 236). On this point, see the chapter on Augustine ("Rhetoric Swallowed up in Hermeneutic") in my *"I Am You,"* 172–90.

219. *De Civitate Dei*, 1.pref., 22.29–30 (*Corp. Christ., ser. lat.* 47:1, 48:856–66).

220. *Conf.*, 2.6.14 (p. 24). See also *De Musica*, 6.13.40 (*Bibliothèque augustinienne*, ser. 1, 4:444: "Generalis vero amor actionis, quae avertit a vero, a superbia proficiscitur, quo vitio Deum imitari, quam Deo servire anima maluit."

221. *En. in Ps. 44, 3* (*Corp. Christ., ser. lat.* 38:496).

222. *De Civitate Dei*, 15.21 (ibid., 48:487).

223. *Ep. 138*, 5 (Migne PL 33:527); *Contra Adimantum Manichaei Discipulum*, 41.47 (ibid., 42:205–6); *De Civitate Dei*, 11.18 (*Corp. Christ., ser. lat.* 48:337). On the song of the universe, see *De Musica*, 6.11.29 (*Bibliothèque augustinienne*, ser. 1, 4:424).

224. *De Nuptiis et Concupiscentia*, 1.23.26 (*CSEL* 42:238–39), quoted in *Contra Julianum*, 6.19.58 (Migne PL 44:857).

225. *Contra Julianum*, 1.8.41, 6.9.25, 6.21.67 (Migne PL 44:669, 837, 864); *De Civitate Dei*, 2.2, 8.3 (*Corp. Christ., ser. lat.* 47:35–36, 218–19).

226. John Calvin, *The Institution of Christian Religion*, 3.24.24, trans. Thomas Norton (London: Anne Griffin, 1634), 480.

Case 2. Herman-Judah's *Account*:
Introduction

1. Salo Wittmayer Baron, *A Social and Religious History of the Jews*, 2d ed., 12 vols. (Philadelphia: Jewish Publication Society of America, 1952–67), 5:112. Surely a slip of the pen. For two other analyses of the *Account*, see Arnaldo Momigliano, "A Medieval Jewish Autobiography," in Momigliano, *On Pagans, Jews, and Christians* (Middletown, Conn.: Wesleyan Univ. Press, 1987), 222–30; Jeremy

Cohen, "The Mentality of the Medieval Jewish Apostate: Peter Alfonsi, Hermann of Cologne, and Pablo Christiani," in Todd M. Endelman, ed., *Jewish Apostasy in the Modern World* (New York: Holmes and Meyer, 1987), esp. 29–35. In Cohen's view, Herman-Judah's objective was not to address prospective Jewish converts but "to publicize among Christians the glorious experience of conversion." Accordingly, his work gives no evident of Hebrew scholarship (p. 31). I am obliged to Professor Robert Lerner for referring me to Cohen's study. Momigliano's prescription of a *grana salis* is well placed: "Hermannus's autobiography, like all autobiographies by converts, raises the problem of the way in which conversion affected the perception of pre-conversion events" (p. 224). For additional bibliographical references, see below, n. 13.

2. G. Miccoli, review of Niemeyer's edition, *Studi medievali*, 3d ser., 7, pt. 1 (1966): 439.

3. J. B. Valvekens, "Hermannus, quondam Iudaeus, praepositus in Scheida," *Analecta Praemonstratensia* 41 (1965): 158. On Professor Avrom Saltman's case for regarding the text as a Christian fabrication, see below, n. 6.

4. J. Stengers, review of Niemeyer edition, *Le Moyen Age* 71 (1965): 612–14.

5. E.g., Gerhoch of Reichersberg, *Tractatus in Psalmum* 64, chap. 122 (Migne *PL* 194:81); Otto of Freising, *Chronicon*, 8.7 (*MGHSSrrG*, 399–400).

6. Avrom Saltman, "Hermann's *Opusculum de Conversione Sua*: Truth or Fiction?" *Revue des études juives* 147 (1988): 31–56. Cf. the argument by Sander L. Gilman that the portrayal in the *Opusculum* could only have been written by a person whose entire thinking was saturated with Jewish patterns of thought (Gilman, *Jewish Self-Hatred: Anti-Semitism and the Hidden Language of the Jews* [Baltimore: Johns Hopkins Univ. Press, 1986]). Professor William C. Jordan directed me to Saltman's article, and Mr. David Nirenberg, to Gilman's book.

7. Saltman, "Hermann's *Opusculum de Conversione Sua*: Truth or Fiction?" 48.

8. Ibid., 52.

9. Professor Saltman's argument allows no equivocations. However, at points, I find ambiguities in the text that the case for pseudonymity does not exhaust or explain. One of these occurs in chap. 6 (*MGH*, 88–90), where the narrator recounts a visit by Herman-Judah to Cappenberg. Professor Saltman reads this passage to mean that Herman-Judah met "the founder, Count Godfrey and his brother, Otto, men of perfect evangelical humility." For him, this is evidence of falsification, since Godfrey must have been dead at the time of the putative visit (pp. 36, 52). However, as I read the passage, what the narrator said he saw was the "religious way of life of the counts and the cenobites." Other allusions to Godfrey can likewise be understood equally well whether he were living or dead. On the allegorical statement that Saul was changed from a wolf into a lamb, see my book *Understanding Conversion* (Charlottesville, Va.: Univ. Press of Virginia, forthcoming), preface, no. 2.

10. The places described in his account are Cologne, Mainz, Worms, Münster

(and the nearby monastery of Cappenberg), and the monasteries of Flonheim (west of Alzay) and Ravengiersburg (west of Bingen).

11. What follows is an abstract of data provided in Gerlinde Niemeyer, ed., *Hermannus Quondam Judaeus: Opusculum de Conversione Sua*, Monumenta Germaniae Historica, Quellen zur Geistesgeschichte, 4 (Weimar: Böhlaus Nachfolger, 1963).

12. But see the reservations about such frequent changes of appointment in Peter Classen's review of Niemeyer's edition, *Zeitschrift für Kirchengeschichte* 74 (1963): 381.

13. The following studies provide essential information bearing on my account. Gavin I. Langmuir, "From Ambrose of Milan to Emicho of Leiningen: The Transformation of Hostility against Jews in Northern Christendom," *Gli Ebrei nell'alto Medioevo*, Settimane di Studio del Centro Italiano di Studi sull'alto Medioevo, 26 (Spoleto: Centro, 1980), 313–68. Langmuir argues that the massacres of 1096 derived from a new form of religion, subscribed to by the Crusaders *en passage* but still unacceptable, or even unknown, to the people they had left at home in their own communities. Lester K. Little, "The Functions of the Jews in the Commercial Revolution," *Povertà e ricchezza nella spiritualità dei secoli XI e XII*, Convegni del Centro di Studi sulla Spiritualità medievale, 8 (Todi: L'Accademia Tudertina, 1969), esp. pp. 284–86. Little sketches the social bases of "progressively deteriorating relations between Jews and Christians" between the early eleventh and the late fourteenth centuries (p. 273). See also the following general studies: Klaus Geissler, *Die Juden in Deutschland und Bayern bis zur Mitte des vierzehnten Jahrhunderts* (Munich: Beck, 1976); Peter Herde, "Probleme der christlich-jüdischen Beziehungen in Mainfranken im Mittelalter," *Würzburger Diözesangeschichtsblätter* 40 (1978): esp. 83–86, with the somber conclusion (p. 94): "Leider endete aber mittelalterliche wie moderne Judenfeindschaft zumeist im Mordern"; Franz-Josef Schmale, "Lebensform und Bedeutung der europäischen Juden in Mittelalter," *Mittelalterforschung*, Forschung und Information (Berlin: Colloquium, 1981), esp. pp. 147–50. See also references cited in Karl F. Morrison, *Understanding Conversion* (Charlottesville: University Press of Virginia, forthcoming), chap. 1, n. 7; chap. 2, at nn. 36, 46, 52, 58, 65; chap. 3, at nn. 16, 23, 24, 27, 66, 72; chap. 5, at nn. 11, 28, 33.

14. On the following data, see *Germania Judaica* 1 (Tübingen: Mohr, 1963): 69–70, 175–81, 437–41.

15. Mainz Anonymous, *The Narrative of the Old Persecution*, in Shlomo Eidelberg, ed. and trans., *The Jews and the Crusaders: The Hebrew Chronicles of the First and Second Crusades* (Madison: Univ. of Wisconsin Press, 1977), 100. On the Jewish cult of martyrdom, and hostility toward Christians, see William Chester Jordan, *The French Monarchy and the Jews: From Philip Augustus to the Last Capetians* (Philadelphia: Univ. of Pennsylvania Press, 1989), 16, 20–22.

16. E.g., *Chronicle* of Solomon bar Simson and *Book of Remembrance* of Rabbi Ephraim of Bonn, Eidelberg, *The Jews and the Crusaders*, 21, 65, 121. For other

allusions to magic (apart from the appeal to trial by ordeal in chap. 5), note the uses of words such as *enchantments* and *incantation* in chaps. 2, 4 (*MGH*, 75, 82–83). Herman-Judah's use of the sign of the cross has a prototype in the story told by Pope Gregory I of a Jew who was driven by the perils of night to take refuge in a temple of Apollo. Though he lacked Christian faith, he protected himself from the assaults of nocturnal demons by making the sign of the cross. They fled from him, since he was a signed vessel, even though an empty one. Subsequently, he submitted to baptism (*Dialogues*, 3.7). The story is repeated by Herman-Judah's contemporary, Giraldus Cambrensis, *Gemma Ecclesiastica*, dist. 1, chap. 29 (ed. J. S. Brewer, Rolls Series, 21, pt. 2 [London: Longmans, 1861], 101–2).

17. Mainz Anonymous, *Narrative of the Old Persecutions*, and Rabbi Ephraim of Bonn, *Book of Remembrance*, in Eidelberg, *The Jews and the Crusaders*, 114, 129. On the avoidance of repeated slaughter when the Third Crusade began, see Robert Chazan, "Emperor Frederick I, the Third Crusade, and the Jews," *Viator* 8 (1977): 83–93.

18. It is enlightening to compare Herman-Judah's account with the analysis of other contemporary texts provided by Chris D. Ferguson, "Autobiography as Therapy: Guibert de Nogent, Peter Abelard, and the Making of Medieval Autobiography," *Journal of Medieval and Renaissance Studies* 13 (1983): 187–212.

19. Chaps. 4, 5 (*MGH*, 83, 87). Cf. his comparison of Jewish and Christian history (chap. 6 [*MGH*, 92]) and his references to the history, or histories, of the Old Testament (chaps. 2, 4 [*MGH*, 74, 80–81]).

20. See case 1 above.

21. On Egbert, see Odilo Engels and Stefan Weinfurter, eds., *Series Episcoporum Ecclesiae Catholicae Occidentalis*, ser. 5, *Germania*, vol. 1, *Archiepiscopatus Coloniensis* (Stuttgart: Hiersemann, 1982), 130–31; Heinrich Borsting and Alois Schroer, *Handbuch des Bistums Münster*, vol. 1, 2d ed. (Münster: Regensberg, 1946), 73.

22. *Germania Judaica* 1: 71–72.

23. The only possible exception is Herman-Judah's reference to the ascetic austerities practiced by the brethren at Cappenberg as "the martyrdoms of such great labors, heavier than death itself" (chap. 6 [*MGH*, 90]). On the community at Cappenberg, see Manfred Petry, "Die ältesten Urkunden und die frühe Geschichte des Prämonstratenserstiftes Cappenberg in Westfalen (1122–1200)," pt. 1, *Archiv für Diplomatik, Schriftgeschichte, Siegel- und Wappenkunde* 18 (1972): 143–289, pt. 2, ibid., 19 (1973): 55–64, 137–50; Gerlinde Niemeyer, "Die Vitae Godefridi Cappenbergensis," *Deutsches Archiv* 23 (1967): 405–67, with references to the quotation from Herman-Judah's account in the older of the *vitae* (pp. 411–12, 464) (a parallel reference occurs in Niemeyer's edition, p. 8); Herbert Grundmann, *Der Cappenberger Barbarossakopf und die Anfänge des Stiftes Cappenberg*, Münstersche Forschungen, 12 (Cologne: Böhlau, 1959).

24. E.g., Gerhoch of Reichersberg, *Tractatus in Ps. 64*, chaps. 119–20 (Migne *PL* 194:79). See also Beryl Smalley, *The Study of the Bible in the Middle Ages*, 3d ed.

Notes to pp. 48–50   169

(Oxford: Blackwell, 1983), 173, and *The Becket Conflict and the Schools: A Study of Intellectuals in Politics* (Oxford: Blackwell, 1973), 83–86.

25. Rupert of Deutz, *Anulus*, bks. 1–3 (Migne *PL* 170:561, 584, 590, 593, 601–8). See Egil Beitz, *Rupertus von Deutz: Seine Werke und die bildene Kunst*, Veröffentlichungen des kölnischen Geschichtsvereins, 4 (Cologne: Das kölnische Geschichtsverein, 1930). See also John Van Engen, *Rupert of Deutz* (Berkeley: Univ. of California Press, 1983), xix, 242–244, 246–48. Van Engen's discussion is also instructive on the range of Rupert's dealings with Jews. On Herman-Judah's suppression of "the marked anti-Jewish invective and theological polemic characteristic of Rupert's writings," see Cohen, "The Mentality of the Medieval Jewish Apostate," 33. A similar linkage of exegesis and religious art occurs in the *Disputatio* of Gilbert Crispin (*Disputatio Iudei et Christiani*, chaps. 152–61 [Anna Sapir Abulafia and G. R. Evans, eds., *The Works of Gilbert Crispin, Abbot of Westminster*, Auctores Britannici Medii Aevi, 8 (London: Oxford Univ. Press, 1986), 50–53]). See Bernhard Blumenkranz, "La 'disputatio Judei cum Christiano' de Gilbert Crispin, abbé de Westminster," in Blumenkranz, *Juifs et Chrétiens: Patristique et Moyen Age* (London: Variorum, 1977), no. 16. See also Bernhard Blumenkranz, *Les auteurs chrétiens latins du moyen-âge sur les juifs et le judaïsme* (Paris: Mouton, 1963), 286. Given Herman-Judah's biography, it is worth noting that the Jew in Gilbert's debate came from Mainz and was well acquainted with Christian as well as Jewish literature. On inhibitions regarding the subjects taken up in Jewish-Christian dialogues, see Jordan, *The French Monarchy and the Jews: From Philip Augustus to the Last Capetians*, 11.

26. Rupert of Deutz, *Anulus*, bk. 3 (Migne *PL* 170:597).

27. *Germania Judaica* 1:71.

28. For the story of bleeding images of Christ, see Giraldus Cambrensis, *Gemma Ecclesiastica*, dist. 1, chaps. 30, 31 (ed. Brewer, 21, pt. 2:102–3). For the story of the statue in the privy, see Matthew Paris, *Chronica Maiora*, ed. Henry Richards Luard, Rolls Series, 57, pt. 5 (London: Longmans, 1880), 114–15.

29. Rupert of Deutz, *Anulus*, bk. 4, quoting 3 Kings 6:29 (Migne *PL* 170:607–8). Compare Gerhoch of Reichersberg's statement that the number of churches was daily increasing, ever more elaborately ornamented with the glitter of golden images (*Tractatus in Psalmum* 64, chap. 51 [*MGH*, *Ldl* 3:461]). See ibid., chap. 169 (Migne *PL* 194:113), for a comparison between true belief and the empty ostentation of a temple with beautiful walls shimmering with much gold.

30. See Gerhoch of Reichersberg on the affective contemplation of a crucifix (*Tractatus in Ps.* 40, 14 and *Tractatus in Ps.* 72, 19–20 [Migne *PL* 193:1486, 194:350]).

31. An interesting parallel exists between Herman-Judah's dramatic portrayal of the sentence of death that the Jews issued against him and the portrayal of the capital judgment proclaimed by the "Prince of the Synagogue" at Damascus against the Apostle Paul in the *Play of the Conversion of St. Paul* (from the Fleury

playbook) (Karl Young, *The Drama of the Medieval Church* 2 [Oxford: Clarendon, 1933]: 221-20).

32. Young, *The Drama of the Medieval Church* 2:221-20.

33. Rupert of Deutz, *Anulus*, bks. 1, 4 (Migne *PL* 170:578, 608).

34. On the adder, Bernhard Blumenkranz, *Le Juif médiéval au miroir de l'art chrétien* (Paris: Etudes augustiniennes, 1966), 64. On the scorpion, see Baron, *A Social and Religious History of the Jews* 5:132. See also Bernhard Blumenkranz, "Juifs et Judaïsme dans l'art chrétien du Haut Moyen Age," *Gli Ebrei nell'alto Medioevo*, Settimane di Studio del Centro Italiano di Studi sull' alto Medioevo, 26 (Spoleto: Centro, 1980), 987-1014; Wolfgang Seiferth, *Synagoge und Kirche im Mittelalter* (Munich: Kösel, 1964), esp. 155-69.

35. On the stereotype of "underhandedness and proneness to cheating," see Baron, *A Social and Religious History of the Jews* 5:131-32; on the alleged Jewish "alliance with demonic powers," ibid., 132; on "laziness," ibid., 132; on the "accusation of Jewish lasciviousness," extorted from rabbinnical teachings on "intensive procreation," ibid., 133-35, and 2:217-23.

36. Chaps. 3, 7, 9, 10, 16, 21 (*MGH*, 78, 93, 97, 99-101, 113-14). On the characterization of Judaism as a superstition, see also chap. 16 (*MGH*, 113): "[At Worms,] introivi eosque Gamalielis sui superstitiosa super vetus testamentum commenta legentes audivi."

37. At least in later generations, Christians openly debated whether Jewish children should be forcibly removed from their families and placed among Christians for education, a prospect that Jews had grounds to fear (Baron, *A Social and Religious History of the Jews* 9:15-17).

38. Chaps. 2, 3, 5, 10, 11, 16, 17 (*MGH*, 74, 76, 83-87, 98-100, 106, 113, 115).

39. E.g., *Chronicle* of Solomon bar Simson, in Eidelberg, *The Jews and the Crusaders*, 42, 50.

40. Herbord, *Dialogus de Vita S. Ottonis Episcopi Babenbergensis* 2.16 (ed. Jan Wikarjak, Monumenta Poloniae Historica, n.s., vol. 7, fasc. 3 (Warsaw: Państwowe Wydawnictwo Naukowe, 1974, 90). With the same elegant attention to decorum, Otto also had incense and other aromatics distributed around the font.

41. Augustine, *De Doctrina Christiana*, 3.37.56 (*Corp. Christ.*, *ser. lat.* 32:115).

42. Cf. ibid., 2.39.59 (*Corp. Christ.*, *ser. lat.* 32:73).

43. Rupert of Deutz, *Anulus*, bk. 2 (Migne *PL* 170:589).

44. Chap. 19 (*MGH*, 120). See also chaps. 2, 6 (*MGH*, 73-74, 89).

45. See case 1 above.

46. J. Stengers, review of Niemeyer ed., *Le Moyen Age* 71 (1965): 612-14.

47. *Conf.*, 8.7.17, 8.9.21, 8.11.27 (*Corp. Christ.*, *ser. lat.* 27:124, 127, 130).

48. See also chap. 6 (*MGH*, 91-92): "Grandis continuo cordi meo de contrariis atque diversis a se Iudaeorum et Christianorum legibus ambiguitatis ortus est scrupulus." Here, again, Herman-Judah was distressed by a legal issue. If God was

pleased with the Jews and their legal observances, why had the Jews been cast out of their homeland and dispersed throughout the world while Christians prospered?

49. *Conf.*, 10.2.2, 10.2.4, 10.6.8 (*Corp. Christ., ser. lat.* 27:155, 156, 158).

50. Chaps. 10, 12 (*MGH*, 98, 108). Chapter 1 (*MGH*, 70) begins the treatise with a confession by Herman of his sinfulness and unworthiness as a priest.

51. E.g., chaps. 14, 15, 20 (*MGH*, 110, 112, 121).

52. Smalley, *The Becket Conflict and the Schools*, 135–37. The *Confessions* was not inventoried in an early thirteenth-century catalogue of an anonymous cleric's library, although other works by Augustine were present (Gerlinde Möser-Mersky, *Mittelalterliche Bibliothekskataloge Österreichs*, vol. 3, *Steiermark* [Graz: Böhlau, 1961], 105). On the question of how widely known the *Confessions* were in the Middle Ages (and the omission of Book 8 from Eugippius's little anthology), see E. Ann Matter, "Conversion(s) in the *Confessiones*," in Joseph C. Schnaubelt and Frederick Van Fleteren, eds., *Collectanea Augustiniana: Augustine, "Second Founder of the Faith"* (New York: Peter Lang, 1990), 25–26.

53. *Conf.*, 12.28–30 (*Corp. Christ., ser. lat.* 27:130–32).

54. See Baron, *A Social and Religious History of the Jews* 5: 128–29, 9:135–92. See also Guido Kisch, "Die Rechtsstellung der Wormser Juden im Mittelalter," in Kisch, *Forschungen zur Rechts-und Sozialgeschichte der Juden in Deutschland während des Mittelalters*, Ausgewählte Schriften, 1, 2d ed. (Sigmaringen: Thorbecke, 1978), 93–106, predominately on the thirteenth and fourteenth centuries.

55. See *Conf.*, 5.9.17, 6.1.1 (*Corp. Christ., ser. lat.* 27:67, 73).

56. Maimonides, *Guide of the Perplexed* 1.33, 34, 3.intro (trans. Shlomo Pines [Chicago: Univ. of Chicago Press, 1963], 71–72, 77–78, 415).

57. One further instance may be helpful. In describing how Bishop Egbert introduced him to allegory, he recalled that the bishop had compared the Jews with brute animals content with chaff (i.e., the literal meaning of Scripture) and Christians with men who, using their reason to attain spiritual understanding, refreshed themselves on the sweet pith of the chaff (chap. 2 [*MGH*, 74]).

The basis for this analogy occurs in Augustine's *Sermo 130* on John 5:5–14 (Migne *PL* 38:725). Asserting that the five barley loaves in John 6:9–26 represented the five books of the Law of Moses, Augustine continued: "The Old Law is barley to the gospel's wheat. Great mysteries concerning Christ are contained in these books. Wherefore, he himself says, 'If you had believed Moses, you would also have believed me, for he wrote concerning me' [John 5:46]. But just as in barley, pith is concealed under the chaff, so Christ is concealed under the veil of the Law's mysteries."

Without being able to recover what Herman-Judah actually heard Egbert say, it is still instructive that he chose this example to recall and, further, that he omitted both the anagogical (or prophetic) reference of Old Testament to New present in Augustine's text and the Father's essential point: namely, that Christ was not only testified to but was actually present in the Law.

58. See Christina of Markyate's willingness to prove her vow of virginity by

the ordeal of hot iron (Anon., *The Life of Christina of Markyate, a Twelfth Century Recluse*, chap. 17 [ed. and trans. C. H. Talbot (Oxford: Clarendon, 1959), 62]). There is also an account of the use of ordeal by a missionary to the Saracens in Spain during the late eleventh century. See Benjamin Z. Kedar, *Crusade and Mission: European Approaches toward the Muslims* (Princeton, N.J.: Princeton Univ. Press, 1984), 45.

59. These include major elements in the narrative, such as the equation between feasting and the search for knowledge (below after n. 56) and the notion of religious study as an antidote to sexual arousal when it came as an affliction from the "abominable one" (chaps. 10–11; cf. Maimonides, *Guide of the Perplexed*, 3.49 [trans. Pines, 608]: "If you feel sexual excitement and suffer because of it, go *to the house of study*, read, take part in discussions, put questions, and be asked in your turn, for then this suffering will indubitably pass away").

Clearly identifiable Jewish elements also include incidental allusions that denote ways of thinking about familial relationships (e.g., children of a paternal aunt [chap. 18 (*MGH*, 116–18)]; cf. Maimonides, *Guide of the Perplexed* 3.49 [trans. Pines, 607]: paternal aunts have the same status as one's father). One can also mention figures of speech (e.g., the Midrashic curse against Baruch [chap. 7 (*MGH*, 28)]: "ground down with a double grinding"; cf. the curse against the Crusader Count Emicho of Leiningen, "May his bones be ground to dust between iron millstones" [Mainz Anonymous, *Narrative of the Old Persecutions*, in Eidelberg, *The Jews and the Crusaders*, 107 (see also p. 108)]); application of scriptural images (e.g., the image of rumination to elucidate mental reflection [chaps. 2, 3, 21 (*MGH*, 74, 77, 125)]). The first citation makes an exact connection with Maimonides' comment on signs of permitted animals: "They are merely signs by means of which the praised species may be discerned from the blamed species" (*Guide of the Perplexed* 3.48 [trans. Pines, 598]), and an emphasis on ritual purity and impurity (chaps. 11, 20, 21 [*MGH*, 105, 121, 126]).

60. On Jews as "servants" or "serfs," see above, n. 54. The allegation of Jews in Mainz that Herman was preparing for conversion by depositing books and money with Christians (chap. 17 [*MGH*, 115]) reflects the general practice either of allowing the property of Jewish apostates to revert to their families or of confiscating it for the civil government. Apostates could expect to be disinherited by their parents (Baron, *A Social and Religious History of the Jews* 9:19–22).

61. See Augustine's explication, which employs the metaphor of the temple, in *City of God*, 10.4–6 (*Corp. Christ.*, *ser. lat.* 47:276–79). See also Augustine, *En. in Ps. 42*, 6 (*Corp. Christ.*, *ser. lat.* 38:479): the human character as image of God consists in the intellect (*intellectus* or *ratio*).

62. Pius Parsch, *The Liturgy of the Mass*, 3d ed., trans. H. E. Winstone (St. Louis: Herder, 1957), 237; Gregory Dix, *The Shape of the Liturgy* (London: Dacre, 1960), 222.

63. The illuminations are reproduced in Frank Neidhart Steigerwald, *Das*

Evangeliar Heinrichs des Löwen (Braunschweig: Rot-Gelb-Grun Verlag, 1985), plates 12, 143.

64. See, for example, chap. 9 (*MGH*, 97): "me... studio cognoscende veritatis actitare videntes"; chap. 10 (*MGH*, 100): "totius pristinae devotionis mee circa inquirendam viam veritatis."

65. Maimonides, *Guide of the Perplexed*, 1.30 (trans. Pines, 64). References to feasting occur in chap. 1 (the first dream), chap. 6 (the ascetic life at Cappenberg), chap. 10 (Bishop Egbert's dinner), chap. 20 (God's vocation of him to a higher place at table, i.e., the priesthood), and chap. 21 (eucharistic feast, celestial banquet, feast for the prodigal son implied).

66. Louis Ginzberg, *Legends of the Jews* 4 (Philadelphia: Jewish Publication Society of America, 1913): 374.

67. Rupert of Deutz, *Anulus*, bks. 1, 2, 3, 4 (Migne *PL* 170:569, 578, 587, 595, 598, 608–10), and *Commentum in Apocalypsim*, 9.14 (ibid., 169:1092).

68. See below, n. 72, on Rupert's interpretation of Genesis 9:3.

69. Chap. 8 (*MGH*, 94); Daniel 10:3.

70. There is one additional point of correspondence in the fact that the narrator and interpreter in one vision wears a belt of gold (chaps. 1, 21 [*MGH*, 71, 124]; Dan. 10:5).

71. Eidelberg, *The Jews and the Crusaders*, 53, 154 n. 155.

72. *Chronicle* of Solomon bar Simson, ibid., 39, 59. Though Herman-Judah recorded one instance of his dining at Bishop Egbert's table, he carefully mentioned that the meal presented to him in charity was bread and roast pike, not among the ritually unclean foods (chap. 5 [*MGH*, 83]). As in many other cases, there is a coincidence here between Herman-Judah's account and the *Anulus* by Rupert of Deutz. In the *Anulus*, when the debaters reached the topic of dietary laws, the Christian recalled God's mandate to Noah and his sons after the flood: "All the fish of the sea are given into your hand, and everything that moves and lives will be food for you. I have given all things to you as though they were green herbs [*olera virentia*], except that you may not eat flesh with blood" (Gen. 9:2–3). The Jew answered: "Therefore, if God says 'every fish of the sea" without distinction... why do you not also eat flesh? Why do you not gorge yourself on frogs and toads?" (*Anulus*, bk. 4 [Migne *PL* 170:608]).

73. Agobard of Lyons, *ep.* 7 (*MGH*, *Epp.* 5, K.A. 3:184). The earliest known prohibition to this effect was issued by the Council of Mâcon (583), which designated attendance by Christians at the feasts of Jews as a crime punishable by excommunication.

74. Gerhoch of Reichersberg, *Tractatus in Ps.* 64, chap. 67 (*MGH*, *Ldl* 3:468).

75. Rupert devoted the eighth book of his great treatise *De Victoria Verbi Dei* (chaps. 1–26) to interpreting Esther as an anticipation of the triumph of Christ (*MGH*, *Quellen zur Geistesgeschichte des Mittelalters* 5:246–70). Especially compare Herman's portrayal of Christ as king with the detailed allegorical parallels that

Rupert drew between Esther's triumph and Christ's (chap. 23 [pp. 266–67]). The principal manuscript of this text (*clm* 14055, fol. 64) is introduced by an initial depicting Esther's feast. A manuscript of the *Glossarium Salomonis* written in Prüfening in 1165 (*clm* 13002) also illustrates the virtue of patience (*longanimitas*) with a representation of Haman leading Mordecai, crowned, on the king's horse and the corresponding vice, with one of Haman on the gallows.

76. See Momigliano, "A Medieval Jewish Autobiography," 226: "The boy had more or less dreamt of himself as a new Mordecai after the death of Haman"; and ibid., 229, on "the Mordecai pattern of the dream." Even here, there may have been a silent allusion to Jewish teachings on gluttony (and lust) as primary sins (see Valerie I. J. Flint, "Anti-Jewish Literature and Attitudes in the Twelfth Century," *Journal of Jewish Studies* 37 [1986]: 47).

77. A black horse, according to legend (see Ginzberg, *Legends of the Jews* 4:435). Herman-Judah was mounted on a white horse (chap. 1 [*MGH*, 71]).

78. Ginzberg, *Legends of the Jews* 4:386.

79. Ibid., 4:372.

80. Momigliano, "A Medieval Jewish Autobiography," 229.

81. Cf. Augustine's parallel comment that his tender infant heart drank in the name of Christ with his mother's milk (*Conf.*, 3.4.8 [*Corp. Christ.*, ser. lat. 27:30]).

82. Wolfgang Giese, "'In Iudaismum Lapsus Est': Jüdische Proselytenmacherei im frühen und hohen Mittelalter (600–1300)," *Historisches Jahrbuch* 88 (1968): 418. See also Baron, *A Social and Religious History of the Jews* 5:113–14. Joseph Kimhi seems to have written *The Book of the Covenant* as "a defense against apostates from Judaism who were trying to evangelize their former coreligionists" (trans. Frank Talmage [Toronto: Pontifical Institute of Mediaeval Studies, 1972], 19).

83. Norman Golb, "Notes on the Conversion of European Christians to Judaism in the Eleventh Century," *Journal of Jewish Studies* 16 (1965): 69–74; Bernhard Blumenkranz, "Jüdische und christliche Konvertiten im jüdisch-christlichen Religionsgespräch des Mittelalters," in Blumenkranz, *Juifs et Chrétiens*, no. 14, p. 269, on Andrew, once archbishop of Bari, whose conversion appears to be recorded in a Jewish text from the Cairo Geniza documents. See Momigliano, "A Medieval Jewish Autobiography," 227: "the story of Andreas's conversion is a problem in itself into which I do not intend to enter."

84. *Ep. 187* (1166), in W. J. Millor and C. N. L. Brooke, eds., *The Letters of John of Salisbury* 2 (Oxford: Clarendon, 1972): 236. On the rule that to be figurative, a scriptural passage must refer to Christ, see Morrison, *Understanding Conversion*, chap. 3, n. 7.

85. For Gerhoch of Reichersberg's similar doubt whether he merited God's hatred or love, see *Tractatus in Ps. 118*, 63 Heth (Migne *PL* 194:773).

86. *Chronicle* of Solomon bar Simson, in Eidelberg, *The Jews and the Crusaders*, 40–41.

87. Ibid., 31, 56.

88. Peter the Venerable, *Adversus Iudeorum Inveteratam Duritiem*, chap. 1 (*Corpus Christianorum, continuatio medievalis* 58:14).
89. *Chronicon*, 5.prol (*MGHSSrrG*, 228).
90. Ibid., 8.35 (pp. 456–57).
91. See case 1 above and my article, "Otto of Freising's Quest for the Hermeneutic Circle," *Speculum* 55 (1980): 207–36.
92. See my essay, *"I Am You,"* 72–81.
93. Chap. 16 (*MGH*, 114). See also chap. 11 (*MGH*, 105): Satan transfigures himself into an angel of light.
94. Rupert of Deutz, *Anulus*, prol. (Migne *PL* 170:561, 570).
95. See the pertinent chapters in *"I Am You."*
96. Rupert of Deutz, *Anulus*, bk. 2 (Migne *PL* 170:587).

Case 2. A Translation of Herman-Judah's *Account*

1. Introduction, at n. 82. On the possible use of this document for proselytizing other Jews, see Introduction, n. 82.
2. Introduction, at nn. 62, 84, 88.
3. Introduction, nn. 70, 74, 76.
4. Introduction, at n. 66 and ff.
5. See below chap. 18 (*MGH*, 117).
6. Introduction, at nn. 21, 38.
7. Introduction, nn. 26, 42, 56.
8. Introduction, n. 59.
9. Introduction, nn. 16, 17 (on Herman-Judah's resort to the sign of the cross as a magical act).
10. Introduction, at n. 22 and ff.
11. Introduction, at nn. 11, 25, 26, 29, 33, 43, 67, 75, 70, 84, 92, 94, 96.
12. Introduction, nn. 17, 24, 34; after nn. 38, 91.
13. Introduction, at n. 25 and ff.
14. Here, the author of the chapter headings used Herman's prebaptismal name. See chap. 19 (*MGH*, 120).
15. Introduction, after n. 25.
16. Introduction, after nn. 28, 84.
17. Introduction, at n. 34, after n. 91.
18. Introduction, at nn. 30, 34; after n. 91.
19. Introduction, at nn. 66, 76; nn. 68, 73.
20. Introduction, at nn. 25, 39, 94.
21. Introduction, at n. 39.
22. A continuation of the passage cited in the Introduction at n. 84 and after n. 86.
23. Introduction, at n. 21.

24. Ibid.
25. Introduction, at nn. 25, 94.
26. Introduction, nn. 21, 92; after n. 62.
27. See the characteristic Jewish curse against Crusaders, "May his bones be ground to dust" (Introduction, n. 59).
28. Introduction, at n. 38; after n. 56; and n. 68 and ff.
29. Introduction, after n. 34; n. 94.
30. Ibid.
31. Ibid.
32. For Augustine's parallel assertion, see Introduction, n. 81.
33. Introduction, after nn. 34, 91.
34. Introduction, after n. 35.
35. Introduction, after n. 54.
36. Introduction, after n. 56.
37. Introduction, after n. 81.
38. Introduction, after n. 34; nn. 50, 51, 93.
39. Introduction, at n. 48.
40. Introduction, after n. 69.
41. Introduction, n. 16.
42. Introduction, after nn. 55, 61.
43. Ibid.
44. Introduction, n. 31; after n. 54.
45. Introduction, n. 62.
46. Deuteronomy 13:6ff. prescribes the stoning of those who try to persuade other Jews to worship foreign gods.
47. Introduction, after n. 43.
48. Introduction, before n. 64.
49. Introduction, nn. 64, 93.
50. Introduction, n. 17.
51. Introduction, n. 60.
52. Introduction, at n. 63.
53. See above chap. 1 (*MGH*, 71).
54. Introduction, n. 40. The Isaac named in the vision may be the same man who provided a carnal interpretation of Herman's first dream (chap. 1 [*MGH*, 71–72]).
55. Introduction, at n. 39.
56. Introduction, after n. 44.
57. In a review of Niemeyer's edition, G. Miccoli compared this striking turn of phrase with a phrase in a sermon by Pope Gregory I (*XI Homiliarum in Evangelia Libri Duo*, 2.32.2 [Migne *PL* 76:1233]): "nudam crucem Christi nudus baiulare" (*Studi medievali*, 3rd ser., 7, pt. 1 [1966]: 441). The parallel with later Franciscan ideals of poverty is obvious.

58. Introduction, at n. 38; after n. 81; n. 84.

59. An interesting parallel occurs in a late twelfth-century biography of Gottfried, the founder of Cappenberg. Before he entered Cappenberg as an Augustinian himself, Gottfried had been married. At his monastic conversion, his wife also took religious vows and entered the community for women founded at the foot of the mountain. When Gottfried died, his wife, who had become abbess, saw him arrayed in amazing beauty and crowned with gold. She asked him where he was going in his crown. He answered that he was going without delay to the palace of the Paramount King, and that, as the son of the King, he was crowned with blessed immortality. See also Introduction, after n. 58. Since Gottfried died in 1127, shortly before Herman's first visit to Cappenberg, this story may have belonged to the growing hagiographical lore that he heard first as visitor and later as member of the community (Anon., *Vita Godefridi Comitis Capenbergensis*, chap. 11 [*MGH, SS* 12:526]).

60. Introduction, after n. 62; nn. 65, 67.

61. Introduction, after n. 46; n. 85.

Case 3. The *Dialogues* of Constantine Tsatsos

1. Pandelis Prevelakis, "Oi 'Dialogoi se Monastiri' tou Konstantinou Tsatsou," *Ekphrasi Timis ston Konstantino Tsatso gia tin Prosphora tou sto Ethnos kai ton Politismo*, Tetradia "Euthunis," 16 (Metamorphosi: Parisianos, 1982), 45, 51, 55; Constantine Tsatsos, *Dialogues in a Monastery*, trans. Jean Demus (Brookline, Mass.: Hellenic College Press, 1986). I am much obliged to the kindness of Professor Theofanis G. Stavrou for making available to me both Prevelakis's review of the *Dialogues* and the pamphlet by Tsatsos mentioned in the next note.

2. See the profound suspicion of militant minorities and antiauthoritarian majorities as inimical to human rights in Constantine D. Tsatsos, *Human Rights* (Athens: n.p., 1978). The essay concludes (p. 23): "An unhealthy spiritual attitude clouds most people's judgment. A spirit of rebellion and distrust prevails, not only among the immature youth, which is only natural, but among many solid citizens as well. . . . If to this phenomenon we add the radical snobbism of the so-called intelligentsia, we begin to understand why free peoples and whole civilizations succumbed so easily to totalitarianism. Not because of the strength of the avowed or at least manifestly totalitarian minority, but rather because of the unwitting enlistment of large numbers of unthinking citizens who, as Lenin so wisely put it, hand the totalitarians the rope to hang them with."

3. Cf., the end of the quest is God (Tsatsos, *Dialogues*, 94).

4. Synesios felt that he had died and become a different man before he entered the monastery, but his friend Ipliksis preceived that he had become more completely what he already was (ibid., 110–111, 115, 117).

5. Cf., "the tragedy of our existence" (ibid., 33).

6. See Karl F. Morrison, *Understanding Conversion* (Univ. Press of Virginia, forthcoming), chap. 6, and *"I Am You": The Hermeneutics of Empathy in Western Literature, Theology, and Art* (Princeton: Princeton Univ. Press, 1988), 99–114.

7. Tsatsos, *Dialogues*, 181. The actual verse is: "Homo sum; humani nil a me alienum puto" (Terence, *Heauton Timorumenos*, 1.1.25). I cannot here consider the important consequences of Tsatsos's similar use of a conventional misquotation of Tertullian, "Credo quia absurdum," instead of the correct statement: "Certum est quia impossibile est" (*De Carne Christi*, 5; Tsatsos, *Dialogues*, 16). The replacement of certainty with belief and of impossibility with absurdity has very considerable implications for Tsatsos's argument, which are only magnified by recalling that when he also used the conventional "Credo" misquotation, Werner Jaeger, claimed as a teacher by some participants in the *Dialogues*, equated the *absurdum* with death (Werner Jaeger, *Humanism and Theology*, Aquinas Lecture, 1943 [Milwaukee: Marquette Univ. Press, 1943], 11).

8. This is another point of contact with Jaeger. Cf. Werner Jaeger, *Paideia: The Ideals of Greek Culture*, trans. Gilbert Highet, 2d ed., 1 (New York: Oxford Univ. Press, 1945): xxiii.

9. Ioanna Tsatsou, *My Brother, George Seferis* (Minneapolis: North Central, 1982), 10.

10. Ibid., 245–46; Ioanna Tsatsou, *The Sword's Fierce Edge: A Journal of the Occupation of Greece, 1941–1944*, trans. Jean Demos (Nashville: Vanderbilt Univ. Press, 1969), 6–9, 112–13.

11. Tsatsou, *My Brother, George Seferis*, 197, 221, 227, 234.

12. Ibid., 66.

13. Tsatsou, *The Sword's Fierce Edge*, 34, and *My Brother, George Seferis*, 177, 188, 243.

14. Cf. the comment of Theofanis G. Stavrou that "the fate of Greece and Hellenism 'wounds' [Ioanna Tsatsou] as it did her brother, George Seferis," and C. A. Trypanis's remark that "eternal problems of mankind . . . wound and inspire" her (Ioanna Tsatsou, *Poems*, trans. Jean Demos (Minneapolis: North Central, 1984), vii, x.

15. Nikos Kazantzakis, *Report to Greco*, trans. P. A. Bien (New York: Bantam, 1966), 346.

16. Chester G. Starr, *Individual and Community: The Rise of the Polis, 800–500 B.C.* (New York: Oxford Univ. Press, 1986), 4. Ioanna Tsatsou's account of a maritime pilgrimage commemorating the nineteen-hundredth anniversary of St. Paul's missionary journey to Greece refers to the ship on which she and Tsatsos (then minister of education) were passengers as a "floating monastery" (*My Brother, George Seferis*, 227–28).

17. Tsatsou, *The Sword's Fierce Edge*, 112, 117–18, 157.

18. One should also note the references to Diotima, Socrates' teacher in Plato's *Symposium* (Tsatsos, *Dialogues*, 26, 125).

19. *The Times* (London), 6 Oct. 1978, p. 11. The threat came from the Metropolitan of Florina. The Assembly of Bishops objected to the law on the theologically neutral ground that it would accelerate the decline in the Greek birthrate.

20. A threefold censure, against women, the young, and Asians, appears in Tsatsos's objection that "nowadays . . . most women teeter along like Chinese, a woman who writes iambs and trochees with her body" (Tsatsou, *Dialogues*, 128).

21. Jaeger, *Paideia* I:xxv.

22. Frank Smothers, William Hardy McNeill, and Elizabeth Darbishire McNeill, *Report on the Greeks* (New York: Twentieth Century Fund, 1948), 4.

23. Calvos, Cavafy, Palamas, Sikelianos (see Tsatsos, *Dialogues*, 54, 70). The omissions of Seferis, Solomos, and Myrivilis are notable in view of their known personal relationships with the author.

24. Cf. Frantz Fanon, *The Wretched of the Earth*, trans. Constance Farrington (New York: Grove, 1968), 219, 246.

25. Synesios recalled quite a different outcome of a love affair in his account of a man in whom "a woman [had] killed passion" (Tsatsos, *Dialogues*, 83).

26. *Sunday Telegraph* (London) 10 Dec. 1978, p. 2.

27. Ernst Cassirer, whose great study *The Philosophy of Symbolic Forms* testifies to a point of view similar to that expressed by Tsatsos, also described these divisions as a wound. Recounting the achievements of humanistic disciplines since the Romantic era, he commented: "But, in the face of all these triumphs of knowledge, achieved within the course of a single century, there loomed a serious defect, an internal wound. Even though research was able to advance continually in each of these fields of study, the inner unity of each became ever more problematic. Philosophy was unable to contend for this unity, nor was it able to put a stop to the growing fragmentation. Hegel's system is the last great attempt to comprehend the whole of knowledge and to organize it by virtue of one ruling idea" (Ernst Cassirer, *The Logic of the Humanities*, trans. Clarence Smith Howe [New Haven: Yale Univ. Press, 1967], 87).

28. Cf. Tsatsos, *Dialogues*, 76: "What we refer to as if it were one crisis is really the many crises of our time . . . and they do not constitute a single picture."

29. Given its place in the structure of the *Dialogues*, the programmatic statement on language, ethos, and spirit at the end of chapter 4 must be read ironically.

30. From a conversation with Christian Zervos (1935), in Herschel B. Chipp, *Theories of Modern Art: A Source Book by Artists and Critics* (Berkeley: Univ. of California Press, 1968), 267. Cf. the reference to discussion by Synesios and Nouty on abstract art, Tsatsos, *Dialogues*, 100.

31. For a contrast between the attitudes of contented self-absorption in the *Dialogues* and a missionary zeal for Greek philosophy, expressed in the organization of discussion circles (some constituting networks), the collection of libraries, research, and the establishment of journals, see Paul R. Anderson, *Platonism in the Midwest* (New York: Temple Univ. Publications, 1963).

32. Martin Heidegger, "The Thinker as Poet" (*Aus der Erfahrung des Denkens*),

in Heidegger, *Poetry, Language, Thought*, trans. Albert Hofstadter (New York: Harper and Row, 1971), 11.

33. Kazantzakis, *Report to Greco*, 15.

34. Cf. Tsatsos, *Dialogues*, 174, Synesios's comment on his conversion to monasticism: "God inspired me to make the final leap."

35. Cf. ibid., 162: "Life is a divine work or it is nothing."

36. Augustine, *Conf.*, 8.11.27–8.12.30, 13.23.34 (*Corp. Christ., ser. lat.* 27: 130–32, 261–62).

37. Thomas Aquinas, *Summa theologiae*, Ia–IIae.q.66.a.6.r.1.

38. Cf. the reference to the life after this earthly existence as noble and true (Tsatsos, *Dialogues*, 87).

39. Cf. the exchange in Kazantzakis, *Report to Greco*, 204. When Kazantzakis and his friend arrived at the monastery of St. Paul on Mt. Athos, the doorkeeper greeted them:

" 'What do you want here, morons?' he asked with a laugh.
'We want to do obeisance, old man.'
'Obeisance to what? Are you in your right minds?'
'To the monastery.'
'What monastery? There is no monastery—it's finished! The world, that's the monastery. Take my advice and go back to the world!' "

40. Erwin Panofsky, "Et in Arcadia Ego: Poussin and the Elegiac Tradition," in Panofsky, *Meaning in the Visual Arts* (Woodstock, N.Y.: Overlook Press, 1974), 303–4, 319.

41. Nikos Kazantzakis, *Travels in Greece (Journey to the Morea)*, trans. F. A. Reed (Oxford: Bruno Cassirer, 1966), 12.

42. Tsatsou, *My Brother, George Seferis*, 10, 20, and passim. Although Tsatsos visited Paris in 1918–19, his major residence outside Greece was during his student years at Heidelberg (1924–28).

43. Smothers, McNeill, and McNeill, *Report on the Greeks*, 135, 146, 148.

44. Tsatsou, *The Sword's Fierce Edge*, 85.

45. The argument attributed to Umberto Eco that there can be no "art of forgetfulness" corresponding with the "art of memory," which latter was much cultivated in the Renaissance, leaves out of account the exquisite care with which forgetfulness was cultivated and written about in the ascetic tradition. See the account of Eco's remarks, "Die Kunst des Vergessens," *Frankfurter Allgemeine Zeitung*, 16 June 1987. I owe this reference to the kindness of Bruce Brasington.

46. Cf. Kazantzakis, *Report to Greco*, 377: "More than wine or love, more underhandedly than ideas, art is able to entice man and make him forget." In the *Dialogues*, Basset describes the pleasure that he derives from reading Montaigne at bedtime: "Some of his phrases, before I fall asleep, calm me and make me forget" (p. 169).

47. Ioanna Tsatsou, "Execution," in *Poems*, 36.

48. This shift may be allegorically represented by the passage of Synesios from the monastery of Agathon (the Good), his first ascetic home (p. 117), to that of the Transfiguration.

49. *Sunday Telegraph* (London), 10 Dec. 1978, p. 2.

50. Cassirer, *The Logic of the Humanities*, 115–16.

51. Tsatsou, *My Brother, George Seferis*, 45, 67, 152.

52. Octavio Paz, "Edith Piaf among the Pygmies," *New York Times*, 6 Sept. 1987 (book review section).

53. See my study *"I Am You."*

54. Tsatsou, *The Sword's Fierce Edge*, 34.

55. Tsatsou, *My Brother, George Seferis*, 158, 168.

56. Ibid., 166, a comment by George Seferis; Tsatsos, *Dialogues*, 71.

57. Tsatsou, *My Brother, George Seferis*, 180.

58. The French translation is also specific: "non loin du golfe Myrtoon" (Constantin Tsatsos, *Dialogues au monastère*, trans. Octave Merlier [Paris: Société d'édition Les Belles Lettres, 1976], 8).

59. Tsatsou, *My Brother, George Seferis*, 207.

60. Plutarch, *De defectu oraculorum*, chap. 17.

61. Cf. G. R. S. Mead, *Thrice-Greatest Hermes: Studies in Hellenistic Theosophy and Gnosis* 1 (London: Watkins, 1949): 186.

Summary

1. See above, case 3, after n. 30.

2. James Joyce, *A Portrait of the Artist as a Young Man* (London: Granada, 1983), 160.

Index

I am greatly obliged to Mr. Michael Cavey and Mrs. Anne C. Morrison for assistance in compiling this index.

abortions, 123
Abraham, patriarch, 70
actors, 74, 142. *See also* theater
Adam, protoplast, 61, 94
affects, 2, 21, 24, 25
Africa, 133
aistheton, 138, 139, 140, 141. *See also* esthetics
Akiba, rabbi, 70
Alexander, Herman-Judah's father-in-law, 94
allegory, 53, 54, 67, 79, 94, 112
altar, 50, 62, 64, 65, 69, 83, 84, 111
Alypius, 11, 27, 28, 57
Ambrose, bishop of Milan, 5, 8, 16, 18, 21, 26, 29, 33, 163 n. 194, 165 n. 213
angel, 24, 30, 32, 35, 56, 109, 110
animality, 25, 79, 123, 171 n. 57, 172 n. 59
Anthony of Egypt, 4, 10, 18, 28, 57
Antiquity, xiv, 115, 118, 142
anti-Semitism, 40. *See also* Jews: stereotypes
Apollo, 168 n. 16

apostates, 44, 70, 95, 103, 174 n. 82
Apostles, 12, 107
Arabic, xii
Arcady, 135, 142
archetype, x
Arians, ix
aristocracy, xv
Aristotle, 125, 133
artisans, 23
arts, xii, xiii, 5, 47, 49, 73–74, 99, 117, 120, 121, 134, 139, 145; work of, 2, 35; and religion, 137. *See also* music; painting; sculpture
ascetics, xii, 4, 74, 85, 88–89, 126–27, 129, 134, 139, 140, 146, 168 n. 23, 180 n. 45
Asiatic, 133, 136
Assyrian, 67
Athens, 120, 143
Augustine, bishop of Hippo, frontispiece, viii, ix, x, xi, xii, xvi–xix, 1–38, 39, 40, 41, 42, 44, 45, 46, 48, 54–60, 71–74, 75, 110, 115, 117, 119, 146, 147, 148, 171 n. 52, 171 n. 57

INDEX

Augustinian order, 42, 46, 52, 88, 110, 177 n. 59
Aztecs, 133

Babylon, 65, 66
banqueting, 50, 62, 64–65, 66, 67, 74, 77, 85–87, 96, 110–13
baptism, ix, x, 6, 11, 23, 32, 39, 41, 42, 43, 44, 47, 48, 51, 52, 53, 55, 57, 58, 60, 62, 67, 69, 71, 72, 73, 75, 86, 96, 101, 102, 107–9, 110, 167 n. 16
barbarians, 133, 134, 135, 136, 138
Bari, archbishop of, 68
Baruch, Herman-Judah's custodian, 78, 80, 91, 92
Basset, 122, 136
beauty, xiv, xvi, 36, 37, 115, 123–24, 129, 147, 158 n. 82
Being, 132, 136
belt, 77, 110, 111
Benjamin, 68
Bertha, ascetic of Cologne, 61, 68, 100–101
bibliomancy, 19, 28
bishop, 9, 11, 12, 41, 72–73
Blake, William, 1, 2, 3, 22
Blake, Mrs. William, 1
blasphemy, 49, 65, 104
blindness, 20, 74, 85, 102, 105
Bonn, 42
Buddhism, xii, 146
Byzantium, 135

Calvin, John, 38
Calvinism, 136
cannibalism, 122
canons, 9, 109. *See also* Augustinian order; Cappenberg
Cappenberg, 40, 42, 46, 62, 67, 72, 74, 88–89, 110, 175 n. 59
catechesis, 58, 106

catechumen, 106
celibacy, 14, 19, 57, 100
charity, 29, 36, 55, 68, 85, 87, 94, 96, 104, 106, 110, 112, 131, 134, 138, 173 n. 72
chastity, 20, 56, 111, 112, 157 n. 72
childhood, 41, 49, 55
children, 13, 16, 17, 24, 27, 32, 75, 77, 89, 98, 102, 145, 148, 170 n. 37, 174 n. 81
China, 133
Christ, x, xii, xiv, 19, 24, 43, 52, 58, 62, 67, 69, 75, 76, 87, 93, 96, 104, 107, 109, 111, 117, 132; body of, 5, 34, 36; as bridegroom, 16; city of, 70; crucified, 14, 63, 69, 80; images of, 49–50, 80, 83, 169 n. 28; as king, 62, 63, 65, 69, 80, 102, 110, 111; members of, 4; as nurse, 16; as Pantocrator, 142; passion of, 50, 83; second coming of, 22, 40. *See also* cross; crucifixion; images; imitation; Jesus; king
Christianity, ix, xii, 135
Christology, 19, 62, 68–69
Church, ix, xi, xii, xvi, 12, 18, 19, 53, 60, 63, 72, 80, 102, 104, 109, 130; bowels of, 93
Cicero, Marcus Tullius, 21, 119, 124
codex, 28–32
coins, 77, 78, 110
Cologne, 41, 42, 43, 47, 49, 58, 77, 91, 100, 106; bishop of, 43
combat, 75, 84, 98; naked, 75, 84, 98
composition, 37, 120, 130
concealment, xii, xiii, xv, 6, 44, 50, 71, 73, 171 n. 57. *See also* hiddenness; evidence (suppressed)
conscience, xv, 56, 99, 128
continence, 12, 17, 18, 55, 56, 98, 111
cosmos, x, xii, 28, 29, 122, 133
creation, viii, 6

Creator, viii, x. *See also* God
cross, 43, 49–50, 63, 69, 80, 83, 84, 99, 105, 106, 107, 167 n. 16. *See also* Christ; crucifixion
crown, 177 n. 59
crucifixion, 69, 82, 83, 87. *See also* Christ; cross
Crusade, First, 41, 43, 44, 47, 49, 66, 70, 166 n. 13; Second, 39, 40, 43, 70; Third, 168 n. 17
cults, xiii, 49
curiosity, 8, 13, 24

Daniel, prophet, 52, 55, 59, 65–66, 67, 68, 70, 92
David, king and prophet, 77, 104
David, father of Herman-Judah, 77
dead, revival of, 10
death, ix, 6, 12, 24, 61, 83, 123, 130, 137, 138, 139, 143, 147, 168 n. 23; sentence of, 50, 52, 103, 169 n. 31
debates, 42, 48, 49, 64, 66, 74, 75, 81–85, 93, 94, 101
democracy, 116, 120
demons, 24, 38, 108, 109, 177 n. 16. *See also* Devil, Satan
demythologizing, xiv
Devil, 12, 14, 38, 51, 56, 73, 75, 94, 96, 99, 109, 110; diabolic, 105; "the Enemy," 8, 75, 76, 105. *See also* demon, Satan
Diana, 45
Dido, 13
diet, 62, 64, 65, 66, 67, 173 n. 72
Dionysus, 120
discipline, ix, x, xii, 71, 137, 140
divinization, 116. *See also* transfiguration; transformation
Donatists, 8, 9, 12, 13, 14, 33, 48, 54
Donne, John, 45
dreams, 13, 47–48, 49, 52, 59, 64, 65, 67, 110–12

ear, 6, 13, 20, 74, 85, 97
Eden, Garden of, 70
education, xii, 23, 24, 41, 170 n. 37
Egbert, bishop of Münster, 41, 46, 47, 78, 85–87, 91, 171 n. 57
Egypt, 61, 73, 102
election, 59, 113, 138
Eliezer bar Nathan, rabbi, 43
Elisha, prophet, 108
eloquence, 36, 37
empathy, 22, 60, 72
emperor, 78, 110
enigma, 22, 54
enlightenment, x, 22, 45, 48, 52, 53, 56, 57, 60, 92, 101, 146
Epicurus, 133
eroticism, 5, 14–17, 26, 55, 71, 72, 128, 133
Esther, queen, 64, 66–67, 68, 173 n. 75
esthetics, xiv, 2, 26, 116, 134, 136, 142. *See also* aistheton
Eucharist, 48, 62, 64, 65, 69, 74
Eve, protoplast, 59, 61, 64, 94, 101
evidence, suppression of, 6, 10–11, 18, 46–47, 169 n. 25
evil, 37, 133
excommunication, 95, 173 n. 73
exegesis, 6, 7, 25, 44, 48, 49, 54, 55, 59, 61, 69, 79, 82, 93, 98–99, 171 n. 57
existentialism, xvi, 114, 118, 119, 127, 134
exorcism, 60, 65
eye, 4, 13, 14, 17, 22, 23, 24, 85, 92, 105, 164 n. 204
Ezekiel, prophet, 49

fables, 94
faith, ix, x, xv, 41, 60, 68, 71, 75, 86–87, 112, 119, 130, 132, 133, 134, 138, 178 n. 7

fasting, 42, 65, 92–93, 99, 107
Faust, 146
fear, 24, 36, 132. See also terror
fecundity, 6, 17, 53, 55, 107
fiction, xiii, xvi, xvii, 41, 82, 115, 145, 147, 160 n. 119
fish, 12
flesh, 6, 12, 18, 19, 20, 21, 24, 78, 92, 97, 98, 109, 110, 117, 123, 131
Flonheim, 106
France, 94
Franciscan order, 176 n. 57
fraud, 39, 99, 108
French, 125, 136, 140
friends, 55, 57, 59, 63, 65, 77, 78, 106, 130
friendship, 16, 19, 24, 27, 29, 55, 124

Gallicanism, 136
Gamaliel III, talmudist, 54, 104
games, 8, 27, 28, 142
gender, ambiguity of, 16–17, 123
Gentiles, 56, 65–67, 70, 99
German, 136, 141, 142; Germans, 121, 123, 124, 125; German Romantic tradition, 135
gladiators, 13, 27
Glismut, ascetic of Cologne, 61, 68, 100–101
glory, 76, 94, 107
goats, 79
God, vii, x, xiii, xviii, 1, 6, 7, 29, 30, 32, 52, 59, 66, 67, 72, 81, 82, 83, 84, 85, 86, 103, 104, 128, 129, 130, 131, 132, 133, 134, 138; as audience for Augustine's *Confessions*, 6; debate with, 89; eyes of, 56; favor of, to Jews, 52; feasts, 64; rewards and punishments of, 90; source of art, 23; suckles infant, 16; supernatural power of, 59; as torturer, 7, 13–14, 47; vengeance of, 70. See also Creator

Goethe, Johann Wolfgang von, 128, 132
Gottfried, count of Cappenberg, 46, 88–89, 177 n. 59
grace, viii, ix, x, xii, 3, 13, 18, 58, 59, 60, 68, 76, 77, 97, 101, 111–13, 138–39
Greek: language, 120; people, 15
Gregory I, pope, 168 n. 16, 176 n. 57
Gregory, bishop of Nyssa, 117, 125

Haman, 174
Harrer, 122, 132
hatred, 68, 128, 132, 174 n. 85
hearing, sense of, 74, 97, 101
heart, viii, xii, xiii, 6, 7, 103
Heaven, Kingdom of, xiii, 64, 79, 93, 101–2, 111, 137
Hebrew: language, 64, 102; books, 79, 83
Hegel, Georg Wilhelm Friedrich, 179 n. 27
Heidegger, Martin, 118, 119, 122, 131, 135, 144
Helen, 134
hell, 63, 70, 91, 96, 107
Hellenic Republic, 116
Hellenism, 135
Henry V, emperor, 77
Henry the Lion, duke of Saxony, 63
Herman-Judah, x, xi, xvi, 39–115, 119, 146, 147
hermeneutics: circle, xiv; doctrines of, ix, xiii, 37, 115, 119; gap, 47–48, 53, 67; methods of, 42, 53, 60–71; program, xv, 47; scenario, 42; strategies, 48, 71; varieties of, 48
hiddenness, 13, 24, 26, 49, 89, 131, 137. See also concealment; secrecy
history, xiii, 36, 39, 44, 46, 71, 79, 83, 85, 129, 138, 139, 144, 148
Hitler, Adolf, 135

Holy Spirit, viii, 29, 44, 107, 110, 111
Homer, 134
homosexuality, 16
horse, 77, 78, 110, 111
humanism, 134, 135
humanity, 132
hunt, 8, 9, 11, 24
Hypatia, 123

iconoclasm, 49
idolatry, viii, 42, 47, 49, 53, 65, 66, 67, 70, 75, 82, 83
idols, 42, 80, 127
ignorant, the, 59, 134
image, x, 1, 4, 5, 22, 23, 26, 31, 32, 36, 49, 73, 82, 83, 169 n. 29, 171 n. 49; in synagogues, 47, 73; for the uneducated, 82
imagination, 13, 32, 44, 131, 136, 145
imitation, 18, 37, 74, 85; of Christ, 47, 87. *See also* Christ; mimesis; mirror
India, 133
inebriation, 25, 26, 62, 64, 112
Innocent III, pope, 116, 117
interpretation, 36, 47, 53, 69; of dreams, 47, 76, 110–12. *See also* exegesis
Investiture Conflict, 46
Ipliksis, 122, 123, 126, 128, 132, 133, 136, 137, 139, 140
Isaac, kinsman of Herman-Judah, 34, 77, 106
Isaiah, prophet, xiii, 88, 107
Islam, xii
Israel, 67, 97, 98, 102; Israelite, 68, 84

Jaeger, Werner, 122, 124, 135, 178 n. 7
James, apostle, 85, 101
Jaspers, Karl, 135
Jerome, ix
Jerusalem, 32, 34, 35, 65, 66, 84
Jesus, 79, 106, 112, 131. *See also* Christ

Jews, 15, 39, 48, 50–51, 57, 60, 73, 75, 76, 77, 90, 94, 98, 103, 109, 111, 113, 121, 122, 133; abuse of, 81, 87; fasts of, 92; fear of, 50; feasts of, 64; legal proceedings of, 95, 102–3; mutilation of images by, alleged, 49; plots by, 102; as persecutors, 75; punished by God, 70; ritual self-slaughter by, 51; scholasticism of, 48; slaughter of, 47, 66–67, 70, 168 n. 17. *See also* Judaism; stereotypes
Job, 94
John of Salisbury, bishop of Orléans, 69
Jordan, 54, 67, 108
Joseph, patriarch, 66
Joyce, James, 117, 119, 141
Judaism, x, xiv, 76; judaizing, 48. *See also* Jews
Jupiter, 45, 163 n. 183
Justina, empress, ix

Karavounis, Christos, 136
Kazantzakis, Nikos, 120, 132, 135
kidnapping, 51, 52, 61, 72, 102–3, 105
Kierkegaard, Søren, 119
kinesthesia, 23, 26–27, 28, 74
king, 58, 63, 65, 66–67, 77–78, 110, 111. *See also* Christ
kingdoms, 7, 66, 71. *See also* Heaven, Kingdom of
Kingsley, Charles, 148

language, xv, 5, 15, 42, 72, 80–81, 117, 120, 126, 127, 128, 129, 131, 137, 140, 142, 144, 146; deficiencies of, 2, 20–22, 140. *See also* words
Last Judgment, 12, 116
Latin, 42, 52, 72, 110
laughter, 7; laughing-stock, 13, 52, 108
law: canon, 9; civil, 116, 123; divine, 16; Old Testamental, 64, 73, 79,

law (cont.)
  80, 81, 82, 83, 85, 90, 93, 98, 100, 104, 108, 111, 171 n. 57
Leo I, pope, 148
leprosy, 54, 67, 108
Levirate, 69
light, viii, x, 25, 26, 36, 59, 68, 76, 80, 83, 99, 138
likeness, x, 37
Livy, Titus, 31
loan, 41, 46
Logos, 132
Lotario dei Segni, cardinal. See Innocent III
Lothar III, emperor, 77, 78
love, 7, 8, 16, 24, 25, 35, 36, 52, 59, 69, 73, 76, 83, 85, 88, 104, 111, 117, 123, 125, 128, 130, 131, 133, 134, 140, 174 n. 85; interchangeable with terror, 1–2, 3
lust, 13, 14, 96

machine, 128
Mâcon, Council of, 173 n. 73
madness, 13, 82, 95, 99, 106, 108
magic, xiv, 60, 65, 80, 85, 167 n. 16. See also witchcraft
Maimonides (Moses ben Maimon), talmudist, 59, 64, 71, 73, 172 n. 59
Mainz, 41, 43, 78, 102, 103, 105, 172 n. 60
Manhorst, 131
Manichees, 8, 9, 10, 14, 18, 19, 21, 48, 54
Marathon, Battle of, 143
marriage, 7, 15, 16, 17, 42, 47, 56, 78, 94–98
martyrdom, 43, 47, 89, 168 n. 223; martyrs, 13, 16, 33
Mary, Virgin, 49, 61. See also virgins
masculinity, xv, 15, 16, 26, 123. See also men; virility
medicine, 14, 19

memory, 4, 6, 10, 22, 23, 24, 25, 26, 30, 31, 33, 73, 180 n. 45; stomach of, 23, 79
men, 76, 81, 97, 122, 123, 126, 127, 146. See also masculinity; virility
merchants, 78, 101
metaphor, vii, xiii, 23, 26, 29–30, 32, 64, 73, 74, 75, 147
metaphysics, xvi, 72, 73, 115, 116, 132, 136
Milan, 5, 9, 57
mimesis, x, xiv, xv, 5, 26, 27, 31, 36, 37, 75. See also imitation, mirror
mind, 13, 15, 22, 23, 24, 25, 30, 73, 116, 123, 124, 132, 137
miracle, ix, 86–87
mirror, 4–5, 22, 32, 33, 35
misinterpretation, 49, 53
missions, xii, 171 n. 58, 179 n. 31
mockery, 7, 13, 27, 52, 75, 81, 108
monasticism, x, 42, 58, 89, 106, 111, 116, 119, 133, 134, 135; profession of, 53, 117, 122, 125. See also monks
Monemvasia, 135
money, 78 n. 106
Monica, mother of Augustine, ix, 5, 7, 10, 11, 15, 16, 17, 19, 25, 26, 29, 32, 57, 58, 59, 115
monks, 40, 126, 127, 133, 134, 137. See also monasticism
Mordecai, 66, 67, 68, 174 n. 75
Moses, lawgiver, 21, 36, 98
mothers, 77, 102, 105, 106, 109; breasts of, 67, 95, 174 n. 8
music, 4–5, 21, 26, 30–33, 38, 45, 74, 134, 137, 139, 145, 148, 158 n. 82, 162 n. 176, 163 n. 194. See also psalmody; song
Muslims, 70, 171 n. 58
mysteries, xiii, 59, 72, 92, 99, 107, 108, 111, 112, 125, 135, 137, 171 n. 57; mystic, xii, 138, 140
mysticism, 71, 117, 122, 124, 131, 142

Mystra, 135
myths, xii–xiv

Naaman the Syrian, 50, 54, 67, 108
narrative, viii, 10, 33–34
Nathan, prophet, 106
Nathaniel, 17
nature, xii, xv, xvi, 22, 24, 27, 115, 116, 118, 138; human, 56, 58, 59, 72, 116, 118
Nazis, 136
Nebridius, ix, 24
Neoplatonism, 72, 115, 135. *See also* philosophy; Platonism
Newman, John Henry, vii, 147–48
Nicaea, 9, 117
Nicodemus, 50, 101
Ninevites, 67
Noah, 173 n. 72
Norbert of Xanten, 42
Nouty, 122, 123, 125, 129, 130, 137, 140

ordeal, 70, 86–87, 171 n. 58
Ostia, 11, 59
Otto, bishop of Bamberg, 53, 170 n. 40
Otto, bishop of Freising, 70–71, 73
Otto, count of Cappenberg, 46, 88

pagans, 45, 62, 64, 76, 80
painting, 2, 49–50, 51, 61, 69, 74, 80, 82, 145, 156 n. 44, 158 n. 82. *See also* picture
palace, 77, 111, 177 n. 59
Palestine, 43
Pan, 140, 142–43
pantheisms, 131
papyrus, 29–30
parable, xiii, 10, 44, 128, 137; pearl of great price, 50, 101. *See also* prodigal son; sower
paradigm, xv, xvi, 136

Paris, 136
Patricius, father of Augustine, ix, 7, 10, 11, 15, 19, 26
Paul, apostle, xi, xiii, xiv, 2, 3, 10, 18, 19, 20, 22, 28, 45, 50, 56, 62, 68, 69, 70, 80, 85–86, 91, 98, 102, 103, 111, 117, 122, 131, 138, 169 n. 31, 178 n. 16, 180 n. 39; maternity of, 159 n. 106
Pelagius, 12
penitence, xi, 10, 27, 46, 67, 88, 89, 90, 99–100, 109
peripety, 3
persecution, xi, 9, 12, 75, 80, 91
persona, 105, 127, 140, 142
Peter, apostle, 39, 106
Pharaoh, 66
Pharisaism, 55
philosophy, xii, xiv, 24, 45, 46, 120, 137, 141. *See also* Existentialism; Neoplatonism; Platonism
picture, 23, 31, 32, 73, 130. *See also* painting
piety, 24, 36, 55, 67
pilgrimage, 23, 35
Plato, 37, 117, 125, 137
Platonism, 115, 118, 128. *See also* Neoplatonism
play, xiv, 24, 27–28, 36, 38, 64, 74–75, 142, 145; metaphors of, 74
Plethon, George Gemistos, 135
Plotinus, 117, 125, 138
poetics, xi, xvi, 136, 144, 146
poetry, 37, 120, 125, 129, 134, 136, 137, 139, 142
Pomeranians, 53
poverty, 176 n. 57
prayer, 34, 58, 61, 68, 70, 92–93, 99, 100–101, 103, 104
predator, 8, 17, 24, 27, 38
predestination, 59
Premonstratensian order, 42
Prevelakis, Pandelis, 115

INDEX

priest, 9, 52, 66, 68, 69, 77, 80, 110, 112, 113, 171 n. 50
Prodigal Son, 10, 50, 64, 65, 113, 156 n. 59. *See also* parable
prophecy, 3, 7, 49, 53, 72, 88, 93, 98, 104, 107, 108
psalmody, 5, 32–35, 74. *See also* music; song

Quintilian, Marcus Fabius, 10

Ravengiersburg, 106
reading, 28–35, 41
reason, 62, 69, 81, 83, 126, 132, 172 n. 61
redemption, x, 36, 62
rhetoric, ix, 4, 7, 8, 9, 12, 13, 15, 18, 21, 27, 57, 138, 147, 158 n. 83
Richenza, queen and empress, 102
Richmar, 85–87
ritual, ix, 42, 43, 56
Rome, ix; Empire, 45, 114; Church, 148
running, 22, 35, 74, 89, 90
Rupert, abbot of Deutz, 42, 48, 49, 50, 54, 64, 66, 67, 68, 69, 81–84, 173 n. 75

sacraments, ix, 7, 9, 72–73, 80, 108, 112
sacrifice, 4, 7, 14, 43, 47, 62, 68, 69, 70, 83, 84, 113, 124, 139
saints, viii, 20, 84, 101, 107
salad, 64, 77
Samuel, prophet, 104
Saracens, 42
Satan, 57, 64, 74, 75, 93, 108, 122, 172 n. 59. *See also* demon; Devil
scepter, 106
Scheda, 42
scholasticism, 48

Scripture, 4, 5, 14, 18, 21, 22, 25, 26, 39, 44, 48, 49, 57, 61, 64, 69, 72–73, 79, 81, 82, 93, 98, 107, 117. *See also* exegesis
scroll, 28–32
sculpture, 49, 51, 80, 82
secrecy, 58, 65. *See also* hiddenness; concealment; evidence (suppression of)
Seferiades, Stylianos, 120, 136, 142
Seferis, George, 121, 141
semi-Christians, 64, 68, 69, 75, 100, 105
senses, bodily, 4
sensuality, 55, 124
Sephora, mother of Herman-Judah, 77
serf, 58, 100, 172 n. 60
servility, 58
sexuality, xv, 12, 13, 14–17, 18–19, 26, 51, 54–55, 123, 126, 159 n. 102, 172 n. 59
sheep, 10, 79, 80, 97, 109, 123
sickness, 57, 97, 158 n. 83
silver, 78, 111
simple (=uneducated), 83, 89, 101
sin, x, 9, 10, 30, 38, 42, 43, 56, 69, 70, 83, 85, 90, 98, 109, 117
slaughter, 41, 43, 53, 167 n. 15, 168 n. 17
Solomon bar Simson, rabbi, 43
song, ix, 4, 37. *See also* music; psalmody
Sophronios, 116, 136, 142
soul, ix, xvii, 6, 16, 59, 116, 124, 127, 128, 129, 133–34, 138
sower, xiii. *See also* parable
space, 126, 128
spectacle, 75, 86. *See also* theater; actors
Speier, bishop of, 43
Spinoza, Baruch, 131
stereotypes, 40, 49, 51, 52, 60
suffering, xiii–xiv, 7, 12–14, 15, 18, 19, 27, 54, 62, 97–98, 119, 121–

22, 125, 126, 131, 137, 141–42, 147, 172 n. 59
supernatural, the, ix, xi, xii, xvi, 3, 20, 22, 27, 38, 46, 71, 115, 117, 132, 138
superstition, 28, 51, 67, 82, 95, 96, 99, 104, 113, 170 n. 36
Suzman, Helen, 162 n. 179
sweetness, 26, 32
synagogues, 47, 48, 50, 51, 63, 70, 75, 93, 95, 102, 104
synesthesia, 160 n. 130
Synesios, abbot, 116, 117, 122, 123, 125, 128, 129, 130, 131, 135–36, 137, 139, 140, 142
Synesios, bishop of Ptolemais, 123, 135

Talney, Ronald, 164 n. 204
temple, 42, 45, 61, 62, 80, 102, 167 n. 16, 169 n. 29
Terence (Publius Terentius Afer), 118, 131, 163 n. 183
terror, 5, 25, 51; interchangeable with love, 1, 3
Tertullian, 178 n. 7
theater, 4, 7, 13, 24, 27, 28, 50, 74, 75, 142. *See also* actors; spectacle
theft, 37–38
theodicy, xvii, 14, 72–73, 90–91, 158 n. 82
Thomas, apostle, 87
Thomas Aquinas, O.P., 133
Thomas à Becket, archbishop of Canterbury, 57
time, 6, 30, 33, 72, 126, 128, 142, 148
tomb, 43
Torah, 59
tradition, xi, xii, xv, 78, 82, 91, 93, 104, 114–15, 123, 142, 146, 180 n. 45
tragedy, 37, 137, 141

transfiguration, 105, 116, 134, 135, 137, 139, 141, 142, 143
transformation, xiii, 116, 118, 142, 143, 146. *See also* divinization
translation, ix, xiii, 119, 120, 137, 139–40, 142
treasure, xiii, 44, 79
Trinity, 107
truth, 7, 21–22
Tsatsos, Constantine, xi, xvi, 114–43, 144, 146
Tsatsou, Ioanna, 120, 123, 136, 142

understanding, 3, 26, 36, 56, 60, 127; mystic, 59; visual, 4, 28; understanding understanding, 3, 22–35, 36, 58–81, 82
usury, 78

Varro, Marcus Terentius, 28
vengeance, 43, 62–63, 67, 69, 70, 75, 84, 90, 91
Victorinus, ix, 8, 10, 12, 18
Virgil (Publius Vergilius Maro), 28, 31
virgins, xiii, 42, 61, 94, 109, 170 n. 58. *See also* Mary, Virgin
virility, 16, 123. *See also* masculinity; men
vision (apparition), 1, 4, 41, 48, 49, 52, 53, 54, 58, 59, 62–64, 66, 77–78, 91, 92, 106–7, 112, 138, 156 n. 61
vision (sense), 4, 22, 32, 74, 164 n. 204
vocabulary, viii–x, 39
vocation, ix, 59, 69, 138, 139

Welanheim, 106
wheel, 49
Wilamowitz-Möllendorff, Ulrich von, 122
will(s), 7, 56, 59, 72
wisdom, 116, 127

witchcraft, 8. *See also* magic
Wolkwin, 102
wolves, 80, 135
women, xiv, 15–16, 26, 49, 55, 58, 61, 67, 68, 76, 79, 94, 95, 98, 100–101, 123–24, 126, 133, 137, 177 n. 59, 179 n. 20, 179 n. 25

words, 36, 37, 126, 127; iron cages, 140; poetic, 138, 140; portmanteau, xi, xii, xiv. *See also* language
World War II, 122, 125, 142
Worms, 41, 43, 104

xenophobia, 133

www.ingramcontent.com/pod-product-compliance
Lightning Source LLC
Chambersburg PA
CBHW022012300426
44117CB00005B/150